PRAISE FOR *YOU'RE IT*

"Whether the situation you're facing is ordinary or extraordinary, *You're It* can equip you with the tools to lead people effectively through times of change and turmoil."

— Doug Conant, founder and CEO, ConantLeadership, and former CEO of Campbell Soup Company

"A practical how-to manual for those who must exercise leadership in crisis situations. *You're It* is a highly readable, essential primer for anyone who is called to lead when people need it most."

— Janet Napolitano, former Department of Homeland Security secretary, president of the University of California, and author of *How Safe Are We?: Homeland Security Since 9/11*

"Every leader dreams (and agonizes) about his or her 'leadership moment'—that singular crisis or challenge that will test our character and define our legacy. *You're It* shows what it takes to prepare for that moment. Its insights, frameworks, and genuinely riveting stories will prepare leaders in any field to seize an opportunity or avoid disaster. Read this book, take its lessons to heart, and get ready to lead."

— William C. Taylor, cofounder of Fast Company and author of Simply Brilliant

"The real beauty of this highly readable book is that today, we all find ourselves leading through crises at work, in our families, and in our communities. And it is packed with fresh, new ideas about leadership that are brilliant, practical, and relevant. The authors' model for how to think, what to do, and how to unite people when extreme crisis hits works, and they've got excellent research and fascinating stories from real life to prove it."

—Annie McKee, bestselling author and senior fellow, University of Pennsylvania

"Combining meticulously engaging theory with heart-stopping anecdotes from the top crisis leaders of our times, *You're It* provides all of us with what to do, and what not to do, when it matters the most. This is a book that takes us beyond the clichés of leadership literature, and provides tools that will make us smarter, more self-aware, and better prepared when we are tested."

—Juliette Kayyem, former assistant secretary, Department of Homeland Security, and faculty chair, Harvard's Kennedy School of Government Homeland Security Program

"*You're It* is a comprehensive resource for individual and organizational preparedness leadership. As a governor, I faced several disasters, natural and man-made, and came to realize that being prepared is not just having plans and designated resources, but it is building trust and working together for an organic, agile, and effective response. This work shows us that pathway, meta-leadership, arming future generations with the tools, knowledge, and the ability to reach beyond themselves when destiny says, 'You're it.'"

—Ernest "Ernie" Fletcher, former member, US House of Representatives, and former governor, Kentucky

"In a world where both challenges and opportunities are increasingly complex and simultaneously nuanced, leaders navigate ambiguity at every turn. In *You're It,* readers will find practical insights and illuminating stories about what it takes to make hard choices when the future seems more chaotic than clear. Readers will also find inspiration and understanding of what it takes to succeed in a crisis whether it is local or international. *You're It* is the crisis playbook for the twenty-first century."

—Farah Pandith, author of *How We Win: How Cutting-Edge Entrepreneurs, Political Visionaries, Enlightened Business Leaders, and Social Media Mavens Can Defeat the Extremist Threat*

"Drawing on the experience of dozens of leaders during times of crisis, *You're It* breaks new ground in our understanding of leadership performance when disaster strikes. Its compelling narrative identifies practical ways leaders can prepare in advance of calamity. This book is a must read for those who want to understand how improving leadership skills can drive better outcomes."

—Alice Hill, former special assistant to President Obama, senior director for Resilience on the National Security Council, and author of *Building a Resilient Tomorrow: Preparing for the Coming Climate Disruption*

"*You're It* is an essential prep course for leaders and leaders-in-the-making who are at risk for ending up on the frontlines of a crisis. Whether used as an individual guide to personal and professional development or a comprehensive curriculum for risk management team planning, *You're It* fits the bill."

—Julie Louise Gerberding, MD, MPH, executive vice president and chief patient officer, Strategic Communications, Global Public Policy, and Population Health, and former director, US Centers for Disease Control and Prevention

You're It

Crisis, Change, and
How to Lead When It
Matters Most

YOU'RE
IT

Leonard J. Marcus, Eric J. McNulty,
Joseph M. Henderson, Barry C. Dorn

Foreword by David Gergen

PUBLICAFFAIRS
New York

Cover design by The Book Designers
Cover copyright © 2019 Hachette Book Group, Inc.

PublicAffairs
Hachette Book Group
1290 Avenue of the Americas, New York, NY 10104
www.publicaffairsbooks.com
@Public_Affairs

Printed in the United States of America

First Edition: June 2019

Published by PublicAffairs, an imprint of Perseus Books, LLC, a subsidiary of Hachette Book
Group, Inc. The PublicAffairs name and logo is a trademark of the Hachette Book Group.

The Hachette Speakers Bureau provides a wide range of authors for speaking events. To find out
more, go to www.hachettespeakersbureau.com or call (866) 376-6591.

The publisher is not responsible for websites (or their content) that are not owned by the
publisher.

Print book interior design by Amy Quinn.

Library of Congress Cataloging-in-Publication Data

Names: Marcus, Leonard J., author.
Title: You're it : crisis, change, and how to lead when it matters most / Leonard J. Marcus, Eric J.
  McNulty, Joseph M. Henderson, Barry C. Dorn. Other titles: You are it
Description: New York : PublicAffairs, [2019] | Includes bibliographical references and index.
Identifiers: LCCN 2018053723| ISBN 9781541768031 (hard cover : alk. paper) | ISBN
  9781541768055 (ebook : alk. paper)
Subjects: LCSH: Crisis management. | Leadership.
Classification: LCC HD49 .M366 2019 | DDC 658.4/056—dc23
LC record available at https://lccn.loc.gov/2018053723
ISBNs: 978-1-5417-6803-1 (hardcover); 978-1-5417-6805-5 (ebook)

LSC-C

10 9 8 7 6 5 4 3 2 1

To you, our readers:
You're it!

CONTENTS

FOREWORD

Nearly every Baby Boomer can remember exactly where they were and what they were doing when they heard that President John F. Kennedy had been shot, just as nearly every Millennial can remember when word reached them that airplanes had crashed into the World Trade Center, the Pentagon, and a field in Pennsylvania. There were many similarities between the events: the sense of horror that gripped at Americans' throats, the fear that we might be under a sustained attack, the worry about loved ones. Each of these tragedies helped define a generation.

But there was one significant difference between the two: America was much better prepared for the 9/11 disaster than for the Kennedy assassination. The presidential assassination was a bolt from the blue, something we had not experienced since 1901, something we had never witnessed before on live television. And as we saw when Lee Harvey Oswald was shot, the locals were simply not ready.

By contrast, an earlier attempt to blow up the Trade Center prompted officials in New York City to make themselves ready. Officials many times practiced what they would do if terrorists struck again; the fire and police forces knew what to do and were prepared to sacrifice their lives in order to spare others; even as the Secret Service moved President Bush into temporary seclusion, New York Mayor Rudy Giuliani stepped forward and, in his finest hour, calmed the nation. Readiness matters.

Even if officials were prepared to act, events surrounding 9/11 also had a ripple effect across the country. Soon after the attacks, as described in this book, the Centers for Disease Control's first Director of the Office of Terrorism Preparedness and Emergency Response met with Lenny Marcus and me to see what could be done to strengthen national response leadership. Shortly thereafter, government leaders along with faculty from across the university gathered at Harvard to inaugurate the National Preparedness Leadership Initiative—or NPLI—in the early 2000s. They together foresaw that the country and world might be entering an era of turbulence when terrorists might hit Anywhere, USA, and they wanted to partner to develop an executive education platform that would study and train first responder leaders from local, state, and federal offices in emergency preparedness. They recognized that to make the country safer, leadership matters. And as this book shows, they also recognized that these same lessons apply to business leaders of all kinds as they face their own crises—whether it's a product recall or a media controversy.

The NPLI was on a roller coaster in its early years. It turned out that starting an education program across government agencies and across jurisdictions was harder than it looked, and getting different parts of a university to collaborate could be even more challenging. Money had to be found in different corners of government to pay for training. No one knew whether it would survive periodic budget cuts.

But over time, as results piled up, NPLI gained traction and now has reached its fifteenth year. It has a proud record of training thousands of senior leaders—from government, humanitarian organizations, and businesses large and small, and from across the country and around the world—to meet a wide variety of emergencies. That training includes bringing leaders to the Harvard campus twice over a six-month period, the first time for intensive training by faculty from across the university and the second as a follow-up to see how lessons from the classroom have played out in the field. Importantly through this work, officials from different departments and different levels of responsibility have formed a close network of colleagues and friends who are there for each other. In the midst of any big emergency, there are frequently several NPLI alumni working across boundaries with each other, pulling on the leadership knowledge, skills, and practices they've gained during their time at Harvard.

One of the strengths of the program has been its adaptability. When it comes to disaster relief, the NPLI initially focused on responses to terror, but as weather-related disasters have grown ferociously in recent years, classes now turn more frequently to the effects of climate change. And in their private-sector training, they've added a focus on cyber security, and are help-ing corporations identify the moments of crisis more quickly as the speed of technology demands. No doubt, they will continue to evolve in the future.

Of course, no one would argue that NPLI is a panacea. Preparedness is an all-hands-on-deck requirement in addressing emergencies. In the battle against Hurricane Katrina, for example, Admiral Thad Allen and his Coast Guard contingent—who assumed leadership late in the response—were val-iant in saving lives and inspiring confidence. By contrast, the local leadership in New Orleans was widely seen as ineffectual and over its head. Clearly, every jurisdiction in the country now has an interest in training up its top people and its responders to meet once-in-a-hundred-years storms or the ravages of uncontrolled fires.

What the NPLI can do that is very hard in government is to play to its strengths: discovering and amassing knowledge, sorting out best practices, teaching others—the lifeblood of universities. There are definitely lessons to be learned about emergencies, both from the American experience and from the experience of others.

I well remember when the chief of London police visited an NPLI pro-gram several years ago. In Britain, the police—not a national team—are re-sponsible for dealing with terrorist incidents. The London chief outlined how the officer in charge of first responses would have at his side someone with equivalent experience to his own to be a second pair of eyes and ears for the chief. The officer in charge, said our London visitor, might be so focused on one aspect of the response that he or she would miss the big picture. The companion is there to be a quiet voice in the ear of the leader. Listening, I was reminded of a short film that is popular in universities: it shows a half-dozen students with a basketball and asks students to count the number of times the ball is thrown quickly back and forth. After the film ends, the teacher asks students how many passes occurred. Guesses vary. Then the teacher asks the students if they saw anything else in the film. At least a quarter of viewers (I remember; I was one of them) say no. What they miss is that while the ball was flying back and forth, an upright gorilla walks through their midst. Aha, I thought, that's why the Brits have a second ob-server for emergencies. Notice what might be obscured by the circumstances. Point well taken.

As this valuable book shows, the NPLI team has developed a number of concepts and tools that apply to emergency preparedness and response as well as to the requirements of everyday leadership. One of the most important is the idea of "meta-leadership"—the concept that in complex systems, a big part of leadership is the capacity to work well with and help steer organizations beyond one's immediate circle. They start with "who are you?" as a leader, the person, and how do you adjust your sights to assess the situation at hand. Then, building connectivity: How can different groups work together toward a common goal? How do they forge the coordination of effort that allows them to leverage what each knows and can do? How do they unify large groups of people to work together toward that common purpose, what they call in this book "swarm leadership?" Examples are countless, and emergency leaders and business leaders find meta-leadership training to be foundational. The authors have compiled their years of research and teaching into this volume.

A related focus central to this book is crisis training. In an emergency, attention pivots quickly to the person in charge. "You're It!" the leader suddenly finds, and it's too late to go back to the classroom for answers. Crisis leaders have to be psychologically and physically ready to act on a moment's notice. And as our soldiers and sailors discovered on the beaches of Normandy over seventy years ago, the person in charge may not make it—and the second in command realizes, "Hey, you're it now." The historian Steven Ambrose believed that the US forces succeeded that day because so many soldiers, as "sons of democracy," had grown up behind a plow, were independent in spirit, and weren't afraid to lead.

President Kennedy once said after the Bay of Pigs fiasco, "Victory has many fathers while defeat is always an orphan." There was a time years ago when NPLI looked like it might go down, but a wonderfully strong team pulled it together. Once a near-orphan, it now has many fathers. The single most important—the man who has carried the program on his broad shoulders since the beginning—is Lenny Marcus. He not only was the chief creator of the program but has year after year steered it forward. Lenny is the "It" of the NPLI. I was proud to work with Lenny years ago in helping to get things off the ground.

Fortunately, he has had great partners along the way—Joe Henderson, long a leader at the CDC, and the guy that got the original ball rolling, has recently retired from federal service and is now investing more of his talent into the NPLI, along with Eric McNulty, who is bringing so much intellectual strength to NPLI leadership thinking and practice, as well as Barry Dorn, the wise sage who was with the program from its inception.

Writing on behalf of the Harvard Kennedy School of Government, I want to express my gratitude and shared pride in the everyday contributions these leaders, and our alumni, are making to the safety of our country and its challenges ahead. First responders across the nation have certainly benefitted from the lessons of NPLI, as will others who now read this valuable new book.

David Gergen
Center for Public Leadership,
Harvard Kennedy School of Government

INTRODUCTION

It was a relaxing spring day on Cape Cod. Staring out at the ocean, Lenny Marcus whispered to his wife, "People on the Gulf Coast look at this same scene and have to worry about the oil hitting their shores." It was May 2, 2010. Twelve days earlier, the Deepwater Horizon oil rig erupted, killing eleven workers and threatening the Gulf of Mexico ecosystem with the largest oil spill in history.

It was a busy weekend for crisis leaders. The day before, a mammoth water main break west of Boston interrupted service to two million people. Massachusetts officials were coordinating with local leaders to ensure a safe water supply for the metropolis. The night before in New York, vigilant Times Square street vendors spotted a suspicious car and alerted police, thwarting what would have been a deadly terrorist explosion. Lenny knew that alumni of the crisis leadership program he codirects at Harvard were active in each of these incidents.

Suddenly, his phone rang. The screen read "Peter Neffenger." Quietly, he said, "Sorry, I need to take this one."

Peter was a captain in the Coast Guard when he completed Harvard's National Preparedness Leadership Initiative executive crisis leadership program. Afterwards, Peter and Lenny stayed in touch. Peter had been promoted to admiral and led Coast Guard operations on the Great Lakes. "Lenny, Thad Allen [commandant of the Coast Guard] asked me to head to New Orleans and serve as deputy national incident commander for the oil spill response. I want you to come down and observe what's going on."

Lenny sat up. He had gotten calls like this before. When H1N1/swine flu erupted the year before, Joe Henderson at the Centers for Disease Control and Prevention (CDC) called, and Lenny was quickly on a flight to their offices in Atlanta. During the Hurricane Katrina response in 2005, the director of the Federal Emergency Management Agency (FEMA), Michael Brown, emailed him from New Orleans: "You want to study leadership? Come on down."

By Friday, May 7, Eric McNulty and Lenny Marcus (two of the four authors of this book) were also in New Orleans to observe Admiral Neffenger as he assumed duties as deputy national incident commander. The next day Peter, his staff, Lenny, and Eric were flying over the oil spill in the Gulf. Barry Dorn later joined the national incident commander, Admiral Thad Allen, in New Orleans. The inquiry about leadership of the spill response would stretch all the way from the Gulf to Washington as they observed both the government interagency collaboration and the wrangling that marked the crisis response. There were frequent update calls to discuss ongoing leadership quandaries.

From one crisis to the next, the "come on down" calls continued. Each at a pivotal moment. Each when it mattered most.

Your leadership moment. The curtain rises and everyone looks to you. They count on you. A solution must be found. You take the helm. You're it.

Some situations you anticipate. Others come as a surprise. Whether you are a crisis leader professional, an organizational leader, or an unsuspecting bystander, in an instant you can be leading a crisis response or leading a part of it. Suddenly, you are responsible. What do you do?

The pages ahead chart steps for those crisis moments: ideas, methods, and pragmatic tools that will guide you as you guide others. Bringing those lessons to life are examples of real-life leaders in crisis scenarios: a terrorist attack, a pandemic, an oil spill, an active shooter, hurricanes. Crises, large and small, will happen. Financial shortfall, sexual harassment allegations, product liability—you as a leader must be prepared for whatever comes.

We, your authors, believe that you'll be most likely to embrace and execute the crisis leadership practices you'll learn about in this book if they are rooted in your everyday leadership and relationships. At the crisis moment, you'll pivot, using the same practices already deeply embedded in your leadership tool box. With precision, you seamlessly adapt what you do to the situation at hand.

Leadership moments and complex problems routinely arise. Workplace leaders face situations demanding change. At home, there are personal issues, life-and-death decisions, disappointments, and transitions. Then there are the life-changing crises—you find yourself in the midst of an active shooter scenario, a terrorist attack, or a weather-related disaster. No matter the situation, when you are the leader, others await your direction and instructions. They count on you to have the confidence to respond effectively.

You own your thinking, behaviors, and actions. Refining them—as you become the leader you hope to be—is the theme of this book. Your life and your career traverse a wide range of human dilemmas, crises, and opportunities. And the way forward isn't simply through the words you find here. You are the starting point for exploring and enhancing your capacity to lead. It's important to be continually reflective and intentional about who you are, what you do, and how you do it. We turn the attention and responsibility upon you, the leader.

Fulfilling your potential as a leader requires a keen awareness and understanding of how your personal experiences—your decisions, stumbles, and triumphs—got you to where you are now. Each prepares you for the moment when "you're it."

Meta-Leadership

The theme of this book—and what we hope you'll achieve—is meta-leadership. This framework and practice method we developed is key to your expedition. You will learn to look at problems, opportunities, and solutions from a "meta-" perspective.

The overarching prefix "meta-" encourages you to seek a bigger picture. You perceive beyond the obvious toward an understanding for how multiple connected factors act and interact with one another. With that, you begin to grasp the complexity of what is going on and you take action. A lot is happening and it demands your attention.

Meta-leadership consists of three dimensions for shaping this holistic view of your leadership:

1. The *person*—you the leader
2. The *situation* in which you lead
3. *Connectivity* in the network of stakeholders you lead

You will learn to use the three dimensions to define the complexities, relationships, and interdependencies that determine your success or failure, and that of the others on your team. The practice method incorporates strategic concepts and practical tools for engaging these stakeholders. Once you master it, you'll work on exercising your leadership effectively throughout your expanding network of influence. Meta-leadership is a force multiplier for all that you and others hope to accomplish together.

The "you" in "you're it" deliberately has a double meaning. On the one hand, "you" is singular, a reference to one person, as in "*you* are the leader." Singular "you" highlights your personal leadership responsibility, accountability, and opportunity. It points to your development, experiences, and learning. The meta-leader is personally willing to assume the challenge of thinking and acting broadly. You are intentional about leading with both depth of understanding and breadth of perspective.

On the other hand, "you" is also plural, referencing the many other people with whom you lead—as in, you *all* share a problem, opportunity, or challenge in which you choose to engage. Together, "you're it." Your meta-leadership manifests in convening people to work collectively on a matter of shared purpose. Plural "you" also refers to being part of following, leveraging, or contributing to others who share complementary objectives. Rallying and engaging people to that meta-purpose emerges from your relationships, mission, and accomplishments and from the trust you build.

In this way, "you're it" is a mutual endeavor to do more than you could do by yourself or as separate entities working in isolation (often called *organizational silos*). The practice of meta-leadership is about forming the plural "you" to achieve the objective. Not everyone grasps the benefit. The meta-leader understands what motivates these many stakeholders and aligns those motives to shape the common you.

This premise shapes our definition of leadership: *People follow you.* And when circumstances require the opposite, the phrase can be reversed: *You follow people.*

Astute meta-leaders grasp this double meaning, which defines and animates both the personal "me" and the collective "we." Your meta-mind-set is one of personal responsibility combined with the strength and advantages of leveraging a wider crowd.

The meta-leadership framework and method grew out of our observations and research conducted with leaders during times of crisis and change, as well as from our own experience leading in routine, day-to-day situations. As a physician, Barry Dorn led the response to life-and-death events and made decisions as a hospital executive. Joe Henderson, following the 9/11 attacks, was a key national leader of CDC bioterrorism preparedness efforts and was later instrumental in reorganizing CDC operations. Eric McNulty and Lenny Marcus have studied numerous US and international crises and change situations. Together we integrate practice realities and academic perspectives into a tool box designed to advance your meta-leadership development.

Through our research, we were given the rare opportunity to accompany leaders—or catch up with them as quickly as possible—as they faced momentous disasters and maneuvered to cope with them. Some leaders rose to the challenge. We learned a great deal from them, and what you read here is a compilation of those insights. We also learned a great deal from leaders who stumbled. From the outset, we never judged an individual as a "good" or "bad" leader. Effectiveness is often circumstance-contingent. Instead, we identified the pitfalls along with the opportunities that leaders and others can expect to face in the midst of a crisis or significant change.

Our work is based at the National Preparedness Leadership Initiative (NPLI), a joint program of the Harvard T. H. Chan School of Public Health and the Harvard Kennedy School of Government's Center for Public Leadership. The NPLI was established shortly after the 9/11 attacks. The federal government asked Harvard University to invest intellectual resources and research in studying and teaching leaders in crisis. Lenny Marcus and David Gergen of the Kennedy School were the founding codirectors. The mandate was to "join the country on the steep learning curve of preparedness and response leadership." Hence, the case illustrations you find here stem from our work in "joining" leaders in the midst of crises.

Our work began with an after-the-fact study and analysis of the 9/11 attacks. Early field research also included on-site observation of the response to Hurricane Katrina in 2005. We later watched our students put the meta-leadership lessons learned into action. Alumni from our NPLI executive crisis leadership program were schooled in meta-leadership and led the CDC response to the first stages of the 2009 H1N1 influenza pandemic in the United States, as well as the response to the Deepwater Horizon oil spill in the Gulf of Mexico in 2010, Super Storm Sandy in 2012, the Boston Marathon bombings in 2013, the domestic response to the outbreak of Ebola virus cases in the United States in 2014, the transformation of the Transportation Security Administration (TSA) in 2016, and the series of devastating hurricanes in 2017. We also observed and interviewed students in the public, private, and nonprofit sectors on their use of meta-leadership in response to more localized crises or predicaments. These were crucible moments for the organizations and communities affected, and certainly crucible moments for the careers of these leaders.

This research took us from practice to theory, not the other way around. We studied the disaster preparation and crisis response actions of leaders in high-stakes, high-pressure situations, as well as during the normal give-and-take of organizational and interpersonal problem-solving. The circumstances through which they led and their openness to our analysis allowed us to observe and assess both their thinking and their actions. From those investigations, we formulated the three dimensions of meta-leadership that can improve the performance of leaders. These dimensions are not a simple checklist or set of characteristics. They are pathways to knowing yourself, the context in which you lead, and the full range of assets, resources, and relationships necessary to succeed.

From Everyday Leadership to Leadership During Change and Crisis

Although meta-leadership was developed through the lens of crisis leadership, its value extends to everyday routine and transformational situations as well. Like Olympic athletes, meta-leaders do not begin their practice and performance on game day. For you, this book is a guide to both the ordinary and the extraordinary.

There is another distinction between meta-leadership and other approaches to leadership. We begin with the belief that no two meta-leaders are identical. Some are introverted, some extroverted. Some are left-brain-dominant, others right-brain-dominant. Whether you work in an entrepreneurial start-up or an established organization, the three dimensions help you fully inhabit yourself as the leader you are truly capable of becoming. We don't believe there's such a thing as a "born leader." Rather, we find that certain personal characteristics can be cultivated and leveraged to enhance your capacities. The most important—and perhaps the most obvious—is your willingness to lead. Combining that with development of your own expansive meta-leadership outlook, you will grow to understand how you—not some mythical perfect leader—can act quickly, confidently, and with maximum effectiveness.

The author and systems theorist R. Buckminster Fuller once asked, "If the success or failure of this planet, and of human beings, depended on how I am and what I do, how would I be? What would I do?" Although you might not cast your endeavors in such grand terms, ask yourself a parallel question: When everything is on the line, how will I be? What will I do? The three dimensions of meta-leadership are a guide to answering these questions in terms distinctly suited to you and the many tests you face as a leader.

To be sure, there are those who, acting in isolation and with detached authority, believe themselves to be "leaders." These individuals believe that the formal authority of a lofty title or position confers the mantle of leadership. They order and they command, viewing their work in transactional, self-serving terms. They expect the world to conform to their expectations. They employ boasting, fantasy, and self-promotion to reaffirm their perceived position. They lie and lack integrity. These people aren't leaders—they're autocrats. We've met and worked with such persons, and no doubt you too have your own book of experiences with the type.

There are others who genuinely perceive, engage, connect, and generate influence far beyond their span of formal authority. They earn the designation of "leader" from their followers. They are authentic. They know and understand themselves and help others do the same. They perceive themselves as part of a larger system. They think deeply. They practice leadership expansively. They grasp a puzzle, shape a strategy, and courageously guide others on a path barely seen.

It is these remarkably captivating people we call *meta*-leaders. You will encounter them throughout this book. You too can choose to be one.

Becoming a Meta-Leader

We, your authors, have woven our perspectives and experiences into the concepts, tools, and stories in this book. The real author of your leadership experience, however, is you. Experience the book. Don't simply read it. If you passively peruse these pages without actively integrating what you learn into your mind-set and practices, you will not derive the full benefit of the time and effort you invest.

Leadership is active, not passive. So too is the process of expanding your leadership capacities and capabilities. We suggest that you keep a journal—a record of your thoughts, experiences, victories, and challenges. It will be a powerful exercise in reflection and revelation as you explore what meta-leadership means to you. We get incredibly positive feedback from our students once they try it. When you keep a journal, you reflect on yourself in ways that are both surprising and reaffirming. You take responsibility. This is part of what "you're it" means.

Your journal doesn't need to be a fancy leather-bound volume, and your entries don't have to go on for pages. You may only jot down a few bullet points at a time. The aim is to learn more about yourself by taking a moment in time to document your experiences as a person and as a meta-leader.

To help, we provide you open-ended questions at the end of each chapter to launch and inspire your thinking. Ideally, you will ask yourself throughout the reading: What am I learning about myself? What am I missing that hinders my ability to accurately assess what is happening around me? How can I learn best from the mistakes I've made? These are tough questions, and many leaders avoid them because they are embarrassing and sometimes painful.

The journal is just for you. It is a gift you give yourself. If our questions don't motivate you, ask yourself different ones. There are no right or wrong questions. Make this book your own, a guide and a challenge to develop knowledge and ways of being a meta-leader when it matters most.

ONE

102 HOURS IN CRISIS

The Boston Marathon Bombings Response

Monday, April 15, 2013, 2:49 p.m., Boston, Massachusetts. It is a mild, sunny day—perfect for running a marathon. The elite runners finished the course a couple of hours earlier. Now the rest of the runners are making their way down Boylston Street to the finish line in front of the Boston Public Library. The flags of every nation with a participating runner flutter above the cheering crowd.

Suddenly, there's a flash and a deafening sound: as a bomb detonates in front of a running store across from the library. The explosion reverberates through the city's historic Back Bay neighborhood. People scream. Others, shocked and confused, are silent. Smoke billows into the air. Fourteen seconds later, a second bomb blast, one block west. Windows shatter. Shrapnel flies. The injured fall to the ground. Everyone realizes that something is horribly wrong. The crowd panics. First responders leap into action.

On Friday, April 19, at 8:42 p.m.—102 hours later—the second of two suspects in the bombings is captured in suburban Watertown, nine miles west of Boylston Street. After an exhaustive manhunt, the terrifying story comes to an end.

In between, 102 hours of grief, grit, heroism, and resilience have passed—102 hours that tested leaders and their followers.

The bombs on Marathon Monday instantly killed three people and injured 264, many with life-threatening wounds. Survivors were dispatched to waiting trauma centers for urgent care. On Tuesday and Wednesday, hospitals treated the wounded, an investigation began, and Boston remained in shock. On Thursday, April 18, law enforcement officials released grainy photos of the suspects, their faces obscured by the brims of their baseball hats. Hours later, the two launched a crime spree, murdering an MIT police officer.

The attacks were the work of two brothers, Tamerlan and Dzhokhar Tsarnaev. Early Friday, Tamerlan died during a wild shoot-out with police officers in Watertown in which another police officer was grievously wounded. Dzhokhar vanished into the night.

The next day a voluntary shelter-in-place directive was issued for the metropolitan area. Boston was a ghost town populated only by law enforcement officers. The exception to the quiet was Watertown, where heavily armed officers worked door-to-door, looking for the younger Tsarnaev. After a daylong manhunt, he was apprehended huddled in a boat stored in the owner's backyard.

There was great tragedy that week. For those who lost loved ones and for those injured, the pain endures.

Leadership Lessons

We studied the leaders of the response to the Boston Marathon bombings, a number of whom were either graduates of the NPLI executive crisis leadership program at Harvard or had participated in meta-leadership seminars we offered locally. These people were eager to share what happened, what they did, how they applied meta-leadership lessons, and what they learned from their experiences. Our research uncovered valuable lessons that can be applied to both crisis and routine conditions. Our interviewees included law enforcement and emergency response officials, political leaders, businesspeople, and citizens—in other words, those who shaped those turbulent hours.

We sought to understand what happened in the response, why it happened, and what impact it had. Our work was exploration. From the outset, we were not sure what we would find.

There were stories of remarkable leadership and courage. Amid the tragedy, there were successes. Despite staggering injuries, all who survived the initial bomb blasts lived, a remarkable achievement resulting from diligent planning and practice by medical responders, care providers, and their leaders. The suspects were captured in 102 hours, ending an ordeal that gripped the city. And Boston was resilient. "Boston Strong"—the slogan that rang through the city and beyond—meant something. That strength was modeled by astute leaders in their behavior and in their interactions. They methodically worked together, exemplifying the principles and practices of meta-leadership. The decisions and actions of these leaders together rallied a city reeling from shock and eager to help.

We opened all our interviews at the same place: the minutes just before the attacks. "It's 2:45 p.m. on Monday, April 15. Where are you and what are you doing?" we asked. And then, "What happened next?"

The responses portrayed an extraordinary series of triumphs. These people had intentionally prepared themselves to lead. What they achieved was by no means an accident. For years, major public events in Boston—Independence Day, New Year's festivities, championship celebrations, and the Marathon itself—had served as practice drills to test system strengths and weaknesses. What if calamity struck? How well would the many different responding organizations and their people work together? These exercises had given leaders the chance to build relationships as they pondered the dire circumstances they might face together. The deliberate exercises readied them to lead.

Their collective experience translated into a sense of leadership confidence. We heard over and over that, with the initial news of the bombings, there was a quick moment of shock. Then, in an instant, their training and preparation rang reassuringly in their minds: *I can do this.* As they moved into action, their faith in others and the system resonated as well: *We can do this.* And they got to work.

Exemplary meta-leadership practices were evident during the event, providing us with important real-world examples and lessons. While you likely will not guide the response to a terrorist attack, these lessons apply to coordinating the high-stakes work of many different people and organizations when both the process and outcome of your combined work is unknowable. The response we observed in the extreme circumstances of the Boston Marathon bombings can inform day-to-day leadership scenarios as well. We found consistent principles and practices that you can harness to increase the collective success of the endeavors you lead. We share and explore these findings in later chapters of the book.

Leadership Is Personal

Boston Emergency Medical Services (EMS) director Jimmy Hooley was in the city-block-long Alpha medical tent just beyond the Marathon finish line. "I heard the first explosion, and I thought it was a propane tank from one of the street vendors, or maybe a car backfiring. Then I heard the second explosion and I knew right away it was an attack," he told us.

Shortly before the Marathon bombings, Jim Hooley and Lenny Marcus had one of their periodic conversations about Jim's leadership. He had moved up the ranks of Boston EMS from paramedic to chief. A quiet, hardworking guy, Jim leads more by example than by charisma. During that conversation, Jim shared that being a leader is work for him. "Sometimes, if I am at a mass casualty event, I have to remind myself to assume that leadership position. My instinct tells me to get on the ground and treat people. That's what I do and what I am good at. Leading for me takes effort."

Leading EMS is a complex endeavor. Some ambulances are part of the city fleet, while others belong to a variety of private companies, all using a central 911 dispatch center. Having learned from bombings elsewhere in the world, Hooley knew that it was critical to distribute the injured across the multiple trauma centers in the city lest any single hospital become overwhelmed. He also knew that those with minor injuries were likely to get themselves to hospitals—and in advance of the ambulances with more serious cases. Coordination was required with police and fire officials. He also knew that the confused and panicked crowds would present a constant risk of distraction.

Fortunately, Hooley and other leaders had thought through the decisions they would need to make. Plans were in place and they had rehearsed their actions, so they all understood what was expected of them and what they could expect from others. They had built trust-based relationships with each other. On that April day, all that planning, practice and persistence paid off.

Eleven days after the bombings, Jim and Lenny met up again. That prior conversation was still fresh. After exchanging greetings, Lenny merely asked, "So . . . ?" "I was the leader," Jim replied. "It was tough, but I realized we had to get this right. One of the people was dying, and I had this urge to get on the ground and work on her. But I didn't. Somebody had to keep the eye on the big picture and that was me, the leader. We had to get those people out of there and in the right order, and I was on top of that. I was also thinking, *What if there is another bomb?* I had to figure out what we would do next. Yeah, I stayed the leader." This was Jim Hooley's "you're it" moment. He grasped the responsibility. He led intentionally.

Boston Strong

Our research on the leadership response to the bombings exposed stirring examples of heroism, goodwill, discipline, humility, and trust. People were purposeful. Themes of collaboration, big-picture understanding, and personal grit emerged as we reviewed what happened and sought to understand why. Our goal was to learn about those leaders and their meta-leadership. We sought principles that could be applied more broadly in other leadership settings.

A bond was created among these agency and political leaders. The power of "Boston Strong" arose from the shared and united purpose that radiated from these leaders to the community and back. Yes, there were rivalries that could have created distractions and led to miscalculations. Boston relishes competition: between law enforcement agencies, across academic medical centers, and among federal, state, and local authorities. This is not to say that there was not some of that. However, competition did not define those 102 hours. These leaders transcended their differences, intuitively recognizing that they would be stronger and more effective if they worked together—and that they and the city would be weaker if they worked independently or at cross-purposes. They set a tone early on and sustained it throughout that week. In simple yet profound terms, the terrorists—the bad guys—were "them." Everyone else was "us." The response drew its strength from that embracing sense of interpersonal connection, assistance, and reassurance.

Within minutes of the explosions, a makeshift emergency operations center was set up at the nearby Westin Hotel. Hundreds of emergency responders gathered. Governor Deval Patrick and key senior leaders convened in a smaller conference room. There were important decisions to be made, among them: who leads the investigation? The governor later explained to us, "I come from a prosecutorial background. I knew there needed to be someone in charge of the investigation. And everyone needed to be behind that person."

There were potentially sensitive city-state-federal jurisdictional frictions in play. Governor Patrick therefore wanted to get the leaders on board together. He first informally polled those gathered around the table. There was consensus that the investigation should be led by the FBI special agent in charge, Rick DesLauriers. Then, like a flight attendant addressing passengers seated in the exit row of a plane, the governor looked each leader in the eye and asked, "Are you okay with Rick DesLauriers leading the investigation?" He waited for a verbal yes and then moved to the next person. Everyone said yes. DesLauriers was in charge of the investigation.

We later interviewed DesLauriers about his experience that week. As we systematically progressed through the sequence of activities, we came to the key decision to keep the public transit system open that Monday, just after the bombings. "Where were you?" we asked.

"I wasn't there," he replied.

"But the governor said you were in charge," we observed.

"I was in charge of the investigation, not the overall operation."

"Then who was in charge of the operation?" He pondered the question for a moment and then answered—himself somewhat puzzled—"Well, I guess no one."

That response perplexed us. We had conducted numerous studies of leaders in times of major national crises, and there was always an identified leader in charge of the operation. During Hurricane Katrina, it was the director of FEMA, Michael Brown. During the H1N1 crisis, it was Dr. Richard Besser, acting director of the CDC. And during the Deepwater Horizon oil spill, it was Coast Guard commandant Admiral Thad Allen. We had observed and interviewed these leaders in the midst of those crises.

As we reviewed our notes about the Boston bombing response, we realized that DesLauriers was right. There was no one identified operational leader in charge of the whole the event. Governor Patrick was a strong, respected political presence with expansive authority over some agencies, although many entities were beyond his purview. He succeeded in establishing the tone of collaboration from the get-go that became the standard for the group of leaders working together. Numerous agency leaders were responsible for the work of their individual organizations; however, there was no one leader who consistently was in charge of everything. How could that be? Without an overarching incident commander, how was the response as successful as it was?

Swarm Leadership

As we puzzled through our interviews and notes to find an explanation, Eric walked into Lenny's office and simply said, "Swarm intelligence."

What is swarm intelligence? Briefly here (in Chapter 8 on connectivity, we go into more depth on swarm leadership), swarm intelligence describes how creatures intuitively accomplish remarkable tasks when no one of them is in charge. Operating in a defined structure, such as a colony or flock, they follow a consistent, shared set of innate rules and social cues that guide decision-making and actions. Picture birds flying in a formation. No one bird directs the flock, and yet they fly in synchrony. Fish swimming in schools are similar. Ants and termites find and build elaborate nesting sites. Each ant operates according to a uniform set of innate, hardwired behaviors. The Harvard sociobiologist E. O. Wilson has written: "If you look at all the species that have ever lived on planet Earth, the most successful were ants, termites, bees and people. Why? Because they're the greatest cooperators."

Although much has been written about organizational design and other structural approaches to encouraging positive connectivity, we discovered that there has been little investigation into the behavioral elements of crisis leadership. So we reviewed what we learned about leaders during the Boston bombing response, looking for patterns to explain their thinking and actions. We were able to discern pieces of a complex puzzle about order and control, following the clue that DesLauriers shared. What explained the heroic acts to save lives after the blasts? How was it that competing organizations cooperated so well? How did they come to so tenaciously trust one another given all the risks and difficult decisions of the week? Were there intuitive principles and rules that guided these leaders and followers? Might there be an innate human force that mirrors the behavior and interactions of simpler creatures?

Then we discovered that each interviewee's experience followed a specific sequence of events characterized by five key points. The first was a focus on saving lives, a theme that captured the *unity of mission* motivating the leaders we interviewed. Rescuers, civilians, and investigators were willing to risk their own lives to save others. The second was the *generosity of spirit and action* pervading their actions. They assisted others and others helped them. The third was how the organizations interacted by *staying in their own lanes.* Each set of responders knew what their own job was and what the others' jobs were. They did not intrude upon others' scope of responsibility or authority; rather, they helped one another succeed. Fourth, people would later describe the leaders' respectful behavior and interactions as *no ego—no blame.* And finally, they relied on the strong, long-term, *trust-based relationships* that were already in place before the bombings.

We combined these observations into the five principles of swarm leadership during the Boston Marathon bombings response. We then shared our observations with the leaders we interviewed. Rick DesLauriers of the FBI typified their reactions: "Yes, that describes exactly what we were doing, though I didn't realize it at the time."

The Three Dimensions of Meta-Leadership

Had any one of the leaders sought to assert control over other leaders, the process and outcome could have been very different. Yes, each leader oversaw his or her own organization and its chain of command. However, the connectivity in how they worked together created leverage that exceeded what any one leader could have accomplished alone; connectivity fostered order beyond control.

These leaders together were able to find and achieve a complex equilibrium that extended to the broader community, emanating to those who were part of the official response system—law enforcement, health workers, and government officials—and out to volunteers, businesses, and citizens who willingly aligned with the game plan. In the face of a terrifying event, they generated a shared commitment and bountiful goodwill. Drawing on a collective impulse, leaders of the response set a tone and sustained it.

How do the actions and outcomes of the response to the Boston Marathon bombings reflect the thinking and practices of meta-leadership?

"Meta-" means "transforming," "beyond," "above," and "at a higher level." These leaders functioned with a wide, meta-awareness of what they were doing. Though each operated from the base of his or her organization's authority and responsibilities, everyone's overriding commitment was to the shared mission and the enterprise-wide collaboration that could get it done. What they did together illustrates the workings of meta-leadership.

As mentioned earlier, there are three dimensions of meta-leadership practice. The first is *the person*. In Boston, the leaders' emotional intelligence and capacity to engage bonded their work in unity of purpose. Though "no ego—no blame" emerged late in our interviews, many commented that without it, the necessary collaboration would have collapsed. These leaders were grounded and shared an overriding commitment to the tasks at hand. They were keenly aware of their personal responsibility in the challenge that faced them.

The second dimension of meta-leadership is *the situation*. These leaders faced a "VUCA" scenario: Volatile, Uncertain, Complex, and Ambiguous. Another attack could have happened at any time. It was not clear who were the perpetrators: self-styled terrorists working alone, or members of a larger cell planning further attacks? Leaders had to be ready for what could come next with little notion of what it might be. The bombings were bad enough—what if the response didn't measure up? Numerous agencies and organizations were involved, and the task of coordination was enormously complex. And for many major decisions, there were no obviously correct answers. Leaders did their best to anticipate how the situation would evolve and the decisions and actions that lay ahead, while also preparing themselves to pivot depending on what occurred. With the bad guys on the loose, they had to be ready for anything.

These leaders had two crises on their hands. Both situations were dangerous and required that leaders account for numerous unknowns. On day one, the crisis was a terrorist attack on Boylston Street—a scenario they had drilled for. On day five, the crisis was a massive manhunt in Watertown—an unforeseen scenario. The word *chaos* was not mentioned in their accounts of day one. Most everyone spoke of "chaos" in describing the confrontation and manhunt on day five.

The third dimension of meta-leadership is *connectivity* of effort. There was a brief hesitation as leaders got together on day one; everyone was first concerned with checking in with their colleagues. By day five, these leaders had learned that the better and more quickly connected they were, the better coordinated, responsive, and adaptive the operation would be, no matter what happened. As the manhunt unfolded on day five, the leaders immediately convened. Forging that connectivity enabled them to effectively *lead down* to their reports, *lead up* to their bosses, *lead across* to colleagues within their organization, and *lead beyond* to people outside their organization's chain of command. They were together. Connectivity marked the operation.

Despite the enormity of the extraordinary circumstances they faced, they unleashed "swarm leadership" that defined their work together. The spirit of their collaboration radiated out to the public, fortifying the resilience of a stricken city—the essence of "Boston Strong."

How might you incorporate these principles and practices into your own meta-leadership? That is the theme of the coming pages.

Questions for Journaling

➤ Have you been involved in situations in which the principles and rules of swarm leadership emerged? It need not have been a crisis: a sports team, place of worship, work group, neighborhood, or family can all exhibit swarm qualities.

➤ Have you been in situations in which swarm leadership could have emerged, though it was frustrated by a violation of one of the principles—for example, "no ego—no blame"?

➤ Reviewing what the leaders accomplished in the response to the Boston Marathon bombings, what are your observations on the dimensions of meta-leadership in practice: the person, the situation, and connectivity of action? Have you observed a similar scenario of "order beyond control"?

TWO

· · · · · · · · · · · · · · · · ·

SEIZE THE OPPORTUNITY

You're It!

As a kid, "you're it" was a designation in a game of tag. You ran. You avoided getting tagged. You moved quickly. And what happened when you became "it"? In that moment, your perspective changed, your view of others shifted, and your strategy was instantly transformed. There was a physical and emotional shift. You were suddenly the center of attention.

If you dreaded being "it," this transition was unnerving. If you relished showing your speed and agility, however, you jumped at the opportunity. You felt a burst of adrenaline as you charged off to tag someone else.

As a leader, "you're it" has a differently nuanced meaning: You are responsible for more than just yourself. People are counting on you, from your subordinates to your boss, from your peers and your collaborators to your customers, your suppliers, and perhaps even the general public. *You* guide and inspire the action. *You* gather and sift complex and contradictory information. *You* seek clarity. *You* craft a vision. *You* make decisions.

It's up to you to achieve success. If things don't go well, you fail. Everyone is looking to you.

There is more than one way to become "it." Often you are "it" by virtue of title and job responsibility. Sometimes, it is more by circumstance than by label; you might just be at the right place at the right time. When the moment comes, you seize it. There is no one else to do the job. You shirk neither the responsibility nor the opportunity. You are the leader and everyone depends on you. You truly are "it."

Just as in the game of tag, when you are "it," your perspective and strategy must change. There is a task to achieve, a challenge to overcome. Your understanding of what is at your disposal and how to best leverage it needs to evolve quickly. You learn to think and see beyond the limited options on the table. You find alternatives that others haven't. Then you figure out what has to be done and chart a path—along with others—to get there.

If you are a true meta-leader, you don't shy away from being "it." If you are part of a team of people, you are all "it" together. You leverage both the singular and plural meanings of "you." You can be many people leading together. You will be ready when a crisis inevitably arrives. And when that happens, it will be up to you to pivot and lead.

The "You're It" Moment

April 20, 2010, Washington, DC. In just one month, Admiral Thad Allen, commandant of the United States Coast Guard, was due to retire, ending a storied four-decade career with the service. Allen had risen through the ranks and weathered numerous crises along the way. Years earlier, President George W. Bush had asked him to assume command of one of the worst disaster management debacles of modern times: the troubled Hurricane Katrina response in 2005. *Time* magazine later called him "the hero of the Gulf" for his leadership.

Late that evening, in the Gulf of Mexico, an explosion ripped through the Deepwater Horizon oil drilling rig leased by BP. Eleven men lost their lives immediately. The explosion dislodged the pipe below the platform, which spewed oil and gas uncontrollably into the waters of the Gulf. Coast Guard crews responded to the fire on the drilling platform, and a regional response began. Leaders in the field soon sensed that this event might be bigger than just another rig accident. In the days ahead, those fears proved to be prophetic.

Fast-forward to April 30. Allen's home phone rang late that night. It was Department of Homeland Security secretary Janet Napolitano, calling on behalf of President Barack Obama, to ask for his leadership. With the oil leak undiminished and the ecosystem imperiled, a political crisis was brewing. The next day, May 1, Allen was named national incident commander for the Deepwater Horizon oil spill response. His job: coordinate the many federal, state, and local government agencies involved and ensure that the legally designated "responsible party"—those who did the drilling—took the necessary steps to clean up the mess. Allen became the public face of the massive effort.

"'You're it' describes exactly how I felt," Allen told us later. "It was a crisis that demanded meta-leadership." Allen is an enthusiast for the meta-leadership framework, as it captures much of his own leadership practice throughout his career. The admiral first met Lenny Marcus as he was taking over the Katrina response. Admiral Allen became a frequent speaker at the Harvard National Preparedness Leadership Initiative executive crisis leadership program.

Allen explained that the oil spill itself was the most straightforward part of the operation. They had identified BP, which had suffered its own losses, as the "responsible party." Paradoxically, BP was both at fault and in sole possession of the technical knowledge and equipment needed to correct the situation. Meanwhile, Washington elected officials and every governor along the coast, as well as many local officials, wanted to show themselves to be protecting their constituents. They were pressing for fast resolution of the crisis. Besides the political pressure, the media was primed to stoke emotions and to headline any missteps.

"In the midst of all that," Allen recalled, "we had to figure out how to link everyone to get things done, [plug] a well five thousand feet underwater— far away from any human contact—and [calm] political sensitivities. I was aware throughout that there was no guarantee that we would accomplish the hoped-for ending."

The most troubling realization hit just as they were about to cap and seal the blown well head spouting oil at the bottom of the Gulf. Scientists estimated a 20 percent chance that the compressed pressure of the surge might crack open the surrounding ocean floor, unleashing a colossal and uncontrollable mass of oil into the sea. Catastrophe was on the horizon. Admiral

Allen understood well that possibility and the limited actions he or anyone else could take to prevent the worst from happening. Admiral Allen was "it." And so he led.

Influence Beyond Authority

Meta-leadership is a strategy and practice method designed to expand the impact of your leadership. It is both conceptually rigorous and intensely practical. It guides being, thinking, and doing.

Meta-leaders build an intentionally wide and deep understanding of themselves and the situations they face. They are self-aware and curious. They develop a 360-degree, multidimensional perspective on the people around them and on their relationships with those people. Seeing connections and interdependencies everywhere, meta-leaders foster this same consciousness in those who follow them. With this understanding of the surrounding complexities, they have a long reach as they lead followers to overcome challenges and seize opportunities.

Meta-leaders wield influence well beyond their formal authority. They not only understand the problem or opportunity itself: they grasp the different meaning it has for each of the many people involved. They weave together significant themes, clarifying overall purpose and values to keep an array of people aligned in synchronous motion. Those who follow meta-leaders discover that they are part of a mission and purpose larger than any one person or organization alone. It is inspiring to follow such a leader.

To lead means that people follow you. For your followers, "you're it." They are part of "it" because they are with you. They are looking for a leader, and you can be that leader with or without a formal title or authority. People will follow you if they believe in you and in what you hope to accomplish— and if they have confidence that you believe in them. They trust that, together, you will achieve the shared goal. Through both process and outcome, you can help them bring meaning into their lives.

To lead is more than just managing or commanding. Leadership is defined through behavior and attitude, not role or rank. Successful organizations large and small have leaders dispersed throughout the ranks and intentionally invest to develop those leaders throughout their careers.

Former Coca-Cola CEO Muhtar Kent described it this way: "I learned that everyone has the innate capacity to lead. Leadership isn't just a trait found at the very top of an organization. I have seen truly extraordinary leadership at all levels of our organization and from all types of people." Coca-Cola is hardly unique in this regard. No matter where in your system you sit now, you can lead.

Is this daunting? Sure. The meta-leadership perspective helps you comprehend the whole of a leadership puzzle as well as its parts. These skills and the mind-set can be learned.

Ultimately, you'll be able to apply the principles of meta-leadership to your own circumstances and persona in a way that works best for you. It's not a single set of prescribed steps. Think of it more as a way to better perceive yourself and what is happening around you; to more fully assess the meaning and implications of your leading; to more accurately identify patterns of activity and better predict what could happen next; and then to reach decisions and take action. You embed these proficiencies into your everyday leadership repertoire so that when you're hit by crisis, change, or any moment that matters, you are ready, like Admiral Allen, to pivot into action. What works for you on a routine day is ready when the routine shifts to the unpredictable.

The Three Dimensions of Meta-Leadership

There are three dimensions to the discipline of meta-leadership—you the leader, the situation, and connectivity. You lead many stakeholders: those who report to you, others to whom you report, and all the other necessary individuals, partners, and entities over whom you may have little or no formal authority. Meta-leadership derives its strength from seamlessly weaving together these dimensions. And when "you're it," these three dimensions together are a rich resource for charting both your challenges and your opportunities.

The first dimension of meta-leadership is you the person—you as the leader. How well do you know yourself? How do you make sense of all that surrounds you? How do you define yourself as a leader? What do you do as a leader, and what don't you do?

Your emotions come into play. Do you display emotional intelligence? What do you do about the emotions of others whom you lead? Can you exercise self-discipline in the ongoing task of seeking balance? When "you're it," events move rapidly and everyone is counting on you. There is much to grasp and many in need of guidance. And not everyone and everything is on your side. There are those who hope you will fail. Being "it" is rarely easy, and yet it can be very rewarding.

The second dimension of meta-leadership is the situation—the objective reality of what is happening "out there." The situation is the context and environment in which you must lead and in which you and others must face uncertain circumstances, demands, and dilemmas. When "you're it," you are handed a situation that, more often than not, is a bad one. You are expected to grasp and understand it in all its complexity. And then you're expected to change that situation, by improving it, overcoming it, defeating it, or making the most of it. Situations are often dynamic. There is much to accomplish, and time is usually of the essence.

The third dimension of meta-leadership is connectivity, which has four facets. Each facet has distinctive power and authority dynamics.

The Dimensions of Meta-Leadership

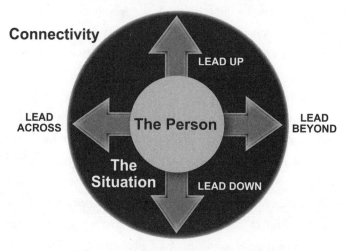

Connectivity

LEAD UP

LEAD ACROSS — The Person — LEAD BEYOND

The Situation — LEAD DOWN

"How can I make you a success?"

The Four Facets of Connectivity

The first facet of connectivity is *leading down*—that is, directing and supervising others. The bulk of the literature on leadership is about how to better motivate and manage the performance of those under your authority. Many leaders expect obedience and can't figure out how to get it. Meta-leaders appreciate that to gain the commitment and loyalty of subordinates, they must first be committed and loyal *to them*. When "you're it" for people who call you "boss," the first question should be, "How can I make each of you a success?" If the people you supervise succeed, then you are much more likely to succeed in what you're all trying to accomplish together.

The second facet reverses this equation: *leading up* refers to your own boss or the constituency to which you are responsible. If, like most people, you work in a hierarchical organization, it is clear who is boss. If you are an elected official, your bosses are hard-to-please voters. If you are a CEO, your bosses are the directors on your board, your company's investors, *and* your customers.

The person or people you report to will have expectations for your performance. They have ways in which they would like to be treated and kept informed. They know what decisions they want to make and what decisions they prefer that you make on your own. Your job is not only to figure this all out—that alone would be relatively simple. You must also intentionally influence and actively participate in the framing of the relationship. Influence well beyond your authority depends in part on your ability to persuade your boss, or bosses, to support you and champion what you hope to accomplish, leveraging their influence, decisions, and actions.

The third facet of meta-leadership connectivity is *leading across* to the departments, business units, and other parts within your institutional base. These are filled with people who operate within the same hierarchical and governance structure as you. Here, your intraorganizational efforts extend across different internal boundaries and functions. Each of these offices, departments, and functions, and each person within them, operates within a formally linked structure. In many organizations, there is some shared measure of control and authority as all involved presumably work toward common purposes. Despite that system, you may face specialized groups—such as innovation units, field operations, or legal functions—that prize autonomy over broad collaboration. Silo-based reward and recognition incentives foster rivalries that impede teamwork. Peers compete to rise within the hierarchy. And there are grabs for finite internal resources. You discover how to work—and sometimes fight—inside your castle walls to advance your objectives while respecting larger organizational goals.

Your first commitment is to the unit you lead or manage—your "home team"—just as you also contribute to companywide activities. Your one piece of the bigger organizational picture contributes to the "meta-success" of your enterprise. In business, this means that marketing, production, and distribution must work together if a company expects to deliver success.

The fourth and final facet is *leading beyond* the four walls of your organization to reach the people, institutions, and communities that are part of or important to your overall endeavors. This is *enterprise* meta-leadership. The interorganizational meta-leadership challenge is to find or create a compelling common purpose among people not connected by the same formal reporting chain or governance structure.

The power and authority dynamics differ greatly between leading across and leading beyond. In leading across, the stakeholders are united by shared interests, including reputation, share price or other metrics, and allegiance to the same chief executive. That formal linkage is not present with those you lead beyond.

Leading beyond requires that you understand, respect, and acknowledge the legitimate interests of a variety of stakeholders. It's important to build common purpose, leveraging your influence in the absence of authority over others. For example, Paul Bulcke, then CEO of Nestlé and now chairman of the board, called in 2015 for a broad, multi-stakeholder strategy for global nutrition and food security. In an opinion piece published by the World Economic Forum, he argued that collaboration is the only potential solution to a system-scale challenge that includes wide-ranging issues such as nutrition, health care, housing, and climate change. The stakeholders are governments, nonprofits, communities, and businesses, from massive global companies like Nestlé to small farmers. He committed Nestlé to playing a leadership role in that larger enterprise endeavor by providing "a robust framework for farmer livelihood and community development" as well as investment in rural education.

No one controls all the many facets, relationships, and people that make up a complex system. No one can directly command all those who can be brought together to achieve something extraordinary or tackle an overwhelming problem—not even presidents or chief executives. That challenge requires order beyond control.

To coordinate the efforts of all these people is a profound challenge. Forging the collective "you" requires building connectivity of effort across many different sectors, leveraging influence well beyond whatever formal authority is invested in a single person or position.

Meta-leaders craft the unifying mission for an array of different constituencies. They build a compelling narrative and create conditions that animate shared values, motivating goals, and each participant's view of himself or herself as a necessary and meaningful contributor. Meta-leaders know that optimal progress does not happen on its own. Someone must see the opportunity and engage others to see it as well.

Connectivity in Practice

Meta-leaders align organizational strategies, operations, and frontline work. If done right, connectivity becomes deeply embedded in organizational culture. Both philosophically and pragmatically, when you are simultaneously leading down, up, across, and beyond, you forge enterprise thinking, acting, and assessment, within your organization and beyond.

Southwest Airlines offers an example of this sort of alignment. Its vision for success is built on top-notch customer satisfaction. Their stock symbol is LUV, reflecting their love for their customers as well as their original home at Love Field in Dallas, Texas. Southwest's standards are exemplified in its slogan: "Warrior's Spirit. Servant's Heart. Fun-Loving Attitude."

Southwest executives know that travelers' experiences with people such as gate agents and flight attendants are critical to the company's success. Travelers don't interact with the CEO—it's the frontline employees who transmit the values of the company. This is why Southwest has committed to treating employees the same way it expects them to treat their customers.

At Southwest, people are an asset, not a cost. Flight attendants are empowered to lead within their domain as much as executives lead from headquarters. Happy, engaged employees treat customers well and solve problems autonomously. Ticket pricing is straightforward and fees for extras are minimal, reducing stress on both customers and employees. There is clarity of purpose, values, and performance expectations. Leadership flows from vision through operations and logistics. At Southwest, "you're it" is about everybody. Results flow as well: Southwest has long been the most profitable of the US air carriers.

How does meta-leadership fit into your other leadership learning and experiences? As you'll see in the pages ahead, we have integrated our work with both classic and contemporary thinking about leadership. We are grateful for and acknowledge the contributions of countless researchers, educators, and executives. However, much of the existing literature and research—as much as 85 percent by one estimate in the *Harvard Business Review*—focuses on leading in hierarchies. An understanding of hierarchical leadership alone is too narrow to inform many of the practical situations that leaders face today.

The most common and daunting leadership opportunities and challenges now arise amid the complex systems and networks of diverse organizations. Each organization accomplishes one piece of the product service or deliverable. Supply chains are global. It takes dozens of companies to piece together your smartphone. Organizations rely on freelancers, contractors, and outsourced vendors. Strategic alliances are common. Communication, commerce, and operations are increasingly conducted digitally. The many different organizations, people, and problems encompassed by these systems are not, by their very nature, calibrated to work together smoothly. This is why the concepts of connectivity and leverage are central to meta-leadership. Although people and situations cannot always be controlled, they can be aligned into a productive order.

This central idea of a widely cast net of connections is why we chose "people follow you" as the definition of meta-leadership. To illustrate, we return to the Gulf of Mexico and the Deepwater Horizon spill.

Admiral Allen had little choice. To successfully prevail over the disgorging oil with all its ecological, political, economic, and social implications, he would have to create a collective "you" out of the many people and organizations reluctant to see themselves on the same side of this problem.

When he stepped into his leadership role, there was much to overcome. The public was angry. One typical sign seen in Grand Isle, Louisiana, derided BP: CANNOT FISH OR SWIM: HOW THE HELL ARE WE SUPPOSED TO FEED OUR KIDS NOW?

Yet Allen couldn't simply demonize and discount BP executives. He needed them on his side to help clean up the mess. He knew that it would be impossible to stop the leak without the company's experience, equipment, and expertise.

Governors of the affected states, all Republicans, were fighting to snatch the finite protective resources being overseen by the Democratic Obama administration. The attitude was, "Get a boom on *my* shoreline." In Louisiana, Plaquemines Parish president Billy Nungesser was among the vocal local leaders deriding the entire federal response, saying, "These guys have no clue and no ability to think outside the box." He was a regular guest on the national news shows. The fishing and tourism industries lamented the millions of dollars of business they were losing every day. One local real estate broker called the spill a "sucker punch" as coastal property sales and rentals ground to a halt.

Not only was Admiral Allen "it," he had to convince everyone who was part of or affected by the operation to see that they were critical to the solution as well. As a meta-leader, he had to overcome the shortsighted belief that only he, the official national incident commander, could surmount all the problems involved in countering the oil spill. BP was both the legally designated "responsible party" and an ally to engage. So too were the governors, local leaders, and the many federal agencies that were part of the mammoth response. Engaging all of these people constructively was more vexing than the enormous engineering challenges involved in stopping the spill. These were the very people whom he needed within the collection of followers, and getting them to work together was the essence of the meta-leadership challenge.

Eventually Admiral Allen succeeded. The hole at the bottom of the Gulf was plugged, and the ecological damage, though significant, was more limited than it otherwise could have been.

Why Do You Lead?

Why do you lead? Everyone has a different answer to this question. Most speak to what makes life meaningful. Making meaning is at the heart of the human experience. For some, life's meaning comes in finding a purpose and trying to make a difference in society. For others, meaning is measured in money and market dominance. Meaning can be about achieving power, becoming recognized, righting wrongs, overcoming strife, finding excitement, preserving a tradition, or molding a new one. Some people embrace an organization's mission as their own. What is your answer?

Meta-leaders are distinguished by the passion and commitment they bring to their quest for meaning: it motivates and engages others.

People follow leaders because they help in that search for meaning. It might be a political leader, a spiritual leader, a business leader, or an artistic leader. People rally behind these leaders even though they may not pay their wages or supervise their work. Picture the leaders who inspire you and whom you follow. You believe in them and see your aspirations in theirs. You appreciate that they recognize your value. You do more than simply show up when such leaders motivate and acknowledge your efforts. You share and amplify their passion.

There is something extraordinarily fulfilling in following people who effectively and creatively shape solutions and who, at the same time, really care about those around them. Such leadership motivates performance and loyalty that exceeds any job description or evaluation. Meta-leading in this way is synergistically meaningful. It is satisfying in its accomplishments for you, and it is equally satisfying for the people you lead. We found just that when we met and later followed Dr. Suraya Dalil.

It takes enormous commitment and courage to stand up and be the leader.

Every year during Harvard's January winter session, we teach an intensive leadership class for graduating master's students. On day one, we tell students that after lunch they will present an introductory speech as the highest-ranking professional official in their state or country. It is their first day on the job, and in five minutes they are to review their background, their objectives for the job, and how they will achieve them. Afterwards, students and faculty critique each speech and offer comments. We videotape the session and its discussion, and after class students are expected to watch their performance. It's an intentionally challenging assignment and experience.

One year, as students stood up to head for lunch and their speech preparation, Dr. Suraya Dalil, a physician from Afghanistan, approached us. She was annoyed. "How can you expect me to give a speech as the public health minister from Afghanistan? Can't you see? I am a woman. No woman would ever be in such a position in my country." We asked her to give it a try, suggesting that she think of this leader position as an aspiration.

After lunch, Suraya reluctantly went through the motions. Her speech was mechanical. Her ambitions for improving health in her nation were narrow. She was thinking from the perspective of a single clinic rather than a country. She was nervous and showed little confidence in herself and the vision she had for the job.

On Friday, as the weeklong class comes to a conclusion, students once again give a speech. This time they choose who they are and who they are addressing as their audience. By that point in the class, they have experienced and learned the whole of the meta-leadership curriculum through interactive exercises, lectures, and discussion. We often find a new sense of leadership confidence and commitment among the students.

That Friday, Suraya again introduced herself as the new Afghan minister of public health. This time she belted out her speech with a bold vision for maternal and child health for the nation. She had a plan to raise health standards for the whole of the population. She was definitive, directed, and pragmatic.

These speeches are ultimately evaluated by a simple criterion: Will people follow you? As Suraya concluded, the classroom of students and faculty cheered and jumped to their feet in a standing ovation. Four months later, at the 2005 Harvard graduation, it was announced that she would soon return to her country and become Afghanistan's deputy minister of public health. Five years later, when the position became available, she was promoted to minister. Dr. Dalil served from 2010 to 2014, and in 2015 she was appointed the Afghan permanent representative to the United Nations, the first woman in the post.

Dr. Suraya Dalil was transformed into a devoted advocate for the health and well-being of the war-torn population of her country. Recognizing the importance of presence despite the dangers, she regularly traveled to areas hard hit by devastation and terrorist attacks, both to learn what happened and to support survivors in their recovery and resilience.

She later told us, "I realized that it is so easy to trap into day to day activities, like signing papers. They are easy, they don't question you a lot. Or doing the easy things that don't challenge you because you are comfortable with them. But then I realized, what did you produce? The number of signatures on a piece of paper? So I . . . made a commitment to myself to do one thing every day that scares me. That I normally don't do it. Or that I am not very comfortable doing it. But they are important. They are important for decision-making. They are important for that job. They are important for the people."

Commitment and courage.

Meta-leadership is both a skill and an art.

Here you'll find the model, methods, and thinking that can help you enrich your skills and understanding. How you incorporate all of this into your personal and professional repertoire is a matter of your unique style, your character, and the artistry of how you lead.

There is much to learn from leaders who have mastered the art of motivating and engaging people to do and accomplish far more than they otherwise could have dreamed. Much can also be learned from mistakes and failures. This lesson in part explains Dr. Suraya Dalil's transformation from day one of that winter session class to the last day. And in how she transformed her academic learning into real-life leading.

What can meta-leadership mean for you? Seek to find what others cannot. Galvanize your courage. Imagine. Dream. And then bring others along for the adventure.

You're it. It is time to lead.

Questions for Journaling

➤ Why do you want to lead? What do you hope to accomplish?

➤ Recall a situation when you were "it." What did you learn from the experience?

➤ Similarly, recall a moment when someone else was "it." What happened with that person, and why? What does this memory mean for you?

THREE

COMPLEXITY IS . . .

Okay, pardon a bit of hometown baseball pride as we (Eric, Barry, and Lenny) recall the 2004 Boston Red Sox. (Unfortunately for the rest of us, Joe is a Yankees fan.) It was the year when the team broke the eighty-six-year-long World Series losing streak known as the "Curse of the Bambino," a reference to the 1920 sale of legendary baseball star Babe Ruth by the Red Sox to the New York Yankees.

All professional baseball teams have the same number of players. The 2004 Red Sox roster did not represent an outsize number of superstars. In fact, team members described themselves as a "bunch of idiots." Yet together they overcame a seemingly insurmountable three-game deficit against the archrival New York Yankees to win the American League Championship Series and then swept the St. Louis Cardinals in four games to win the World Series.

For Joe and our readers who are not Red Sox fans, we note the contrast in the 2012 team. Red Sox management spent lavishly to put together what appeared on paper to be a dream team. They finished in last place, twenty-six games behind the division-winning Yankees.

What was the difference between those two teams, and what does it have to do with meta-leadership? It was the relationships between the players that were different, not simply the talents of the individuals.

Every team, organization, community, or swarm you lead is a complex adaptive system. To lead, you must grasp three basic concepts: systems, complexity, and adaptive capacity. In this chapter, we introduce these concepts, show their relationships, and apply each to meta-leadership thinking and practices. As you read, consider how they apply to the work you do.

Systems, Complexity, and Adaptation: Keeping Track of All That Is Going On

A *system* is a collection of connected parts that work or move together. Shift one piece and others are affected, some subtly and others profoundly. A new law, a different leader, or a shocking disaster exposes how one changed component of a system affects the others. By shifting priorities, these new factors redefine what is important, what gets attention, and what does not. Actions and events are connected even if the moderating dynamics are not readily apparent.

Complexity characterizes the multiple and varied interactions between the parts in a system. Change one relationship and the cascading effects are hard to trace. Some of that complexity is visible, while other, intricately related aspects are difficult, if not impossible, to perceive. No one person or entity is in charge of a complex situation. Many factors affect what happens. A perfect example of complexity in action would be the stock market, whose gyrations are driven by national policies, individual company actions, analyst predictions, and investor attitudes.

A situation becomes more complex when human factors, idiosyncratic phenomena, and difficult-to-know forces are in the mix. Bosses, subordinates, and colleagues are often puzzling and unpredictable, and all the more so when difficult personalities interact.

Adaptive capacity is the ability to change in response to fluctuating conditions and pressures. To adapt, you need to recognize what has changed as well as the effects of those changes. Adaptive capacity is closely linked to the survival instinct. Those able to adapt, survive. Those who can't adapt, do not. For example, changes in technology, the economy, the market, and the population require businesses to adapt. Organizations that adapt to survive often enhance their place in dynamic markets. Organizations that fail to recognize and respond to a changing situation shrink, collapse, or are bought out by competitors. Newspapers that deftly shifted operations online and adopted new business models survived, while those that could not adapt, folded. Resistance is the opposite of adaptive capacity, while resilience is the expression of it.

Together, these phenomena comprise what is known as a complex, adaptive system. It is a collection of numerous parts, actions, interactions, and reactions. There are inputs that affect what happens. There are outputs that result from decisions and actions. Relationships among these individual components change over time. For example, in 2014 the pharmacy retailer and benefits provider CVS Caremark changed its corporate name to CVS Health to reflect its expanding role in providing health care services at its locations. Adapting to be consistent with its new wellness theme, the company simultaneously removed all tobacco products—a source of significant revenue— from its stores. It was the first national community pharmacy chain to do so.

The contrast to a complex adaptive system is a *simple, linear system*. A watch provides a classic example. Each part has one role, one purpose, and a finite, well-defined connection to the next part. Remove one part and the watch does not fully function. There are no parts without a purpose.

Even though a watch is linear and the systems used to manufacture it are linear, if its design, pricing, functionality, and marketing don't keep up with the market, it will eventually become obsolete. Remember the now-extinct personal digital assistant, the Palm Pilot? At one time, the Palm Pilot was the standard in its market. However, its functionality stagnated, better devices emerged, and the Palm Pilot disappeared. Simple, linear systems and complex adaptive systems affect one another.

Simplicity is part of complexity. Breaking down a large and complex problem into easy-to-understand and easy-to-execute tasks is a management responsibility of effective leaders. As a meta-leader, it is important for you to see both the complex big picture and the simple parts and pixels which create it.

Herman Miller provides an example of a company that has balanced the complexity-simplicity equation. The company, an innovative manufacturer and retailer of furniture, is best known for its ergonomic Aeron chair. As a manufacturer reliant on global supply and distribution chains, it focuses on optimizing processes for assembling and shipping products. Yet it also gives designers free rein when they are conceiving a new product. Manufacturing efficiency never constrains design creativity.

Brian Walker, the CEO, described achieving this balance as putting "principle above protocol." In other words, don't follow a rule that breaks a core principle. Change the rule. Herman Miller's principles have evolved over time, with input from individuals throughout the company. Articulated as "things that matter to us," these principles currently include relationships, transparency, curiosity and exploration, design, and inclusiveness. Herman Miller has a leadership culture that embraces complexity while remaining mindful that value can be derived from simplicity.

More recently, Herman Miller executives realized that their growth goals would require moving beyond the highly cyclical office furniture environment. They acquired one of their major customers, the retailer Design Within Reach, with the intention of establishing a presence in the consumer market. The company was willing to evolve their *form* beyond manufacturing and business-to-business sales in order to fulfill its *function* as a growing, profitable company providing home and office furnishings to design-conscious customers.

Look inside any organization and you find activities that are simple and linear. Invoice payment is one example. Other activities, such as new product innovations, emerge not simply from formal processes but also from informal networks, ad hoc initiatives, and commitment to experimentation and continuous quality improvement.

Progress—and the new and innovative thinking it requires—leverages complexity. Interactions and decision-making need to be fluid if something fresh and worthwhile is to be discovered. The people involved must be adaptive: recognizing themselves as part of a complex adaptive system, they jump into the flow of change and reorient those forces in their favor. Organizations that leverage complexity are agile and willing to change synchronously with their evolving contingencies and mission.

Let's go back to the 2004 and 2012 Red Sox teams. It is clear that simply plugging individuals into positions, even quite talented people, is no guarantee of outstanding team performance. That's a linear approach to a complex systems challenge. Meeting this challenge requires recognizing that winning games is about more than just individual performance. Kevin Millar, first baseman on the 2004 team, described the chemistry to ESPN Boston: "The group of guys, the family, it wasn't just a team. It was a unit that literally hung out together and ate together and liked each other," Millar said. "You can't buy that." The 2004 Red Sox operated like a swarm.

Just as the 2012 Red Sox stumbled by applying linear thinking to a complex systems problem, the opposite can also occur. Linear thinking has its place, such as the checklists used by pilots and physicians. Instead of relying on unreliable memory, the checklist helps pilots ensure that everything important has been verified before they fly their plane. Similarly, checklists in hospitals safeguard surgical procedures, confirming that the right patient is getting the right procedure, with all the necessary steps done in order. This simple practice helps keep "complex" people from messing up simple, linear processes.

The challenge for you is to distinguish between what is simple and what is complex, then deploying the appropriate solution set. Before checklists were introduced, piloting an airplane or performing surgery seemed too complex to be put into simple formulas. The introduction of "simple" checklists, however, has greatly improved flying and medical safety.

Working with Complexity

If you make it so, complexity could actually be your friend. Complex adaptive systems are best understood by stepping back to look at the whole. Unlike the direct, consistent patterns of linear systems, reactions and responses in complex adaptive systems are more likely to vary, depending on changing situations. A CEO might make a statement during a meeting on Monday that's met with applause, and then the same comment on Friday elicits boos. Actions, reactions, and implications are not static, which can create perplexing ambiguity. You can never know for sure whether what worked before will work now or in the future.

Meta-leaders, because of their focus on both the big picture and its components, better grasp the puzzle that is complexity. With a worldview filtered through the lens of a complex adaptive system, they perceive both the transforming whole and the changing linkages between the parts it comprises. For those who hope to spearhead change, a meta-perspective is essential.

The key here is to look for patterns that help you figure out how to remove obstacles and guide interactions to shape conditions for success. What are the variables—economic, political, emotional—that currently affect what is happening, and why? What is more important, what is less important, and how are your priorities changing? As you leverage connections among the parts, ask: what are people doing, and does it shift how others behave? When you perceive these changes, you better understand where they lead and how they affect what you and others do and accomplish. Sometimes you spark the changes. Other times you go with the flow. And if you succeed, people follow you—or not. Complexity often poses difficult choices.

When you view your leadership through the lens of complexity, you realize that people and actions do not always follow what you initially expect. Seek patterns that clue you in.

Here is a hypothetical example of leading a complex organization, based on our field research. You are recruited as the new executive director of a company. The number-two person hoped for and did not get your job. You question whether to keep her on or find someone else. Is she on your side or acting to undermine your authority and your initiatives? This is not a simple boss-subordinate "do as I tell you" situation.

Becoming a detective, you open a dialogue trying to discern her intentions. She also has institutional knowledge that could be valuable. You'd like to make this arrangement work, so you provide opportunities for her to show what she can do, but she fails to produce. There are problems she is aware of, and she does not follow protocol to let you know about them. After talking to her colleagues, you hear about some negative chatter she generated that others find disturbing. The pattern is clear. You weigh your options and act. It's time to find someone else to do the job.

🔥

It's a common mistake in organizations to attempt to solve complex problems with simple solutions. Constant reorganizations that shuffle the reporting structure and responsibilities fail because they attempt to make the dynamic static. The human brain simply cannot design an organization—particularly one in the ever-changing knowledge economy—that reflects the complexity of its actual functions. There are too many variables to script every interaction.

The people-intensive, linear bureaucracies that created efficiencies and productivity in the twentieth-century industrial age are now being replaced by the predictive algorithms of the twenty-first-century digital age. These technologies expand the automated decision-making that is best left to machines. Increasingly, what is left for humans is creativity, innovation, and knowledge-sharing—all of which burst the bounds of mechanistic rules in their dynamism and variability.

How is this shift reflected in your behavior as a leader? When seeking solutions, you realize that no one has all the necessary information, yet anyone may have some part of it. Ask questions. Analyze. Seek explanations and options that fit the situation at hand, not the situation as you would like to see it. Answers to complex problems do not arrive in simple packages. You observe and assess ever-evolving relationships between the parts because changing outcomes result from those many interactions.

Complexity is. Embracing those two simple words is the first step toward understanding the dynamic environment of leadership. Complexity is not something to be solved. It is not a condition that can be cured. You can't make it go away. You can, however, navigate through it.

Finding Order

Complexity offers choice. The meta-leader promotes order amid complexity and encourages followers to do so as well. Order can be achieved through patterns of communication, decision-making, and action-response arrangements, offering a measure of predictability and stability in a system. With order, you clarify what you expect of others and what they can expect of you. You can then direct how to logically get things done, figuring out who does what, when, and where. Order helps you gauge the delicate balance between complexity and simplicity. How do you best grasp your options to arrive at the best possible choices?

The transformative leader finds patterns in a situation and then takes action to generate new patterns, initiating a fresh and different order. Ideally, your intervention accomplishes the intended changes. For example, a proactive crisis plan establishes order through clear roles and responsibilities, need-based resource allocation, and transparent protocols and actions. In the face of an impending catastrophic hurricane, authorities designate beforehand who will do what, how emergency supplies will be distributed, and how and where shelters will be established. Potential chaos is transformed into order.

How can a better understanding of order help you meta-lead through complexity? Order and disorder lie on a continuum. Our brains order information and emotions to make sense of what we experience. Consider people you know: some are "neat freaks," craving coherent order. Others deride such concerns and are not bothered by their messy desks. These individuals nevertheless have an order to the apparent madness of their environment, assuring you that "I know where everything is!" What they resist is control—order imposed and defined by someone else.

Achieving a measure of order—beginning to discern patterns in a situation—boosts both productivity and predictability. Too much order, however, can stifle creativity, adaptability, and the capacity to engage complexity.

Don't let yourself get frazzled by disorder. One part of your meta-leading through complexity is facing up to disorder as a step toward shaping new order. This is where many leaders fail. They panic, unable to assess the true complexity of what is happening. Disrupting current patterns without a better alternative makes things worse. Change for the sake of change is not necessarily an improvement on what is already in place.

Chaos, residing at the extreme disorder end of the order-disorder continuum, is an unavoidable element of highly complex scenarios. It is the necessary scrambling of order as a system moves from stable state A to stable state B. All change involves a measure of chaos. Chaos can be uncomfortable, confusing, frightening, and often unpredictable. But chaos is not "bad" by definition. Like complexity, it simply is. Some chaos descends upon people as a natural disaster—a hurricane, pandemic, or earthquake.

Other chaos is human-made, such as terrorism, revolt, a market crash, or a budget shortfall.

Leaders with an ambitious change agenda even provoke strategic chaos at times to overcome the prevailing social, economic, or political order. Just as order has its functions, so does chaos. Changing the office floor plan to encourage greater interaction and creativity introduces an element of chaos into a physical work space. Protesters stop traffic in the midst of the holiday shopping season to bring attention to their cause. A senior leader ignores the usual formal reporting chain and meets with frontline workers to learn how things are going. All these are examples of a measure of disorder designed to generate a new order.

There are many ways to assemble or reassemble order. Control is one way. A command-and-control hierarchy maps clear lines of authority. Information technology controls the flow of data, knowledge, and communication. Laws, rules, and procedures likewise seek to assert control over what can and cannot be done. At the extreme, the fear of chaos is leveraged by political and organizational leaders to justify strict or even authoritarian control. Repressive rulers try to suppress complexity by imposing strict control.

No one fully controls a complex adaptive system. The drive for control can actually lessen chances of success. Overbearing controls rarely solve a problem and often make it worse. Rigid business processes, for example, can stifle an organization's adaptability. Political repression often prompts rebellion and further chaos.

Though people appreciate order, few like to be controlled. It generates pushback.

What is the alternative?

Meta-leaders, with their big-picture view of the system, its evolution, and its people, assert control when it advances order. They reduce control when it detracts from order. They find that point of equilibrium in any given situation.

One way to accomplish order is to exercise influence rather than exert authority. You can engage people by shaping and clearly articulating a purpose that rallies their voluntary engagement and action. Engaging people is different from commanding them. When you get their buy-in, people come together because they believe in the mission and want to contribute and be included. They see how to add order, and they do it enthusiastically. In the absence of rigid top-down control, they are free to increase their adaptive capacity to meet challenges. Remember the swarm intelligence that manifested during the Boston Marathon bombings response? It exhibited a high degree of order beyond control.

As a meta-leader, you attract people to willingly follow you. They are encouraged by your character, values, and purpose. The magnetism of such leadership is more compelling than control.

The transformation of FEMA exemplifies what it means to meta-lead a complex adaptive system. In the wake of major disasters, FEMA is responsible for guiding and coordinating federal relief activities—helping to restore order in the midst of chaos.

In 2005, during the aftermath of Hurricane Katrina, FEMA's poorly coordinated response compounded the chaos of the disaster. It was a crucible moment for emerging leadership in the United States. We were on-scene, interacting with leaders. We saw that, while so much had been to done to ready agencies for an event of this scale. Even so, when it mattered most the system and its leaders could not meet the needs of the people in the affected areas.

Changing the culture and performance of FEMA was a priority for the new Obama administration in 2009. From 2009 to 2014, Rich Serino, a colleague and an alum of our NPLI executive crisis leadership program, served as FEMA deputy administrator. While at FEMA, he and Administrator Craig Fugate transformed the focus of the agency's work. The intent was to redefine the agency's mission, its operations, and confidence in the agency. The implicit premise was that restoring order amid chaos required the collaboration of many different agencies, communities, and people. Alignment of their efforts could not be commanded, though it could be coordinated.

The leaders recognized that FEMA needed first to refocus itself and its priorities. Previously, those affected by a disaster were referred to as *victims*. Leaders changed the term to *survivors*. Victims are people who died. Survivors are active participants in the recovery and resilience of their lives and communities. Characterizing the agency as survivor-centric prompted changes in rules, protocols, the redesign of Disaster Recovery Centers, relationships with nongovernmental organizations, and more.

The redefinition of those directly affected by disasters was accompanied by another change in perspective: FEMA reoriented itself to prepare and support the "whole community" during a disaster. This wider meta-view of its mission and operation reordered how FEMA engaged other agencies and communities in times of crisis. By convening rather than commanding the "whole of community," FEMA was better able to connect with and support a vast array of government, business, community, and nonprofit organizations, all eager to assist. FEMA became the connective tissue in the response network, catalyzing these other entities into force multipliers for a wide enterprise of people and organizations. No one did everything and everyone did something to contribute to the whole that was accomplished. Encouraging these partnerships was far different from commanding and controlling. With that, FEMA stimulated greater order and far better alignment of support to survivors. Businesses, nongovernmental organizations, and young people— the new FEMA Corps—wanted in, and the agency was there to welcome and facilitate their meaningful contributions.

In reorienting and revitalizing its purpose, the agency redefined the balance between form and function. In bureaucratic institutions, which tend to cling to form, you often hear comments like, "This is how we've always done it," or, "I don't make the rules, I just work here." The agency had been a typically bureaucratic institution in that form dominated its thinking and operations.

Organizations that deliver breakthrough services and products that truly engage employees and delight customers are open to adapting form to serve function. Their bottom line is: what are we here to do, and what is the best way to get it done? Rather than trying to fit their purposes into rigid structures and rules, they cultivate and choose organizational strategies, decision-making practices, and lines of communication that support organizational objectives. They enable self-organization in the pursuit of those objectives. Function eclipses form.

This is what leaders accomplished at FEMA after 2009. Rich Serino recounted his experience bringing private-sector representatives into the

FEMA National Response Coordination Center (NRCC). Up to that point, they had been excluded. "At least 95 percent of commerce is run by the private sector, and so they had to be in the NRCC to coordinate responses at national, state, and local levels," Serino said. "I was told, 'We can't do that because it's against the law.' So I said, 'Show me the law.' There was no law. Then they said, 'It's a policy.' So I said, 'Okay, show me the policy.' There was no policy. 'It's just how we do things' I was told. So I said, 'Now we're going to do things differently.' And so we brought representatives of the private sector into the NRCC, and it really made a difference."

Rich saw FEMA's role as helping to restore community function for survivors. By the time Rich left FEMA, every rule and protocol was regularly being reviewed for relevancy and usefulness. Those found to be deficient in this regard automatically came off the books.

Forces of Crisis, Change, and Meta-Leadership

In any complex system, there are *forces for you, forces against you,* and *forces on the fence.* The wide meta-view of leadership encourages you to see, understand, and weigh how these many different forces affect what you and others do. Some of these forces you control. Many you don't. That is what makes them so complex.

These forces are both tangible and intangible. Obvious forces, such as finances, assets, and equipment, can help or hinder your efforts. More subtle factors also come into play, such as opinions, friendships, personalities, and external developments, some quite distant. Some forces are even internal to you as leader, such as your knowledge, experience, and emotional intelligence.

The "forces for" include allies, the power of your ideas and information, and the resources, whether of money or goodwill, that you accumulate. These forces amplify your message and efforts, and the more you have, the more energy is available to accomplish your meta-leadership objectives. Be careful, though: misperceiving or embellishing just how much force you have can lead to overconfidence and jeopardize your efforts.

The "forces against" are your enemies and the assets, information, and support they bring to resisting what you hope to accomplish. Your own internal blinders can also work as a force against you if you are unwilling to challenge your own thinking. Other "forces against" include the comfort of the status quo and people who see a loss for themselves in what you hope to accomplish. Together, these forces can stop or certainly frustrate you.

The "forces on the fence" are all those stakeholders and factors not committed to one side or the other. These forces are negotiable, open to persuasion to lean in either direction. These uncommitted forces are often substantial. Recruit the relevant ones and you win. Lose them and you don't.

Driving Your Knowns

These different combinations of forces define the contours of the complexity you face. What you know and what you don't know are both key to deciphering that complexity. Your objective as a meta-leader is building and executing a disciplined, intentional process that drives you and others toward what is knowable. You pursue and gather as much situation-relevant knowledge as possible. You do that grasping that much is unknown in what you face, and also that some of the knowledge you don't have is knowledge you can acquire. Through this analysis, you grasp what you know and commit to the pursuit of additional knowledge.

There are four categories for what you know and what you don't know:

1. *The known knowns:* These are the tangible facts that you are aware of and that you use in your meta-leadership thinking. The more you know, the better your strategy, decisions, and actions.
2. *The known unknowns:* You are aware of what you don't know, the questions to ask, and of whom to ask them. This is accessible knowledge and information that you assemble.
3. *The unknown knowns:* Additional information is available that may be hidden and outside your awareness. Seeking this knowledge is vital; without it, you could unexpectedly stumble.
4. *The unknown unknowns:* These are abstract factors that you may not even think to think about. Imagination is required. Unknown unknowns could include critical knowledge that has bearing on the situation.

DRIVING TO THE KNOWNS

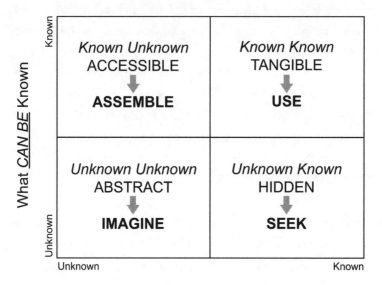

On the afternoon of September 13, 2018, a nearly simultaneous series of explosions ripped through forty structures in three Merrimack Valley towns north of Boston. For the emergency response leaders in the first moments, the known knowns were the multiple 911 calls reporting explosions and fires in rapid succession; the known unknowns were the extent of injuries and the damage to the many affected structures; the unknown knowns were the cause or causes of the explosions and whether they were related; and the unknown unknown was what could happen next. Through a quick and continual knowledge acquisition process, leaders drove accumulating information into the known known. It was soon learned that the cause was an overpressurized natural gas pipeline. Ultimately, the objective of the knowledge acquisition process is to learn fully what happened and then to take steps to ensure that it does not happen again.

Herein lies the mystery of the complexity through which you meta-lead. With a systems view of the puzzle, you seek connections and patterns among all these forces, both known and unknown. Acquiring knowledge is a critical step in navigating complexity, amplifying the "forces for," mitigating the "forces against," and engaging the "forces on the fence." It is through meta-leadership connectivity that you and others accumulate, share, and apply knowledge to the problem at hand. Your objective: to lead your team to the best possible outcome.

What could be hiding the unknowns from you? First, there are the technical problems. You may not have the tools, such as a microscope, or the training and specialized skills to uncover the unknowns. Second, others may hide information from you for their own purposes, which may be hostile. Third, the biggest impediment may be you yourself: narrow, limited thinking may obscure important information. If you exclude others and are not probing for what they know, what could be known to you remains out of reach.

Figuring out what to do with all of this is the adaptive side of complex adaptive systems. What can you do to influence the forces in your favor? What can be changed? How might you move or win over others? At times, you relent on smaller issues in order to prevail on the big ones. Your responsiveness and flexibility are assets that, when strategically applied, realign forces to support and encourage what you hope to accomplish. Get it right and you advance. Get it wrong and you are stopped dead in your tracks.

Begin by mapping the stakeholders and discerning who sits where. Rally those working for you to garner their advice, enthusiasm, and active support. Their spheres of influence can greatly expand yours. Understand those working against you. How legitimate are their objections? Is there a way to overcome or mitigate their opposition? It may be as simple as acknowledging them and genuinely listening to their point of view. Can you turn an enemy into a friend? Engage those who are on the fence to see what it will take to bring them to your side or prevent them from taking the side of your opponents.

These forces exist in all complex systems. As a meta-leader, you recognize the forces, figure out what to do about them, and then work them into your strategy and actions. If you prioritize function—what you hope to accomplish—over form—the structure and rules of your organization—you align the forces with your leadership priorities. This was the lesson of the stories about both FEMA and Herman Miller. Both organizations changed what they were doing and how they did it to better accomplish their core mission. They made the necessary adaptation when operating in a complex adaptive system.

When you bring all this together, you shape and discover *emergence*. Emergence happens when qualities not found in any of its individual components manifest in a system. For example, the flavor of a chocolate chip cookie cannot be tasted in the eggs, flour, chocolate chips, or other ingredients. It emerges when the ingredients are baked together. When you bring together different people, activities, and objectives, your meta-perspective opens up the possibilities and your meta-leadership aligns them in new ways. Emergence was vital to the success of the 2004 Red Sox. Complex adaptive systems have properties that emerge over time from the interactions of components. It turns a group of people into a team, or a problem into a solution.

As a meta-leader, you can encourage leadership among those who are part of your system. That capacity transforms and binds relationships. It is not easy to identify *the* leader of the 2004 Red Sox. Leadership lived in the system and the mantel of leader was worn by different people at different times. The team's historic victory came not from the sum of the individual abilities and actions of its members. It emerged from their personalities, relationships, skills, and motivations. They found shared purpose, which they integrated with adaptive capacity. They complemented and supplemented one another in ways that could not be duplicated by merely inserting other players of similar or even superior athletic prowess.

In August 2012, Lenny met with two NPLI graduates just outside FEMA headquarters in Washington, DC: FEMA deputy administrator Rich Serino and Desiree "Desi" Matel-Anderson, FEMA's newly hired chief innovation advisor. "What if you innovated in the midst of a disaster?" Lenny asked. The theme of the conversation focused on complexity and adaptation. Emergency management agencies often shy away from trying on new ideas or procedures in the midst of a disaster response for fear of distracting from core activities. This rigidity, ironically, can also cause leaders to miss important information, as was seen in the FEMA response to Hurricane Katrina in 2005.

Two months later, Super Storm Sandy hit New York and New Jersey with unprecedented fury. Rich Serino decided that innovation was exactly what was needed to fill the inevitable gaps when responding to a storm of this magnitude. Eager to innovate, Matel-Anderson was soon on her way to support the gaps inevitable when responding to a storm this large. Serino's charge to her, "Solve problems. Don't break the law." A week later, she was joined by FEMA chief technology officer Ted Okada.

Shortly after Super Storm Sandy struck, Eric flew to New York City, where the extent of the devastation was still unfolding. The city had taken a direct hit just seven days earlier. Power was out in many areas, and flooding was extensive. He made a brief survey of lower Manhattan before heading to Brooklyn, where he was to embed with the first FEMA Innovation Team to deploy in the midst of a response.

Dusk was falling as Eric made his way toward the designated meeting point. He expected to find a large emergency operations center, not the residential building before him. Perplexed, he rang the bell. Matel-Anderson ushered him into an apartment where a dozen people were busily at work on their computers. Among them, Eric met Willow Brugh of Geeks Without Bounds, John Crowley of the Harvard Humanitarian Initiative, and Galit Sorokin of the aid crowd-source group Synergy Strike Force. McNulty discovered that the FEMA Innovation Team didn't actually include many people from the government. Most were self-deployed volunteers—designers, programmers, artists, and more—who were young, tech-savvy, and eager to make a difference on the ground.

That evening he watched as the team gathered social media information and confirmed or debunked rumors about the response. They mapped internet connectivity voids based on the absence of geo-tagged tweets. Innovating to expedite survivor assistance, they also crafted blueprints to redesign Disaster Recovery Centers and, alongside FEMA Corps, started using tablets to register survivors. They also tapped into an extensive informal network for ideas, skills, and resources. These were people who had honed their expertise in international humanitarian response efforts. Over the next several days, Eric watched the team applying their expertise and tech talents across New York and New Jersey. Well beyond that, they recruited support and involvement from volunteers across the internet. There may have been few people in that room, though there were hundreds if not thousands across their fast-sprouting network, processing a vast collection of valuable information.

Matel-Anderson later explained that while innovation in a response was new at the federal level, local communities had been doing it for some time. "I am from Milwaukee," she explained. "We never had enough resources. People learned to innovate in austere conditions. I saw that local emergency managers, citizens, innovators of all types could support response and recovery efforts to deliver unconventional solutions in real time to meet the challenges they faced. Now we were trying it on a larger stage."

One of the transformative changes at FEMA was engaging the team to connect the formal government response with informal community-led initiatives. The hope was that rather than working in isolation or possibly at cross-purposes, the formal and informal networks could link and leverage each other's resources and efforts. There was a lack of trust on both sides. Groups like Occupy Sandy were no fans of the establishment, and seasoned professionals at FEMA were wary—these "amateurs" might do more harm than good. The Innovation Team brought information in from the field, enlightening official agencies: "Someone stranded in Brooklyn." They pushed information from those agencies out to people and communities in need of it, such as how to apply for FEMA transitional shelter assistance. Together, they were able to turn important unknowns into valuable knowns. It was unprecedented collaboration.

Building connectivity called for true meta-leadership. Matel-Anderson and the other members of the Innovation Team proved to be adept translators for the array of stakeholders. Fluent in the "languages" spoken on each side, they could explain the camps to each other. Some Innovation Team members looked like straight arrows, and others had interesting collections of tattoos and piercings. The team used appearance to establish "street cred" and manage dissonance in formal and informal exchanges. Most important, they avoided "us-versus-them" situations by showing respect, judging only mission-centric results, and embracing the ethos of "how can we help make you a success?"

"It's about breaking down the barriers by showing that you are there to listen and be useful," Matel-Anderson said. "Empathy is the translator. Being humble, caring, and listening for the heartbeat of the community. People have to be heard before you can help them. Then it doesn't matter what you look like. You're in."

She explained that innovation leaders create physical and psychological space and support people in that space. When deployed, the first FEMA Innovation Team created such a space. "From there, we begin thinking about design. It isn't just brainstorming. It isn't off the cuff. It is quite strategic," she said.

Matel-Anderson has since left government and is now chief wrangler of the Field Innovation Team, an independent nonprofit organization, and CEO of Global Disaster Innovation Group, LLC. She and her teams have been active in responses from refugee camps in Lebanon to Hurricane Harvey to wildfires in northern Spain and Portugal.

"I have always believed that we, as humanity, can do better. The leaders in disasters are not always who you think they are going to be. People step up. I try to lead by example. Leaders walk, they don't just talk," she said. "Listen, solve fast, and make it happen. Less talk . . . more action, listening, and doing . . . more 'we.'"

Complexity is a source of both great challenge and tremendous opportunity. This is the advantage of the meta-view in your leadership. Working with complexity reveals a wider canvas and otherwise overlooked opportunities. You act upon that expanded landscape to link and leverage what you are doing and the forces that can work in your favor. Aware of the complexity through which you lead, you ask more, learn more, and then assimilate all that as you continue to question, be curious, and discover. In that quest, you are more likely to find your answers.

You develop the mind-set and master the tools to effectively navigate complexity.

Complexity is.

Questions for Journaling

> ⊠ In what ways is complexity found in your organization or community? Distinguish a simple task from one that requires complex adaptive *system* thinking and interactions.

➤ What are the critical relationships and interactions that impact your leadership objectives? Have you experienced or observed situations in which swarmlike interactions emerged?

➤ Consider a recent leadership experience. What were the "forces for," the "forces against," and the "forces on the fence"? How did you influence them? How did they influence you? What might you have known or done differently?

FOUR

META-LEADERSHIP THINKING

The Cone-in-the-Cube

Noon, Sunday, April 26, 2009, Washington, DC, the White House press briefing room. Ninety people are dead in Mexico from a mysterious influenza virus. There are reports of the virus spreading into Texas and California. Scientists and policymakers are working around the clock to determine the characteristics of the virus and what to do about it. Some experts believe that a fast-moving and aggressive killer virus is invading the country. An extensive pandemic would devastate vulnerable populations and cause widespread disruptions, jeopardizing the American and Mexican economies. Others believe that, though mysterious, the virus is a milder variant of typical seasonal flu with a much lower risk. If the response is not cued precisely to the magnitude of the risk, overreaction or underreaction will impose a disaster on top of a disaster. There is little time.

This was the beginning of the swine flu, later renamed the H1N1 influenza pandemic.

CDC acting director Dr. Richard Besser, who has advanced training in meta-leadership, follows the president's press secretary, his homeland security advisor, and the secretary of the Department of Homeland Security into the

White House press briefing room for a nationally telecast announcement. The Obama administration has a strategy for combating the virus and keeping the public safe.

Lowest in rank among those on the podium, Besser takes his turn to address the assembled journalists. A physician, public health expert, and accomplished meta-leader, Besser grasps the challenges that lie ahead. He begins: "First, I want to say that our hearts go out to the people in Mexico and the people in the United States who've been impacted by this outbreak. People around the country and around the globe are concerned with this situation we're seeing, and we're concerned as well. As we look for cases of swine flu, we are seeing more cases and expect to see more cases of swine flu. We're responding aggressively to try and learn about this outbreak and to implement measures to control this outbreak."

Soon, reporters are lobbing medical and health-related questions at the group. The others on the podium step aside, and Besser steps forward to lay out what is known about H1N1 influenza, what is unknown, and what scientists are doing to close the gap. His comments are clear, crisp, and—even when so little is known—reassuring.

"I knew that I was 'it,'" he told us later. "And I knew that while we could buy time with the public, we had to be very aggressive in finding everything we could know about this virus and its impact on human health. Science had to drive decision-making, and the sooner we had the science, the better able we'd be able to guide policy decisions and inform the public." Besser's leadership task was to maintain connectivity and communication between the epidemiological investigation, policy decision-making, and the public. There were many different options and opinions about what should be done.

"I felt it was my job to raise the likelihood that together—nationally and internationally—we would be making the right choices," Besser explained.

Ten days later, Besser briefs the president and his cabinet at the White House. When Besser finishes his comments, President Obama declares, "We will follow the science." This is a clear signal to all around the table that the decision-making process going forward will avoid speculation, political consideration, or bureaucratic turf battles. The criteria are and will be derived from evidence-based knowledge.

At this point, Besser is meta-leading across (within his team) and beyond to an array of political and governmental officials and organizations, including state and local public health officials as well as World Health Organization leaders over whom he has no command-and-control authority. Within and between these groups are inevitable rivalries and frictions. Presidential advisors are used to managing political considerations—the "optics"—and for them, the science is not their only consideration. As the personification of the science-based approach endorsed by President Obama, Besser balances these many competing and complex priorities, resources, concerns, biases, perceptions, and personalities as he works to shape the effort. His personal mission is to keep everyone moving cohesively in the same direction.

One point of contention is the question of whether or not to close schools. Those who see a grave danger in the virus genuinely fear that hundreds of thousands of children, rapid spreaders of a flu virus, may die if schools are not shuttered. Others are less concerned about the lethality of the virus, given the preliminary epidemiological data streaming into the CDC. The virus could result in a similar number of deaths (usually in the thousands) as a standard seasonal flu outbreak. Keeping children at home might keep them from catching it, but would also prevent many parents from going to work. Children whose parents have to go to work might be left alone or at a mall or other public place where the virus could spread as fast as it would at school. With the country tumbling into the Great Recession of 2009, economic fallout is a critical consideration.

Different people have conflicting, fervently held beliefs about what is happening and what should be done about it as they look at the same problem from different perspectives. "It's a 'cone-in-the-cube' problem," observes Dr. Carter Mecher, the lead physician policy advisor in the White House. He is right: the swine flu response is what we call a "Cone-in-the-Cube" problem. It is the same type of dilemma faced by leaders confronted by a possible product defect or a customer data breach. So what exactly is the Cone-in-the-Cube, and how does it inform this puzzle?

Integrating Different Perspectives

Consider this metaphor: Two groups of people are assigned the task of describing a shape inside an opaque cube. One group looks through peephole

The Cone-in-the-Cube

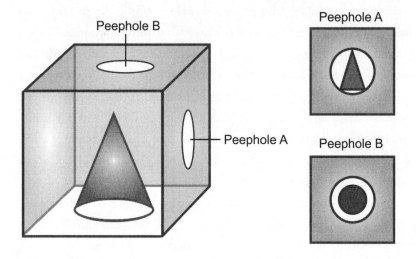

A on the side of the box. They see a triangle. The other looks through peephole B on the top of the box. They see a circle. The two groups fall into conflict about what is in the cube, and each substantiates the validity of its claims based on professed superior experience, values, intelligence, or power.

Discovering that it is neither simply a circle nor a triangle but in fact a cone depends upon the two groups' willingness to share and combine their different observations. As a meta-leadership tool, the Cone-in-the-Cube, of course, is a parable. In reality, there are many peepholes in the "cube" and a much more complicated collection of shapes inside, presenting numerous variations in how people of individual perspectives and dissimilar expertise perceive the same phenomenon and reach divergent conclusions.

This is foundational thinking for meta-leaders. You expect that different people will see and understand the situation from their distinct vantage points. You encourage a meta-view by comparing, combining, and integrating these viewpoints and helping others see the bigger picture as well. The real task is acknowledging and analyzing those distinct perspectives. If it's done right, the stakeholders recognize the complexity—they see that "there is a Cone in the Cube"—and achieve a more blended and balanced perspective. The ultimate mission of the meta-leader is to fuse those streams of thought into a common purpose and a shared narrative to achieve unity of effort among the many involved constituencies.

People view the world through a lens crafted by their distinct experiences, expertise, allegiances, values, and objectives. Recognize that different individuals, even if they have similar backgrounds, can still observe the same phenomena and reach wildly varying conclusions. And especially if the discourse becomes polarized and adversarial, there will be scant curiosity about what others believe to be true and why. It'll be difficult to even ask the simple question, "What do you see from your angle?" Rigidities grow when much is at stake or when someone is in a state of panic.

Cognitive Biases

In the "people follow you" equation of meta-leadership, your job is finding and crafting common ground. There are plenty of reasons why people cling so tenaciously to their limited or fixed perspectives when approaching a problem, even in the face of contradictory information or data. These include blatant selfish interest, self-justifying evidence, spite, and rigid personal stubbornness ("it's all about me"). And don't forget the more earnest reasons of conviction, passion, and well-intentioned advocacy ("it's all about the mission"). The complexity of your situation is animated by a range of diverse and, at times, contradictory attitudes. The more nimbly you identify and work with clashing points of view, the more effectively you'll meta-lead people toward what you hope to accomplish.

Your brain receives a cacophony of information to process—which is perhaps even more likely to happen during a crisis. To enhance efficient processing, that information is filtered into pre-established formulas, attitudes, and beliefs embedded in your thinking. These are known as *cognitive biases*. You see something, and your brain reaches for a quick explanation for what is happening or what it means. Once the impression is triggered, it is hard for your brain to be convinced otherwise, despite both contrary facts and logic. Oddly enough, these filters can sway your brain to perceive just what you expect to see. Cognitive biases can be triggered by what someone is wearing (torn jeans), where they went to school (Harvard), where they work (the government), or how they speak (with a Southern accent). Your brain makes quick risk-and-reward calculations and bases its conclusions on those indicators. "Well, obviously, anyone that (blank) is a (blank)." You fill in the blanks for yourself, and you grasp how others do the same.

Cognitive biases are formulaic pathways for efficient reasoning, and human brains cling to the comfort, ease of decision-making, and conclusions they provide. When something new comes along, the information is forced into a preconfigured pattern. And new data that do not conform to preexisting biases are rejected, serving only to reinforce the rigidity of these bias unless a correction is consciously made. For example: *That person with the ripped jeans just made a brilliant suggestion. Maybe she's smarter than I thought.*

Many times, the shortcuts provided by cognitive biases are helpful. Sometimes, however, they distort your thinking in ways that are incorrect and dangerous. A multitude of biases, shaped by culture, prior experiences, and personal preferences, affect your perceptions of situations and the decisions you make. They can both inform and blind you.

One type of cognitive bias is *confirmation bias,* which causes people to elevate information that validates their existing worldview and discount anything that challenges it. After buying a car, you look for evidence that affirms that you made the right choice. Another common cognitive bias is *availability bias:* overweighting that which comes most easily to mind. For example, after a dramatic plane crash, many people question the safety of flying despite unequivocal evidence that it is the safest mode of travel. *Self-serving bias* interprets information in ways that benefit you. For example, if you give a talk and you get positive feedback from the audience, you may attribute that success to your material and your upbeat presentation style. If the feedback is not so positive, you may decide that because you were scheduled to speak right after lunch, the audience was in a "food coma." Self-serving bias also leads you to rate the comments and opinions of your affinity group—the people in your workplace, culture, or alma mater—higher than those of others. *Judgmental biases* are those based on preconceived notions, including ideas about where people live, their organizational rank, or their circle of friends.

When a cognitive bias overpowers your mental processing or perceptions, you do not recognize a novel situation as such. Emotion clouds your vision and you ignore new information as you handle the situation as though it were familiar. Instead, start by questioning your assumptions. Ask others the simple question, "Am I missing something here?" Take a moment to check yourself. Look for anomalies and teach others to do the same. We met a CEO who appointed someone to his crisis management team specifically to spot cognitive bias.

When alarm or anger sets in, your field of vision narrows from seeing a spectrum of grays to only a stark, black-and-white set of options between good or bad, friend or enemy. Your suspicions about the unknown grow. Cognitive biases can deceive you.

Cognitive biases put enormously powerful and sometimes overwhelming constraints on your thinking and your leadership. These narrow perspectives can inflate vulnerabilities. The more complex and alarming the problem, the more people tend toward simple and reassuring explanations. This can be true even when those perspectives defy logic and common sense.

To address the phenomenon, modify how you deal with yourself as well as with others. If you remain aware of preconceived biases and stay vigilant in combating them, you have a better chance of distinguishing self-serving or convenient fictions from critical facts. And as you remain open to feedback from others, they are more likely to provide insights and advice on what you may be overlooking.

The Meta-Leadership Challenge

There are two sides to the meta-leadership challenge.

First, there is you. Don't be afraid to challenge the limitations that cloud your own view—your biases, experiences, and preferences. At times, leaders are so intensely focused on charging ahead, with everyone else in tow, that they fail to notice their own blinders. If considering other perspectives feels to you like a sign of weakness, you may be making yourself even more rigid and unaware. It is dangerous to be oblivious, and even more so to be unaware that you are oblivious. Avoid traps of your own making.

Second, beyond your own limitations, marshal the patience, sensitivity, and tenacity to gently and persuasively understand the perspectives of others. This is no easy task. It will call upon all your finesse and capacity for empathy, diplomacy, and flexibility. Remember, there are powerful reasons why people see the world the way they do. Expecting them to shift perspective, even slightly, is a tall order. Sometimes it is best to work *with* their cognitive biases rather than try to persuade them otherwise. In the earlier example of H1N1 policy development, Dr. Besser recognized that the presidential advisors, with their focus trained on political considerations, were afraid that shifting the narrative too quickly would make the administration appear erratic and fit the public's confirmation bias about government incompetence. Holding fast to the science, Dr. Besser nevertheless accepted "decisions I could live with" regarding the timing of announcements and policy changes. The simple image of the Cone-in-the-Cube is a useful reminder and metaphor. It can help you and everyone else get beyond the intrapersonal and interpersonal constraints that prevent all of you from building a valuable meta-perspective on the situation at hand.

June 8, 1999, Belgium. Thirty-three schoolchildren became ill after drinking Coca-Cola produced in Antwerp. Some were hospitalized and others reported similar symptoms a few days later. Then some eighty people in northern France reported intestinal problems after drinking Coke produced at a different plant, this one in Dunkirk, France. In total, more than 250 people were stricken. The media exploded, spreading fear of further contamination.

The scare led to the largest product recall in the company's history: 17 million cases of Coke across five countries. Belgium and France banned the sale of Coca-Cola products for ten days. Health ministers in Italy, Spain, and Switzerland warned their populations against consuming Coke, even though the product for sale in those countries was not produced in the suspect plants.

At the time of the outbreak, Douglas Ivester, Coca-Cola's CEO, was in Paris. The leadership actions he took over the next days and weeks are instructive: they illustrate common pitfalls that you may also confront when your next crisis strikes. Ivester had fashioned Coca-Cola into a highly centralized organization. All international group heads were based in Atlanta, so instead of heading to nearby Belgium upon learning the news, he returned immediately to headquarters in Atlanta. While the company sent several dozen executives to Brussels to manage the crisis, its official position was that Coca-Cola products posed no serious health risks. It took two days for the company to provide the necessary information and identify potentially tainted product. Ivester himself made no public statement for eight days. He finally traveled to Belgium ten days after the initial scare, the first of what would become several trips. Yet still he made no public appearances.

Ivester had risen through the corporate ranks and should have been ready to handle such a crisis. He was an accomplished executive elevated to CEO by a unanimous vote of the board of directors, his promotion lauded in the press and welcomed by the markets. He understood the company, having been with Coca-Cola for twenty years before getting the top job. And he was fully familiar with European customers and governments. A decade earlier, his first operating role with the organization was as president of European operations.

Under his direction, Coca-Cola took several proactive steps. The company set up a consumer hotline, offered to pay all medical bills related to the affected products, and launched investigations. They discovered a problem with defective carbon dioxide at the plant in Belgium. In France, they found that a wood preservative used on shipping pallets may have contaminated the outside of the cans. In the thinking of Coca-Cola officials, however, neither of these problems would have created a serious health risk. They went about making their case using evidence they found compelling. They publicized the results of tests and other health data that absolved their products. Eventually, the company and Ivester apologized, even though he continued to believe that his company bore only part of the blame. The rest, in his view, was not his problem.

Despite the evidence presented by the company, Coca-Cola's stock dropped by 10 percent. Sales fell worldwide, and their competitors gained ground. Half a year later, on December 5, 1999, Ivester resigned as CEO. This incident was but one of several missteps that led to his descent.

Ivester's error wasn't lack of concern or unwillingness to take action. It was misreading the situation because he viewed it through a very narrow lens. In the end, seeing only a technical product quality problem, he failed to see the Cone-in-the-Cube. He took steps to diagnose and rectify that problem. When the tests did not correlate the problem to the evidence, he shared those results. He was firmly convinced that everyone else would concur when they saw the same evidence.

What Ivester didn't understand was that consumers and governments were going to have a different view of the problem than he did. They saw sick schoolchildren. They were worried, suspicious, and perplexed, and the problem they saw was as much emotional as technical. The public needed empathy more than evidence. In his mind, Ivester had solved the problem—though only as *he* understood it. He did not solve *their* problem—the public's problem and the problem of consumers of his company's products. He thereby fostered suspicion of his leadership and his product. He may have answered his own question, though he did not unravel the bigger conundrum. And that was the one that mattered.

When you confront a major problem or crisis, consider how each stakeholder views the situation. Your task as meta-leader is to discover and respond to that bigger picture, fusing different perspectives into solutions that work across your range of critical constituencies.

The Meta-Leadership Brain and Problem-Solving

You may well take your brain for granted. Information and experience are inserted and stored in the gray matter. You learn tasks and processes and, with time and repetition, come to perform them reliably. You order information into logical and explainable patterns that elicit clarity and believe with confidence that you can anticipate what will happen next. You presume that you are in control of your brain and assume that others are in control of theirs. It all makes sense because that's what your brain is supposed to do: make sense of things.

It doesn't always work that way.

The brain is a mysterious organ. We actually know and consciously control much less of our brain than we realize. Chemicals and hormones regulate our emotions in ways we can barely sense. There is much that we cannot recognize or comprehend.

Clinical studies have shown that the brain has a narrow focus: its most important function is keeping you alive, and second-most important is perpetuating your genes through your offspring. It perceives only what it thinks it needs to see lest it be overwhelmed by sensory overload. People assume that they know and understand more than they do. Even memories have been shown to be malleable, subject to change over time. False memories can become embedded as accurate recollections.

A dramatic example comes from the Innocence Project at the Cardozo School of Law. They report that eyewitness misidentification played a role in more than 70 percent of convictions overturned through DNA testing. Misconceptions themselves limit what you can know and understand.

Why is this so? You are an ambitious and accomplished individual. You consider yourself to be pretty smart. Your greatest and most valuable asset is your brain. Remember how you scored on that high school test? How you hammered that essay in college? Who is to tell you that you don't know and control your own brain?

Having an appreciation for what you do not know and understand is actually an important step in building broader knowledge and deeper understanding. It is the motivation for curiosity and the springboard for imagination. You become open to thoughts you might otherwise miss. You seek evidence, data, and facts from sources you know to be reliable even if they run contrary to your assumptions and views.

Why can you see more by appreciating what you are not seeing? Because in doing so, you transcend the misconception that what you see is all there is to be seen. You abandon the notion that you and you alone "get it." With a deeper appreciation for your limitations, things previously unseen become more visible. You begin to pay greater attention to others who may alert you to what you have been missing. You remove your own blinders.

Think about this contradiction, as strange as it might be: the power of your brain increases the more you acknowledge its limitations. This is a vital insight for your budding meta-leadership.

The understanding of how the brain works is still relatively new. It is known that the brain grows in both structure and function as a result of experience. It is not a rigid organ. The brain changes over time through a phenomenon called *neuroplasticity,* which accounts for the ability of some stroke victims to regain speech even though the part of the brain that typically controls this function has been damaged. The brain adapts to better accomplish what you ask it to do. The more you "train your brain" to think about multidimensional, Cone-in-the-Cube problems, the more readily it will discern them going forward. The more you practice the meta-leadership mind-set, the more readily you will be able to draw upon it.

The Cone-in-the-Cube is a tool to encourage this wider thinking about problem assessment and solution-building. It encourages robust analysis through discovery of multiple perspectives. In its most basic form, the Cone-in-the-Cube helps you compare and contrast linear thinking and complex adaptive systems thinking, as discussed in the prior chapter.

At times, you see a simple linear problem best addressed by a simple linear solution. We call this a "duct tape problem." Apply the fix and move on. Don't complicate matters by making them more difficult than necessary.

At other times, the wide meta-view will help you discern the complexity of what you face. Embedding the Cone-in-the-Cube into your thinking trains your brain to understand the complexity and to overcome the bias that inclines it toward linear thinking. You will see beyond the parts to grasp the whole. Once you see the larger, integrated picture, your job is to communicate it so that others can appreciate it as well. This is meta-leading, complex problem-solving.

The key point: adapt your thinking to shift between the linear and the complex, between peepholes A and B. Applying a linear solution to a complex problem doesn't work, just as trying to solve a linear problem with a complex solution is a waste of time, effort, and investment. Train your brain to be nimble.

Wider and clearer perception is a way to further guide your thinking and use it to better lead others. Consciously figure neuroplasticity into your mind-set. Learn to expand and tighten your focus, just as an accomplished photographer uses different lenses and settings to accomplish different shots. This will allow you to integrate problems and perspectives. It encourages solutions molded to the matter at hand.

Richard Besser did that when he forged a path for a country and a world intimidated by an invisible and deadly virus. He helped others to understand what lay ahead, and he inspired people to follow, even up to the president of the United States. As he directed his staff in the multifaceted work of investigating and responding to the pandemic, he also gave simple instructions to the public: cough into your bent elbow to minimize the spread of the virus. This both assured people that they had a role in the response and gave them a sense of control to counter their uncertainty. Every media outlet that wanted an interview got the chance to speak with a CDC spokesperson. Dr. Besser wanted the public informed. He wanted the government to be responsive. Dr. Besser leveraged influence well beyond his authority.

By contrast, Douglas Ivester missed the complexity of the problem he faced. His understanding was narrow. It cost him his job—and cost his company market share and revenue.

You have many opportunities to open your own mind and those of others. Use the Cone-in-the-Cube to expand everyone's outlook, including your own. Look into the mirror to challenge your cognitive biases. Find the bigger picture.

It's your moment to think like a meta-leader.

Questions for Journaling

- Think of a Cone-in-the-Cube situation you recently faced. They are common. How was it resolved? What were the frustrations? How might it have been resolved differently?

- Consider a time when you narrowly perceived a complex problem. What constrained your perspective? What were your cognitive biases? What were the cognitive biases of others? What were the implications? Were you able to open up your thinking? What or who helped you?

- Reflect on a time when you saw someone else impose a linear solution on a complex problem.

FIVE

GENERATING LEVERAGE

Influence Beyond Your Authority

April 2006, Leeds, United Kingdom. Harriet Green is named CEO of Premier Farnell, a global, UK-based electronic components distribution company. While the business has roots stretching back to the dawn of World War II, its future looks troubled. It's in dire need of a strategic transformation.

The business is both simple and deceptively complex: an engineer, perhaps designing a new smartphone prototype, orders from Premier Farnell's extensive catalog of parts. The company sources the parts from suppliers around the world and delivers them as quickly as possible. Now though, having lagged in moving its business online, the company is being outmaneuvered by competitors who can deliver more quickly and inexpensively. Its market share and margins are under pressure.

Green's challenge is not simply to drive efficiency and growth. She must also lead the company to a fundamentally different way of thinking about its business: from selling products to being at the center of and facilitating information flows from its suppliers to its end customers. "When I arrived, the business needed to understand who its customers are and then meet their needs, both now and into the future." In her view, Premier Farnell would succeed only if its stakeholders succeed.

Green steps into the corner office with significant authority, knowing that she has the full backing of the board and that everyone in the organization understands that significant change is imminent. She has a reputation as a high achiever who demands results. As CEO, she can set forth her vision, hire and fire whomever she pleases, and direct company policy. However, her actions on that first day do not invoke that authority. Instead, she sends a companywide email asking for help. She says that she knows the company must change to grow and acknowledges that she needs the ideas, energy, and support of the entire organization to make it happen.

"I was careful not to appear to be some know-it-all newcomer from a competitor," she later told us. "Yes, I had ideas about what we needed to do, but there are always limits to what one person can do or make others do. I needed the people in the organization to see themselves as part of the solution. They knew this particular business better than I did—its strengths and weaknesses—and I needed their knowledge and insights. Yes, I knew that there would be people who would be gone in a few months, but I also knew that there would be people who would rise and become significant contributors to our new strategy."

With that simple email, Harriet Green laid the foundation for influence that would extend far beyond her formal authority. Over the next few years, Premier Farnell did transform itself, moving significant parts of its business onto the internet, expanding into new regions around the globe, and growing profitably despite generally unfavorable economic conditions. Employee engagement scores rose. People enthusiastically followed Green because they wanted to, not merely because she commanded them.

Authority Plus Influence Drive Your Meta-Leadership

You may think "you're it" means that you are in charge. Within some limited parameters, you may be. On the whole, however, there are constraints on what you can order your subordinates or others to do. There are bounds on the discretion you can exercise. And there are organizational and legal checks and balances on the actions you can take.

As a meta-leader, you constantly navigate the tension between authority and influence with the people who follow you. Authority is the right to enforce actions from others, to command, or to make decisions. Influence, by contrast, persuades and secures commitment from other people. Combined, your authority and influence drives action and builds momentum. What you get from others is their engagement: the combination of their own authority and influence.

Authority is *given to you* by others. Influence is *built by you* with others. While both can drive accountability, authority is more distant and rational, while influence is closer and more emotional. Harriet Green was given authority by the board of directors who hired her. She could have made changes unilaterally. Instead, she first reached out to employees to involve them in the change, leveraging influence before asserting her authority.

Your hierarchical authority represents what you are officially sanctioned to do in your position as you make decisions and exercise power. It also delineates the limits on what you can do. Your authority is codified in your rank and title. If you work in government or the military, your authority is legally specified and certified. If you work in the private sector, your authority is incorporated into the governance documents of your organization.

Your authority enables you to hire and fire people; approve expenditures; set strategy; enforce laws, policies, and regulations; and even, at the extreme, operate against the will of others. Given the position you hold, you may be invited to speak at prestigious conferences or serve on blue-ribbon panels, engagements that may be less about you as an individual and more about your title, its assumed prerogatives, and the stature of the organization you represent. (Once you lose the title, your stature will probably diminish and the invitations end.)

You have clear authority over your subordinates as you lead down. It is stipulated in your job description and theirs. You exercise this authority to ensure that your unit is productive and achieves its mission. Errors can arise in using this authority either too much or too little. You don't always want to be the "nice guy" who shies away from using authority, nor do you want to be the overlord who exercises formal authority as the only way to get things done. Your challenge is finding just the right balance.

Meta-leaders rarely rely on authority alone, even in circumstances where they have it. The optimal blend of authority and influence depends on the context in which you are leading.

This is particularly relevant as you lead across to peers and beyond to suppliers, regulators, community organizations, and others outside of your organization. You certainly derive authority from your position, credentials, interorganizational agreements and contracts, and the reputation of your company. And yet you have no direct hierarchical authority over these others. For example, a physician may not sit high on a hospital's organizational chart, though can still have significant influence on clinical affairs. No matter the extent or source of your authority, to succeed your efforts are interdependent with the efforts and resources of others. That's when you rely on influence. Whatever authority you have, combined with the influence you generate, equals your capacity to drive dedication and accomplishment.

For instance, you may have the authority to sign an agreement to acquire a key competitor, taking your firm in a new direction. You have a solid financial case to move ahead. However, you don't have the authority to order investors and customers to support the move or to have regulators ignore their antitrust concerns. This is when your meta-leadership matters most. Even within your own hierarchy, you may order employees to integrate with the acquired firm, though, unless you win their heads *and* hearts, they can resist and undermine your best intentions.

We were involved as conflict resolution facilitators in the merger of two large health care institutions. The boards signed an agreement, which was within their respective authorities, though they did so without fully consulting their clinical departments. The boards could not force those clinical units to cooperate and work well together. In fact, clinicians from the different organizations became competitive and hostile with one another. Where there had been two department chiefs in the separate hospitals, with the merger there now would be just one. The chief who got the job asserted his priorities and preferences across the newly integrated departments. Everything from departmental procedures and medical equipment vendors to organizational culture were being imposed upon those who had worked for the other organization. Pushback and resentment ensued. It took significant time and effort to help them find common ground and learn to work together— intangible qualities not included in a formal legal document. (You will learn more about the methods used to negotiate such disputes in Chapter 11.)

As a meta-leader, you aspire to achieve results because people are motivated, not simply required, to do so. Toward that objective, you first listen. Demonstrate that you are interested in finding ways to make the new arrangements succeed. If you want flexibility from others, you must be a role model for that same flexibility and curiosity yourself. In doing so, you exercise influence to reason, persuade, and inspire key stakeholders. What you hope to accomplish together is in their interest as well as yours. If you are leading an organizational merger, seek mutual success: their success in making the merger work can likewise be your success. In the merger of the two health care organizations, the leaders on both sides could have explored each other's priorities in order to embed them into a combined operation. That is a "best of both sides" attitude. This was not the case, and the merger was therefore rife with conflict. Authority is vital, yet it is not a fail-safe.

Unlike a simple machine in which every part is specialized and uniformly fitted, organizations and relationships are complex and dynamic. Humans are emotional, fickle, and self-interested, all in somewhat distinctive ways. Much occurs outside formal chains of command and organizational hierarchies. Any policy manual that attempts to formalize every interaction would be so thick and complicated as to be useless.

Motivating Followers

Recall our operative definition of leadership: "people follow you." They follow you because they believe that you can lead them to a shared goal, be it a sales objective or a humanitarian mission. The example you set is a significant source of your influence. Having influence means people are ready to follow you, willingly and wholeheartedly. You are a role model for everything you want others to do.

Robert Cialdini of Arizona State University is one of the world's fore-most experts on building influence. He and his team found six foundational principles that are valid across cultures, albeit in different measures: *reciprocity,* if I do a favor for you, you are more likely to do one for me—influence derives from benefits that are shared and exchanged; *commitment and consistency,* when people commit to something or someone, they tend to remain consistent with that choice—hence the need to make a good first impression; *social proof,* people are influenced by those they perceive to be "like them" and who are respected by others whom they respect: *liking,* people are influenced more by those they enjoy and admire; *authority* derives from your formal position and power, along with what you do with it (and clearly, authority and influence are not mutually exclusive); finally, *scarcity,* your control of resources, skills, or information that others want.

If this all seems like basic good behavior, it is. Leadership expert Warren Bennis advised, "If you want to be a better leader, be a better person." This can be challenging amid bureaucratic politics, pressures to deliver financial results, and sometimes unclear direction from above. Nevertheless, stick with your principles and values. Your authenticity is at the heart of your influence.

The bounty of influence you accrue and sustain depends on you. You seek it, cultivate it, earn it, and deploy it wisely. When you leave a position, your successor inherits your authority. Your influence—and your way of building it—are yours to take with you. If authority is the power officially given to you, influence is the unofficial power you amass through diligent effort, even with those who hold authority over you. Though there are limits to authority, there is no limit to how much influence you can accumulate.

In physics, physical leverage is created when a rod is used with a fulcrum to amplify energy. That leverage creates the force to lift a massive rock. To wield social leverage, meta-leaders combine authority and influence to achieve their objectives.

Some problems demand command-and-control authority for speed and decisiveness. In an emergency, for example, there is often no time for debate or indecision. By contrast, building the strategic direction of your organization is best achieved through participative processes. Some members of your team may need authoritative direction while others thrive with independence.

You have authority over yourself and your subordinates. You have some limited positional authority leading up, across, and beyond. Influence can be exerted in many directions, often simultaneously. As a meta-leader, you uncover the contours of a situation. Ask yourself: What is the relevant authority you hold? What is the support you can influence? And what are the key points at which leverage can be created and exercised? Map out the people, circumstances, and objectives as you balance authority and influence to deliver the best possible outcome.

Influence and authority: two very different ways to persuade people to follow you. They vary in the behavior and attitudes of the leader as well as in the experiences and the motives of those who follow. The primary distinction is whether followers are with you because they want to be or because they perceive that they have no choice. This is an important question for you: why do people follow you? Different people may do so for very different reasons. The answers inform how you engage them.

This raises another question. If influence is so effective, why don't more leaders exercise it? From our observation of leaders in both high-stress and routine situations, we find that the angrier or less self-confident they are, the more often they tend toward authoritarian tactics over influence strategies. These individuals demonstrate interpersonal antagonism, anxiety, fear, self-doubt, or apprehension as they engage in what is often "my way or the highway" directive behavior. This style can reap short-term success, however, its effects are limited. Consistent authoritarian leadership does not foster the motivation or productivity of followers. It provokes antipathy toward the leader.

The deepest and most genuine followership arises when people choose freely to be with you, whether or not you have authority over them. As leaders share and model their humanity, passion for a common purpose, credibility, confidence of character and loyalty with their followers, they most often inspire the same in return. The result is an authentic enthusiasm that far exceeds mere compliance.

You motivate people and effect change well beyond your formal authority.

Harriet Green used her authority to set high standards and establish rigorous performance measurements at Premier Farnell. She used her influence to gain acceptance for the new strategic direction by inviting input from people throughout the organization. By offering people opportunities to shape and contribute to those moves, Green helped them understand the reasoning behind the changes. She then ensured that the organization supported people with training and other incentives that made them aspire to higher performance. It didn't all go exactly as planned, though working through influence, she helped her people gain the confidence to overcome the obstacles they encountered. And there were consequences for those who would not or could not accept the new direction: they were, as a matter of last resort, moved out of the organization. Judicious use of authority is a path toward greater influence.

Trust is essential to influence. Green created what she called the "trust agenda," the goal of which was for Premier Farnell to be seen as fully trustworthy by each of its stakeholders. The firm created the "Element 14" online community for one of its key customer segments, electronics design engineers. In Element 14, designers can speak freely with each other—even criticizing Premier Farnell if they choose. These engineers often work alone or in small groups, and they appreciated the chance to connect and collaborate with peers from around the world. By providing a useful, secure, and uncensored community, Premier Farnell became a trusted part of that community rather than just another supplier of parts. They built influence with a constituency upon whom their success depended and over whom they had no authority.

Green is currently head of Asia Pacific for IBM, where she is involved in an even faster-moving business involving artificial intelligence (AI) and the Internet of Things (IoT). Reflecting on her more recent meta-leadership, Green said, "I am a believer in lifelong learning, and never has it mattered more. Leaders who don't understand the power and potential of the exponential technology shifts we are seeing are missing opportunities and putting their businesses at risk. They become irrelevant. You gain influence when you're authentically involved and on top of the latest digital knowledge."

She added that, with four generations active in the workforce, leaders must learn from their teams even as they lead them. "The more experience I have, the more I believe in humility: recognizing what you don't know, and the importance of surrounding yourself with people who know more and are better than you." Reflecting on being influenced, she emphasized being open to feedback and, where appropriate, acting on it personally. "Our younger colleagues have so much to teach us about social priorities, speaking up, work-life balance, and finding purpose in all we do."

The Why of Your Meta-Leadership

When discussing Premier Farnell's sustainability initiatives with us, Green said, "People need more than a mission. They need a purpose." Purpose goes beyond slogans, revenue goals, and incentive programs. It is not simply selling a product or service. It is improving people's lives in some tangible way. Purpose articulates the higher *why* of your endeavor. Why are you pursuing this objective? Why are you and your followers together? Why, and how, is each of them essential to success? A compelling purpose captures the positive and significant ways in which all of you, individually and collectively, contribute to the larger system.

Along with a resonant purpose, you need to build the credibility to accomplish it. Who are you, and what do you stand for? What is to be done, and have you marshaled the resources, mandate, and expertise to accomplish the goal? When combined, purpose and the credibility to achieve it are powerful motivators.

When your followers believe in the *why* of the mission, they invest more of their energy and enthusiasm. Just as important, their commitment strengthens when they trust that you value them and their contributions. Aligning with and contributing to your efforts offers them a way to find personal purpose and meaning. They discover that your values conform to theirs. They are impressed by the wisdom of your analysis and understanding. They notice that you encourage contributions from your subordinates and share credit for accomplishments.

Through your influence—and the leverage across the system that comes with it—you can shape your followers' thinking, decisions, and actions. The voluntary nature of influence beyond authority captures the motivations and aspirations of followers. There is more capacity for collective effort because people dedicate themselves so generously to it. This enthusiasm gets people to give the proverbial "110 percent." In your leading down, it manifests in how you supervise, mentor, and encourage your employees. You invest in people and they invest in you.

Our Harvard colleague Joseph Nye coined the term *soft power*. It describes an option that leaders have for attracting or coercing allies and enemies. Your values, culture, policies, and institutions are the currency of soft power. Soft power compels others to "want what you want," even in adversarial circumstances. Originally applied to international strategy to avert the use of military force when other less coercive options are available, soft power is equally applicable to organizational, professional, and interpersonal relations. It is another way of describing the goal of attaining influence beyond authority.

Motivating others isn't only dependent upon position. Every organization has people in the middle and lower ranks who have tremendous influence on what is being or can be accomplished. They often know how to cut through red tape. They include frontline people who interact directly with your customers, clients, and collaborators. What they say and do reflects directly upon you. They understand how to use the informal network that shadows—and sometimes overshadows—the formal organizational structure. They grasp the larger goal and inspire others to strive to achieve it. These people are meta-leaders even if they do not occupy a formal organizational position of overarching authority. Why is this important?

Few leaders accomplish significant objectives solely through their formal subordinates. You recruit peers from other parts of your organization, garner the support of your boss, and engage outside constituencies, including customers, suppliers, politicians, or advocacy groups. As you evaluate your full range of options, you discover that your success is largely dependent on people and organizations over which you have no direct authority. Informal authority and influence may be your most important—and sometimes your only—option to generate momentum.

Collaborative or Competitive?

In our teaching, we conduct a simple exercise to convey a relevant lesson that helps students calculate the balance of their influence and authority. It illustrates how different perceptions of triumph and opportunity affect people's actions and outcomes when engaged in a particular task.

In the midst of a lecture, we stop and ask people to link up in an arm-wrestling position with the person sitting next to them. We tell them that their task, in thirty seconds, is to get the back of the other person's hand down as many times as possible. We then wait five seconds and shout *"Go!"*

The room erupts with commotion. On average, half of the pairs are pushing at one another with all their might. They hear "arm wrestling" and charge into competition. They aggressively employ force. At the conclusion of the exercise, they are tired, sore, and often frustrated. They each perceived a win-lose battle and they fought to win.

Others hear something very different. Figuring that they are both trying to accomplish the same objective—"get the back of the hand of the other person down as many times as possible"—they opt to work together. After hearing *"Go!"* they energetically wave their hands back and forth, each touching the table in turn. At the end of the exercise, they are laughing and feeling quite jubilant.

When the noise in the room calms down, we ask, "How many people got five or fewer?" Those who played the game as an adversarial contest raise their hands. "How many did you get?" we ask. The answers are uniformly "I got one," "I got three," or "I got zero." It is always what "I" got.

Then we ask, "How many people got more than five?" Those who played the game as a collaboration enthusiastically declare, "We got thirty," "We got twenty each," or "We got fifty together." It is uniformly a declaration of what "we" got.

It is this subtle distinction in thinking that the meta-leader understands and puts into practice. The lesson is derived from the field of game theory. Those who see the game as a contest invest great energy in defeating the other side. Once they start pushing, each meets strong resistance from the other. If the two arm wrestlers are of equal strength, they keep each other at a standstill, a zero-zero outcome. This likely reminds you of meetings you've attended.

By contrast, those working together experience the enthusiasm of shared purpose leading to benefits that derive from the combined strength and fervor of both sides. The harder and better they work together, the more they both benefit. Rather than investing effort in obstructing one another—the muscle of the contest—effort is invested in achieving mutual success—the power of the collaboration. A shared win requires trust and unity of purpose. The arm-wrestling exercise is a metaphor for what can be gained when people genuinely work together. Just as the Cone-in-the-Cube symbolizes the meta-leadership perspective, this game theory exercise embodies the aspirational practices and outcomes of collaborative meta-leadership.

At one of our seminars, a young, petite nurse happened to be sitting next to a burly, sixty-year-old surgeon. They paired up for the arm-wrestling exercise. They had never met before. When we said *"Go!"* the surgeon thrust the nurse's arm down. She didn't resist. He yanked her arm up and pushed it down again. Once more, she offered no resistance. At this point, he looked at her quizzically. Without saying a word, she took his relaxed arm and waved it back and forth with hers so that each of their hands quickly touched the table. After two such swings, he exclaimed, "Oh, I get it!" and joined her in furious arm swinging.

Afterwards, the nurse explained, "I knew if I told him beforehand that the point of the exercise was for us to work together, he would reject what I said." She understood that in most professional situations, doctors have greater formal authority than nurses and many times feel that they have greater informal authority as well. "So I let him get two points and then I let him figure out the better alternative on his own. And once he figured it out, he did exactly what I'd hoped for," she concluded. "We nurses learned how to do this a long time ago."

Privately, the surgeon later sheepishly admitted that it was among his most profound life lessons. He commented, "I was so focused on the arm wrestling that I didn't even notice who I was with." Winning does not always require asserting dominance. There are many options for exercising leverage.

The power of this nurse was not in her physical strength. It was in her subtle, calculated influence with her arm-wrestling partner. She knew that *she* could not succeed unless *they* succeeded together. Her actions enabled the surgeon to realize the same thing, deliberately creating the conditions for success to emerge. By offering no initial resistance to the surgeon, the nurse showed him the futility of his reliance on force alone. It is such wisdom and "we-ness" that the meta-leader leverages, building the sense of "we" well beyond the confines of simple professional or organizational authority.

There is prudence in knowing when to assert yourself and when to carefully support others as they take the lead. At times, you plant a seed that grows as someone else's great idea. President Harry S. Truman once said, "It is amazing how much you can accomplish when you do not care who gets the credit." Genuinely helping someone else to successfully solve a problem is a gracious and profoundly effective way to acquire influence.

Now, let's take a moment for some self-reflection. Are you trying to win points for yourself instead of working *with* your stakeholders to achieve your goals? When presented with a challenge, do you automatically kick into adversarial mode? Does your vocabulary include more "I" and "me" than "we"?

If you persist in getting points just for yourself—even after the instructions have been clarified—you are not thinking meta-leadership.

Try this exercise: Go into a meeting committed to paying $10 to others every time you say "I" or "me." It will compel you to pay attention to the kind of language you use and what motivates it. When taken to the extreme, "I" can be blinding. How much did the meeting cost you? If it was $100 or more, think about how you might have achieved your objectives for $60 or even $40. Use this tangible measure to assess and reframe your mind-set to be more inclusive.

Influence beyond authority was abundantly present during the Boston Marathon bombings response, as described in the first chapter. Its emergence encouraged swarm leadership to surface and thrive. Influence set the tone and formed the glue that connected people.

By authority alone, leaders would not have been able to galvanize the generosity of spirit and action in an entire metropolitan area and leverage the massive systemic cooperative effort that delivered exceptional results that week. Government agencies worked together despite jurisdictional complexities. Citizens voluntarily gave of themselves to achieve something that no one government agency could have done alone.

Place into this picture the cooperating partners in the arm-wrestling exercise. They understood that the challenge was not about "me." It was about "we"—the arms jubilantly waving back and forth together. As a meta-leader, you strive to nurture that collective insight and then leverage it to accomplish remarkable results.

Influence is not restricted to one-on-one interactions. The meta-perspective encourages you to think and act on a broad plane of influence well beyond your authority.

Michael Brown is cofounder of the nonprofit international youth service organization City Year. In the cities it serves, the organization builds its profile and influence by having corps members engage in calisthenics in a public place each morning. In their uniforms of bright red tops, khaki pants, and work boots, these young people are hard to miss when doing jumping jacks in a plaza traversed by commuters. After this public ritual, City Year corps members head off to work in public schools. They focus on third through ninth grades, intervening to disrupt the three patterns that foreshadow dropping out of high school: poor attendance, disruptive behavior, and significantly below-average course performance in math and English. Corps members serve as tutors, mentors, and role models.

"By being visible while engaged in a team-building exercise," Brown explained to us, "we show the community that we intend to be positive contributors to their neighborhoods. It allows people to see young people energized and enthusiastic about service. We believe in the power of public rituals and were inspired by Joseph Campbell's work, particularly *The Power of Myth*, as we sought to build the City Year culture and public image." He added that "public rituals, like the calisthenics, build unity of purpose within the organization and send powerful messages to the community at large.

They give people a common experience and story to tell. That is critically important in building influence."

Embedding Influence into Your Meta-Leadership

To cultivate influence, hold a mirror up to yourself. More than the authority of a formal title, influence is about you. You're "it."

No matter how, who, or where you lead, if you hope to build influence, focus on your own behaviors and attitudes. Know that people consistently watch you, taking cues from what you say and do. Be honest, straightforward, and generous in spirit and action. Be just as open to the ideas and perspectives of others as you hope they will be to yours. Take responsibility and be accountable. Share credit, and never shirk blame. Be a positive role model. Be congruent with and consistent about the expectations you set.

Seek out someone who has influenced you as a leader and observe him or her in practice. What feels comfortable for you? President George W. Bush was famous for giving people humorous nicknames that implied a certain intimacy valued by admirers. His predecessor, President Bill Clinton, mastered the talent of making each person with whom he spoke feel as if he or she was the most important person in the room. These are both powerful tools for extending influence. And yet, if these practices do not reflect the real you, they will fall flat. To find your own ways to influence, observe others, observe yourself, be genuine, and then revise and adapt.

Pay close attention to people and relationships. There is great value in the goodwill of authentic relationships. They are the glue that allows organizations and complex systems to progress, adapt, and succeed, all the more so in tough times. Consider a person you value, and ask yourself why you do. Likely it is about loyalty, respect, and trust, along with shared commitments and values. It no doubt also includes a share of camaraderie, humor, and playfulness. Build your other relationships on that same foundation. Ultimately, your measure of influence is reflected in the many people who are convinced that what you are doing and where you are going are worthy of their time and contribution.

Influence is yours for as long as you interact with and lead people who know and respect you. There is no limit to how much influence you can accumulate. The arc of your authority is reflected on your résumé. Your influence is written in your character. It is an enduring life asset offering bountiful dividends.

The influence-authority equation of leadership varies across cultures, generations, and purposes and is always evolving. Ilana Lerman is a community organizer and leader. Hers is an inclusive perspective on the practices of meta-leadership, generational differences, and generational commonalities in championing parallel missions.

Ilana describes herself as a queer white Jewish millennial devoted to sparking change and supporting others to do the same. Both her grandfather and father were social justice leaders, traditions that she carries on. Her grandfather was a union man and ally to the civil rights and American Indian movements. He led a connected and purposeful life as a community organizer, and Ilana was inspired by his commitment.

"As I grew up and came to see and experience injustice," Ilana shared, "I knew that I could have a part, together with others, in creating change." Likewise moved by her late father, Ilana described him as "a goofy, feminist, joyful human. He worked as a prosecutor, but grew angry at the failings of the criminal justice system, so he went searching for alternatives." Her father learned about restorative justice from indigenous people and became determined to bring the process and philosophy to the Milwaukee County court system in Wisconsin. He eventually developed a restorative justice program for young people charged with misdemeanors. His leadership focused on the transformation of systems, communities, and individuals.

This legacy translates into Ilana's social justice leadership. "My grandfather and father led from love. They led in a way that called people into their highest dignity and potential, recognizing people as full beings with a mind, a heart, and a spirit worth fighting for." So how does she see this happening? Through decentralized organizing in "leaderful movements"; capturing the hearts of the public; and cultivating the full self even while existing in an oppressive context.

Decentralized organizing opens the door to creative strategic movements that scale quickly. Once there is a story, strategy, and principles, leaders take ownership and grow with mentorship, guidance, and learning from mistakes. Ilana continued: "When there is an awesome idea, people will replicate it. When there is a need inside the network, people swarm to fix it."

She explained that when decisions have to go through centralized control, the energy, capacity, and creativity of the people involved are often stifled. "We are in a time that we cannot afford to lose people's desires to lead. We are in a time where every person's contribution matters. There are different models of decentralization; my experience is with small bonded groups called 'hives' that are networked with other groups. Relationships are at the core, which hold these groups together through trust, vulnerability, and action."

A "leaderful movement" is one in which many individuals assume the leader role. It encourages people to take intentional risks together and to support those who do. Ilana has been a keen student of numerous leadership teachers, mentors, and role models. "We are in a time when people are moved to act but do not know how to engage. This model of 'one great leader' is intimidating and limiting. I am noticing new generations of organizers are more interested in shared leadership and collaboration: two people at the front of a room leading together, such as collectives and other forms of being together. My teacher Carlos Saavedra says that if you don't have a role, then you're not in the movement. We live in the historic and cultural legacy of European colonialism, a context in which leadership was only open to white men and we have not undone this legacy. We operate inside institutions in which people of color, women, transgender, disabled, LGBTQ, poor, and non-Christian folks are under heightened scrutiny. Their leadership tends to be under higher suspicion and is often attacked. Leaderful movements seek to transform this."

From this perspective, the emphasis is on creating cultural shifts that change both the process and intentions of leading, thus building change into the mind-set of communities in order to foster deep-seated and enduring transformation. Personal and interpersonal shifts occur as well. "How do we make it so compelling that these leaders want to stay? We work to bring our full broken and healing selves. Living in a time of immense separation from ourselves, our bodies, the earth, our histories, and our ancestries, we intentionally build in time to reconnect. The best leaders around me are the ones taking time to heal, to laugh, to keep close relationships, to have spiritual lives, to sing together, to exercise, to slow down, and to reflect. When we make time to truly hear each other's stories, neurons fire in our systems and we cannot unhear or unlove the other. That vulnerability becomes the building blocks for collective change-making. And the more joy and beauty that goes in, the longer we stay.

"This is what both my grandfather and father knew and did. They prioritized human connection and changing the oppressive systems that are the top culprits of disconnection. I am humbled to follow in their footsteps, songs, and tools of the heart towards real change-making."

For some readers, Ilana's story of social justice leadership may seem far removed from their experience. Or perhaps the corporate and government examples here seem foreign. Rather than divergent, we find these different expressions of leadership to be on a continuum.

What connects them? Presence. These are leaders who are less sequestered and more involved than traditional leaders. More broadly, these changes reflect shifts toward distributed leadership, participative decision-making models, and the "hives"—what we here call *swarm leadership*—that are becoming more common across organizations and social movements. What ties together the leaders highlighted in this book is their commitment to presence: physical, cognitive, and emotional. In this chapter, you have seen presence in the stories of Harriet Green, Michael Brown, and Ilana Lerman. These leaders are not superheroes. Their influence emerged through their presence. The meta-leadership framework opens your thinking and practices to be more present, both "people follow you" and "you follow people." How will you enhance your presence?

In the next chapters, we dig deeper into the three dimensions of meta-leadership. Though presented individually, focus your thinking on how the person, the situation, and connectivity fit with and amplify one another. It's important to practice them together.

The dimensions are designed to help you widely perceive more of what is happening within you and about you. Studying dimension one—yourself, the person of the meta-leader—will help you understand who you are, your constraints, and how you can be a better meta-leader.

Dimension two, the situation, helps you understand what is happening around you and eventually what can be done about it. The breadth of perception that is the strength of dimension one (the person) is leveraged in the work of this second dimension of meta-leadership.

We dedicate three chapters to dimension three, connectivity and its facets. These represent the social aspects of meta-leadership, and each facet presents a distinct dynamic of power structures, values sets, economic calculations, expectations, assumptions, individual and institutional histories, cultural norms, alliances, and agendas. Attuned to the multitude of interlocking patterns of behavior and activity among all these people, you begin to predict and shape the course of events.

When you embrace and integrate the three dimensions, your thinking moves ahead of events, much as an expert chess player thinks three or more moves ahead. Anticipating events with more accurate assessment and understanding, you will find better alignment of your decisions and actions. Ultimately, your presence and impact will expand, extending your influence ever more widely.

On to dimension one of meta-leadership: you, the person of the meta-leader.

Questions for Journaling

➤ Think about a time when you or someone you observed tried to solve a leadership challenge using only their formal authority. Then think of a time when influence was the dominant method used. Compare and contrast the processes and the outcomes. How would you calibrate the right balance of authority and influence?

➤ How do you cultivate influence? What could you do to increase your impact?

➤ Why do (or don't) people follow you?

SIX

DIMENSION ONE

Becoming the Person of the Meta-Leader

It all starts with the questions you ask yourself.

Who am I? What motivates me? How do I balance intellect with instinct—the patterns and behaviors fixed into my thinking and actions? What experiences, values, and ambitions drive my passions and aspirations? With deeper understanding, your answers become your meta-leader identity.

We return to our earlier question: why should people follow you? Your character—"who you are"—is one answer to that question. Character combines with the purpose you champion. Is your cause, mission, or objective meaningful enough to motivate others? Dr. Suraya Dalil, whom you met in Chapter 2, exemplified these qualities as she looked forward to assuming leadership of the Afghanistan Ministry of Public Health.

People are attracted to your meta-leadership by numerous personal factors, including your gender, race, culture, religion, nationality, expertise, professional credentials, politics, sexual preference, age, language, physical characteristics, and more. These factors combine in countless ways. One part of "who you are" is how others perceive and define you, sometimes based on factors that are out of your control, such as your nationality. You recognize the perceptions of others, sensitively accounting for them in your interactions. Leadership, after all, is about people with all their many commonalities and differences, affinities and aversions.

In this chapter, we introduce the key factors for better understanding and establishing yourself as a meta-leader. Take some time to reflect on the breadth of the variables that define you—the person of the meta-leader— and how they affect your ability to effectively lead other people. Certainly, the better you understand yourself, the better able you will be to understand others.

Fort Dix, New Jersey, April 1975. The Vietnam War is winding down. It is a beautiful Sunday morning on the sprawling army base. This military training center remains an active staging area for soldiers and equipment readying for battle.

Major Barry Dorn is one of seventy physicians at the base hospital, a facility that serves the routine medical needs of thousands of enlisted trainees and their dependents. Dr. Dorn is on his obligatory rotation as "Officer of the Day." This puts him in charge of everything medical at the hospital and on the base. He finds it tedious because most of the cases are minor injuries or routine ailments. Sundays are particularly quiet. An orthopedic surgeon who relishes the pace and challenges of the operating room, Dorn passes the time reading the *Journal of Bone and Joint Surgery.* He would much rather spend the day with his wife and daughter—anywhere but the sleepy hospital.

On the far side of the base, soldiers move through their daily routines. Powerful missiles are being readied for training exercises in the ordnance "shack"—actually a complex of buildings where munitions are stored and maintained. More than one hundred uniformed troops are busily on duty. As a palette of light anti-tank missiles is lifted, one slips. Its explosive tip is aimed straight at the floor.

BOOM! The missile detonates, sending shrapnel flying. The hot metal savagely slices into nearby soldiers. Other missiles are pierced, triggering cascading explosions. *BOOM! BOOM! BOOM!* Some soldiers stumble away, grasping bleeding wounds. Others are incapacitated. In the chaos, it looks as if the base is under attack.

Barry flips another page in his journal when the phone rings. He hears the screaming voice on the other end even before the speaker reaches his ear, "Explosions! There are wounded everywhere!"

Barry's heart rate and breathing accelerate. His brain ignites. "Where are you? How many casualties?" he demands. He is already calculating the brutal implications of the explosions. "Ordnance shack" is the breathless reply. "Can't count the casualties. Bloody people everywhere." *Click.*

Barry jumps from his chair and runs out to the emergency room, moving faster than he thought possible. The scene there is still calm. "Okay! Everyone—over here! There have been explosions in the ordnance shack. A lot of casualties. No idea yet on numbers or condition. Get ready for anything and everything." Dorn's physical reaction causes the other doctors and nurses to freeze. Eyes open wide, they are overwhelmed by a sense of horror: what happens next?

Minutes later, an Army jeep screeches up to the emergency room entrance. And another and another. They don't stop. The hospital erupts into a scene of injured soldiers screaming and moaning. Blood is everywhere. People scurry back and forth trying to keep up. The injuries just keep coming. The emergency room is getting overwhelmed. Dorn has no idea of the extent of what he has to deal with. The only thing he knows for sure is that he does not have enough: not enough blood, not enough people, not enough of everything for this onslaught of injuries. He begins to panic.

And then, for a brief moment, he pauses to collect himself. He recalls his training. He reminds himself that he has seen every one of these injuries before. He rehearses the sorting protocol. Yes, the numbers are high, but with careful triage, those with life-threatening wounds will get immediate treatment while the less severely injured can be stabilized for later care.

He then engages in creative problem-solving. He has to make sure that everyone avoids the temptation to focus on the walking wounded. They will be okay with just a bit of attention. What can be done for the more seriously injured? He has two operating rooms. He can turn the recovery room into a third and the anesthesia room into a fourth. All medical personnel will be activated. He will get a blood bank going. Bring in supplies from other hospitals. He asserts his self-confidence. "You can do it," he says to himself out loud as he surveys the frenzied activity around him. "Now you just need to get everybody else on the same page. We can do this." With that pivot, he is ready to go.

Near the nursing station, he assembles his senior staff: doctors, nurses, and managers he trusts. He sees their alarm. He is purposeful in projecting calm and determination. "We can do this," Barry tells them. He hands out assignments: One highly capable nurse is made responsible for quickly opening up the two additional operating rooms. A doctor-nurse team is put in charge of triage. The emergency room manager is to perform a rapid assessment of equipment and supplies and then get whatever else they need from nearby civilian hospitals.

"Most important," he instructs his senior staff, "your job is to get everyone else on track, focused, and as productive as possible. We don't have a second to waste. Remind them that this is what they are trained to do. Give concrete instructions. Encourage them—and each other—along the way. Loop back to me. I am here for you." Dorn watches the shift in the faces of his team. There is a powerful sense of shared confidence and commitment to the mission. They stare at him waiting for his next direction. "Okay, go!" he barks. And they do.

Over two days of ceaseless work, Barry and his team treat more than fifty soldiers. There are two amputees. Two other soldiers have serious penetration wounds to the abdomen and chest. Countless stitches are sutured into heads, hands, and legs. And when it is all over, no one has died. Every soldier is saved.

Working straight through with barely a moment of sleep, Barry doesn't return to his office until Tuesday morning. The *Journal of Bone and Joint Surgery* lies open to the page where he left it. *Yes, we did do it,* he thinks to himself. Mission accomplished.

Barry later reflected that it was the moment when he paused to collect himself that was the pivot point. If he had not disciplined himself and his staff, the outcome would have been dramatically different.

Your Meta-Leadership Brain in Practice

You may not find yourself facing a similar onslaught of gruesome injuries in your work. However, you might one day find yourself caught in a vexing organizational challenge or wrenching personal calamity. Alone, isolated, and emotional, you may carry the meta-leadership responsibility for others on your shoulders.

As the rest of us first listened, riveted, to Barry Dorn's story, we recognized many important insights about the first dimension of meta-leadership—the person of the meta-leader. These insights are just as relevant to the mundane moments of life as they are to those rare crises when effective leadership is a matter of life and death.

The workings of your brain provide one of the most exciting frontiers now facing humankind—and one of the most important for understanding the human dynamics of meta-leadership.

Neuroscientists who explore the inner workings of the brain are making valuable discoveries about how it functions and the implications for human behavior, memory, and information-processing. Research into complex cognitive and neurological systems is rapidly progressing, advanced by new imaging techniques that show how the brain internally reacts to external stimuli. Scientists observe the sections of the brain that light up, which neurotransmitters respond, and how different brain regions operate and interact with one another. Among the lessons learned: much brain function—by some estimates 95 percent—is outside of your conscious control.

In our leadership teaching, we set students the paradoxical challenge to become "smarter than their brain." Smarts may seem to derive from the brain, yet the organ has its limitations. For instance, there is the nature-nurture divide: how do instinctual urges affect learned preferences and practices? In the face of overwhelming complexity, the brain creates simple explanations and patterns—the cognitive biases discussed in Chapter 4—that allow it to make rapid, close-enough judgments about risks and rewards. Emotions cloud rational analysis and actions. Understanding these factors helps you better discipline your own leading and better respond to the behaviors of others.

Daniel Kahneman, a Nobel Prize–winning psychologist, describes two systems at work in the brain, one slow and one fast. These systems, with their different cognitive functions and processing, complement and operate together.

The slow system is responsible for complex problem-solving and creative thought: mental challenges for which extra time and effort are required to accomplish more exacting outputs. This includes new learning or discovery. We refer to Kahneman's slow system as the *executive circuits* that are responsible for intricate analysis and execution.

By contrast, the fast system prizes speed and efficiency over precision. This system processes most routine mental activity. It includes practiced tasks that require little attention—such as habitually getting to work—or reactions to immediate threats—such as slamming on the brakes when the car ahead of you suddenly stops. For our purposes, we divide the fast system into two subsystems, *routine circuits* and *survival circuits.*

The routine circuits direct the learned behaviors that you do almost automatically. This includes your rote everyday activities, from how to walk and talk to riding a bicycle. Stored in these circuits is your distinctive collection of practiced procedures, plans, and protocols for your habitual actions. If you are an experienced driver, these circuits mechanically guide you along familiar routes. Meanwhile, your neocortex is otherwise occupied with more complex thinking, such as rehearsing the meeting you will soon have with your boss.

The other fast brain subsystem—the survival circuits—propels your instinctual behaviors. These include involuntary physiological actions, such as breathing and heart beating shared by all species, from reptiles to humans. The survival circuits also include the lightning-fast threat response pathways deeply ingrained in mental processing. Notice how fast you jump when a fire ignites on your stove. It is instant, seemingly without your brain thinking about it.

Our intention here is not to draw a comprehensive map of all the brain structures and processes in the 180 distinct brain regions identified by researchers. Instead, we offer this model of three sets of circuits as a metaphorical framework to explain brain functioning as it's applicable to your meta-leadership practices.

We start with the survival circuits. When your brain perceives a threat, the survival circuits exert quick and instinctive control over your cognitive and physical functions. Adrenaline kicks in, your breathing accelerates, and your heartbeat quickens. Your being and body are in survival mode.

Resting in the center of your brain is the amygdala. This almond-shaped cluster of nuclei processes emotions and serves as your threat alert system. It remains relatively quiet until the instant it senses a threat—often before you are consciously aware of it. Then it immediately and automatically triggers two neural responses, one fast and one slow. The fast reaction instantly ignites your survival circuits, activating your instinctual and protective "triple-F" survival responses: freeze, flight, and fight. The slow response travels a neural pathway to the neocortex, where the available information can be more fully interpreted. The fast survival circuit signal is quicker and preempts other mental processes until immediate safety is assured.

The psychologist Daniel Goleman refers to this activation of the fast survival circuit as an "amygdala hijack." Others refer to it as the "dinosaur brain"

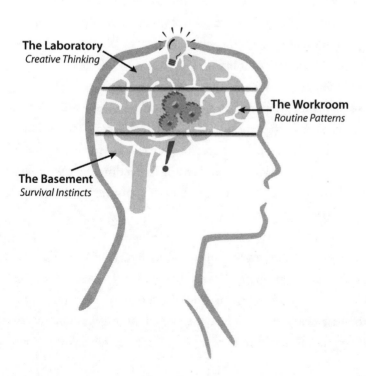

or the "grasshopper" in the brain. Our meta-leadership term is *going to the basement.** This reference has roots in the thinking of Sigmund Freud, who described the deep subconscious as "the basement" of the mind. "Going to the basement" encapsulates the most primal instincts and behaviors. When Barry Dorn got that phone call at Fort Dix and heard about the explosions, he and the rest of his team went immediately to the basement.

The amygdala hijack is a deeply embedded stimulus-response mechanism that saved your ancestors—as well as other species—from threatening predators. The swiftest runners and the best fighters survived. Picture the triple-F impulses of a rabbit you encounter in the wild. When it senses you, a potential predator, it immediately freezes, a response that provides camouflage and lets the rabbit blend into its surroundings. The predator brain is primed to detect movement to identify prey. Thus, the freeze could be salvation for the prey. However, if you get too close, the rabbit doesn't contemplate your intentions. It takes flight, bolting to escape because survival depends on speed. If all else fails and a predator snares the rabbit, it struggles to survive by fighting. When you go to the basement, the same innate, sequential freeze-flight-fight responses are activated in your brain.

A similar phenomenon happens to you when you're threatened. There is an instant physiological response. For a moment, you *freeze*. Your brain is focused on survival. Your heartbeat is signaled to accelerate, and you unconsciously get ready for *flight*. Your breathing is rapid. Hormones surge through your body, preparing you to run. Sensing impending threat, you get ready to *fight*. It is difficult to break this reaction. It is instinctive. It is common to all animal species.

The Triple-F sequence—freeze, flight, fight—can be traversed in seconds, hours, or even days, depending on the situation, your training, and your experience. At Fort Dix, Barry Dorn initially froze at the news of the explosions. How would he treat them all? Might some die? Instantly, he was deep in the basement, and then he remembered: fleeing was not an option. He was a physician with a duty to treat the injured, his fellow service

---

* Dr. Isaac Ashkenazi introduced us to this term.

members. People were counting on him. He would have to overcome his internal fears and fight the external threat.

With the skills and confidence born of medical training and experience, Dorn assumed control of his brain. In disciplined fashion, he ignited his mid-brain, what we call the *workroom* of learned and practiced protocols. His routine circuits triggered his neurological ascent back up from the basement by recalling oft-practiced sequential actions. Triage procedures for determining who to treat first, for example, transform overwhelming crisis into workable directions. When he said, "I can do this," he remembered that he and the staff knew how to set priorities and treat these injuries. He reset his brain the way you might reboot your computer when it freezes. With focus and calm, he led others out of the basement, routine brain circuits firing. He had done this before. The hospital staff rapidly kicked into gear. "We can do this."

With this brain reset, Barry switched on his executive circuits, which enabled him to tackle the complex problems of reorganizing personnel, reconfiguring facilities, and obtaining supplies. He ascended to what we call the *laboratory* of the brain: the neocortex and its executive functions. This highly advanced section of the brain is where complex data collection and analysis occur. To reach this advanced level of thinking, Barry needed first to calm his survival circuits by activating workroom problem-solving. Going from the basement to the laboratory is impossible without convincing the brain that it no longer has to focus on survival. His capacity to regain control of his brain propelled him quickly to strategic decisions and actions. He rallied the wide set of people and resources necessary to meet the situation at hand. It was meta-leadership at work. Lives were saved.

Getting Out of the Basement

Today you rarely encounter the ferocious jungle predators that once stalked your ancestors. Nevertheless, the instinctual mechanism that propels you into the basement is embedded in your mind. During an amygdala hijack, when other functions of the brain shut down, extraordinarily smart people can go to the basement, get stuck in the basement, and say or do the dumbest things, often to their later regret. The hijack could be triggered by an offensive email from a colleague, an argument, or a sudden and devastating cut in the departmental budget. Any perceived threat can ignite the reaction. When the threat is perceived to be big, the fall to the basement can be precipitous.

When survival circuits are in control, your world is simplified: all you perceive is danger and safety, good and bad, friend and foe. Your natural options are limited to primitive survival responses. If screeching brakes send you leaping from the street back onto the sidewalk, you appreciate your fast-system response. In less life-threatening circumstances—including your response to that offensive email—you are better served by disciplining your reaction.

You cannot assert control, however, until you get yourself up and out of the basement. As a meta-leader, you want to help others up and out of the basement as well. Leaders are counted on for their rational thinking and insight. You can't do that when overtaken by the impulses of your survival circuits.

You descend to the basement regularly. If you are a parent, you've been sent there by an incessantly crying infant or a petulant teenager. You are cut off on the highway and you scream in rage, your survival circuits preempting a more measured response. Conflicts and frustrations at work can take a whole group of people to the basement. It is your threat response.

There is nothing fundamentally wrong with going to the basement. It is automatic and instinctual. You have little conscious say in the matter.

Never lead, negotiate, or make major life decisions when you are in the basement. The speech or decision you make when you are in the basement is the one you are most likely to regret. Remember, the problem is not in going to the basement. The problem is how deep you go, how long you are there, and what you do while in the basement.

The good news is that you can control the speed of your ascent out of the basement. You can consciously reset your neurocircuitry and restore disciplined thinking and behavior, thereby activating your routine and executive circuits.

Just as evolution built a high-speed neural pathway to your survival response, you can intentionally form and develop pathways to activate the slower systems that take you to your rational workroom and laboratory. Build disciplined, learned responses that enable you to quickly reassert higher-level thinking. Construct and embed patterns of thinking and acting—experiences—that stimulate your slow-system signal to catch up to and surmount your Triple-F reaction.

This neuro-reset is deliberate and in your control. To reestablish the discipline of your brain's routine and executive circuits, first acknowledge that an amygdala hijack has occurred. At times, you recognize it on your own. "I am in the basement!" shouts your inner voice. At other times, someone else—a colleague, spouse, or friend—alerts you: "You are in the basement!" You might resist ("I am *not* in the basement!"). You do so at your own peril. Your agitated tone and tense expression reveal that you are, in fact, in the basement.

Perceiving and admitting that your thinking has been hijacked is your first and most important step toward reestablishing your resilience. When you remember that you have only partial conscious control over your brain, you're taking a critical step toward getting smarter about your brain.

Getting to the Reset

To start the neuro-reset in your brain, reach for something familiar that prompts self-confidence or composure through demonstrated competence. This could be a practiced task or protocol. This intentional pivot activates your routine circuits and calms your survival circuits with the message, "I can do it." Just as the survival circuits take you to the basement, engage your routine circuits to take you to your brain's workroom. Here you perform learned and well-rehearsed actions almost automatically. The pathway to your workroom is your *trigger script*—your brain reset process.

Your trigger script breaks your basement's grip on you. It could be as simple as counting to ten or taking three deep breaths. It is what you learn to reach for automatically. For example, drivers are taught to steer into a skid to regain control of the automobile. It is the same with your brain.

As you learn to recognize the descent to the basement—the mental skid—so too can you learn to initiate your trigger script to reassert control. When a patient suffers a cardiac arrest in a hospital, an alarm is sounded: "Code Blue!" Someone is dying! That phrase serves as the trigger script for staff to follow preestablished protocols to treat the patient. The medical supply cart is positioned, staff members situate themselves around the patient, and everyone knows exactly what to do. The trigger script and the tools in your metaphorical workroom allow you to reactivate your routine fast brain, deactivate the panicked Triple-F response, and begin your ascent up and out of the basement. You begin to see and perceive more, and things start making sense again. There is the familiarity and comfort of the routine. Your brain is in a different state.

As a meta-leader, you are a role model. Your trained brain functioning encourages the same in your followers. In his discussion of emotional intelligence, Daniel Goleman describes *mirror neurons,* which imperceptibly communicate emotions and responses from one person's brain to another's. One brain can take another out of the basement, just as the process can work in reverse. For example, one petulant person complaining bitterly at a family reunion can put the whole roomful of people in the deepest part of the basement. They've implicitly received the signal: *He's in the basement sensing danger my brain doesn't perceive, so just in case, I should go to the basement too.*

Basement behavior is contagious. When you are leading, people mimic your actions and reactions. If you are panicked and agitated, followers duplicate that behavior, further complicating their return to productive thought and behavior.

By contrast, when you begin guiding the action with calm and confidence, you prompt a similar response from others. Engage people on the common ground of shared protocols or practiced routines to redirect their actions. If they are your followers, your encouragement points them toward joining in disciplined, constructive action. As you lead more and more people out of the basement, you generate a self-reinforcing feedback loop of rewarding momentum and progress that reassures and invigorates your followers. And pragmatically, guiding others out of the basement bolsters your own ascent. This is what Barry did at Fort Dix.

Once your routine circuits and those of your followers are fired up, you are best able to engage the slower frontal cortex executive circuits required for complex thinking and problem-solving. You are in the laboratory of your brain, learning and processing new information. With your analytic executive circuits engaged, you perceive gaps between what is and what could be. You have a clearer grasp of problems and solutions. You detect and create fresh options and alternatives while you navigate complexity, smartly adapting and innovating.

To build the mental muscle of your meta-leadership brain, spend some time learning about yourself. Carefully observe your own actions and reactions, tracing the circuitry of your fast brain and slow brain. What takes you down to the basement? What do you typically do while there? How can you better activate your trigger script and get yourself and others up to the workroom? How can you better calm yourself and others in order to activate the executive circuits and return to the laboratory of complex learning, thinking, and problem-solving? For instance, you may realize that you are more controlled at work—your job is on the line—and more emotionally uninhibited in the comfort of home.

Perspective is also gained by studying others, both those close to you and people at a distance. For example, if you review photographs of the immediate aftermath of the Boston Marathon bombings, you see first responders demonstrating routine rehearsed reactions. Law enforcement officials draw their weapons and scan the crowd for more threats. Emergency medical personnel grab their kits and head toward the wounded. Firefighters race to their trucks to get on scene. Each of these individuals has trained to respond proactively to an emergency. By exercising well-rehearsed steps, they quickly get out of the basement, reestablish control over themselves, and act appropriately given the circumstances at hand.

What helps you reset your brain? Being mindful of what is happening in your brain may feel awkward at first. Soon you will find your awareness of the basement to be second nature. Intentional, methodic brain reset is a meta-leadership skill you can practice and master. The more you do it, the quicker you achieve the thinking needed in the midst of crisis, change, or complexity.

How might this brain circuitry work in a crisis less dramatic than the multiple casualty event at Fort Dix? Imagine that you are heading to the office on Monday morning. You are relaxed after a lovely social weekend. The only task looming is a presentation to the senior management team on a proposed reorganization, and that is not scheduled until later in the week. There is plenty of time to prepare.

You are settled into your seat on the bustling commuter train when your phone rings. It is your assistant. "Have you seen the email?" she asks insistently. You are perplexed. Trying to keep work off your mind until you get to the office, you intentionally hadn't looked at your emails. "Thursday's presentation has been moved to today," she continues. "Eleven o'clock this morning. What are we going to do? We'll never be ready!"

A moment ago there were four days to prepare. Now there are about three hours. You go straight to the basement. "Did you make a mistake with the date?" you demand. "Don't blame this on me," she shoots back. Thoughts run through your mind: Is this sabotage by the CFO, who has his own ideas about reorganization? Was it a mistake not to cancel those weekend plans and work on the presentation instead? What will be the consequences if the presentation falls flat? All of senior management will be there.

First, pause. Recognize that you are in the basement. Stop blaming yourself or your assistant. Time is valuable, too valuable to spend pointing fingers. Go for your trigger script. Take three deep breaths. Feel yourself relax. Apologize to your assistant and ask her to have the team ready in the conference room when you arrive in twenty minutes. Remind yourself that you have successfully presented to this group before ("I can do this"). Remember what made those presentations well received. You'll follow the same patterns and routines, just this time much faster. You have a competent group of staff who know how to work fast ("we can do this"). Emerging from your basement, you go straight to your mental workroom—and get to work with confidence.

Use the remaining time on the train to organize a plan and jot down thoughts you've worked on since you reviewed the last draft of the presentation. When you get to the office, stop before walking into the conference room. Take a moment to ensure that you are out of the basement. When you enter, thank your team and then calmly give direction to help them ascend from the basement. Step by intentional step, turn the preliminary work into a polished presentation. One person can incorporate your notes and finish the slides. Another can proofread the final documents. While your staff members are working, rehearse your presentation, making sure to have a compelling opening and a memorable close. You are now at your highest level of thinking and preparing, with your executive circuits completely lit up. Your brain is under control, and so too is the situation.

Understanding Heuristics and Memory

Your brain's circuitry and information-processing system—the basement for survival, the workroom for routine activities, and the laboratory for executive thinking—shape your leadership behaviors. You become more intentional and disciplined as your awareness of these cognitive processes increases. Your grasp of cognitive limitations is a strength that helps you better understand and influence the decisions and actions of followers.

As we discussed earlier, the brain is subject to cognitive biases that shape your perceptions of what is happening. These biases direct your thinking along preestablished cognitive pathways. They prioritize efficiency at the expense of precision and accuracy. In evolutionary terms, fast and good enough was a better survival strategy than slow and perfect.

These biases shape *heuristics*—the mental shortcuts or cognitive rules of thumb that rapidly direct your actions and problem-solving. Heuristics are the established analytic or action scripts embedded in your thinking. They methodically focus your attention and eliminate distractions, helping the brain and body move fast and deal with the torrent of information rushing in at every waking moment.

The speed and ease of heuristics can reduce the accuracy of your decision-making as you reach conclusions and take action without complete data and rigorous analysis. Heuristics also are useful shortcuts when there is neither the time nor the need to carefully think through a problem. Think of them as naturally occurring brain algorithms. For example, you walk into a colleague's book-lined office for the first time. You don't need to read the title of each volume before you conclude that Sally is probably smart and well read. Your brain automatically connects the data points in a way that is, at least superficially, logical.

Heuristics can be both a solution and a problem. For example, the *anchoring heuristic* is one that causes you to overestimate the significance of the first bit of information you receive. If a car salesperson says that a used auto is worth $10,000, you assess all other valuations in relation to this initial anchoring valuation. In this case, the anchoring heuristic is a solution because it orients you to the range of potential values for the car. It's also a problem because you may overvalue that one data point over a more objective price for the car (especially if the car is really worth only $5,000).

When facing a crisis or urgent situation, you have little time for careful analysis. For example, during an active shooter event, the public is instructed to "run, hide, fight!" This is an easily remembered heuristic. Recalling it can help terrified people get up and out of their basement (their "freeze") to save their lives. Football players apply heuristics when the ball is intercepted and offensive players suddenly are transformed into defensive mode. There is no time for a huddle or strategic analysis. They do whatever is necessary to get that tackle. Heuristics are trigger scripts to get you out of the basement and headed toward productive action.

The *familiarity heuristic* causes you to draw a quick parallel between what is happening now and something that happened before, even if the current situation is very different. For example, there are people who ignore warnings to evacuate during hurricanes because they figure that they survived disasters before and they can do it again. They downplay the specifics of the impending situation.

The way to circumvent heuristics and avoid such misperceptions is to call upon a broad base of data whenever possible. Data will provide you with a more accurate perspective. Ask yourself how heuristics affect your thinking and decision-making. How do heuristics affect the thinking and decision-making of family members, colleagues, or friends? What happens when their heuristics collide?

Heuristics can be a problem when we ignore or dismiss significant information. They can also cause inefficiency and wasted time as they unleash poor-quality decisions and all that ensues. Heuristics are tools. Know them and then apply them with caution and care.

Hidden deep in your brain's subconscious is a vast reservoir of memories, experiences, and facts that are not readily recalled. It could be a childhood experience, a disturbing interaction with a colleague, or a book you read. Though you don't remember details, these memories subtly affect your attitudes and decision-making. They may surface in your dreams, and they also invisibly color your daily interactions. Following are two exercises to help you surface and apply the power of your subconscious.

To gain access to your intuitive wisdom and experience, try this drill devised by the neuroscientist David Eagleman: You face a difficult decision, and you are having a hard time making a choice. Flip a coin. Heads and you take option A. Tails and you go with option B.

The point is not to randomly make a choice but rather to note your emotional reaction after you flip the coin. If you are satisfied with tails, why is that so? If you are disappointed and had hoped for heads, what does that tell you about your hidden predispositions? Think about it.

This exercise give you access to the wealth of hidden information stored in the recesses of your brain. It aids awareness of your true preferences and cognitive biases. Alert to this phenomenon, you may discover hidden factors that likewise complicate the rational decision-making of others, perhaps the result of their own traumatic or profound experiences. Unlocking your subconscious reveals memories and insights that tap into the wisdom of your experience.

Here is another analytic exercise that we have found useful. Who is the greatest leader you have ever known? Not someone you have read or heard about, like Gandhi or Moses, rather someone you've chosen to follow, with whom you've interacted, and whose strengths and weaknesses you know. Likewise, who is the worst leader you have ever known? Again, think of someone you have known, not a Hitler or Mussolini.

These two people you have identified could be a boss, professional colleague, political leader, or friend. Place them on either side of a continuum. Now place yourself right in the middle, between the greatest and worst leaders you have known. How do these three people compare at getting themselves up and out of the basement? How open-minded are they? Are they overly bound by cognitive biases? And how would you rate their emotional intelligence?

By recalling both your greatest and lousiest leaders—the one you aspire to emulate and the one you disdain—you articulate the behaviors and characteristics that shape your own leadership.

Emotional Intelligence

Meta-leadership practice requires an abundance of emotional intelligence. While smart people have a high IQ (intelligence quotient), truly successful people possess a depth of emotional intelligence (EQ, or emotional quotient). You use these attributes every day and everywhere, and they are particularly important when there is opportunity to meta-lead.

Emotional intelligence is a framework popularized by Daniel Goleman. His model details five attributes of emotional intelligence:

1. *Self-awareness* encompasses knowing yourself and the experiences that color your perceptions. Understanding what drives you requires awareness of your hopes and passions as well as the demons and distractions that steer you astray. You can recognize both your strengths and your weaknesses. You cannot know and appreciate the strengths and weaknesses of others if you don't first know yourself.
2. *Self-regulation* is the capacity to control your desires, moods, look, impulses, and interactions with others. You can become the person— the meta-leader—needed in the moment. You have the ability do so in a manner that is both genuine and intentional. And you are able to avoid emotional outbursts when you are upset.
3. *Motivation* is not only what inspires and impels you forward. It is so deeply engrained in you that it inspires and energizes others.
4. *Empathy* is the capacity to understand other people for their distinct experiences, needs, and interests. Empathy requires viewing and appreciating someone else's experience as different from, yet equally valid as, your own.
5. *Social skills* enable you to be comfortable with other people and to make other people comfortable with you. These skills are particularly important and potentially challenging when interacting with people from other cultures, professions, organizations, or walks of life. The

capacity to find and forge connections across differences is part of the engaging talent of the meta-leader.

With these five attributes of emotional intelligence in mind, how would you compare and contrast your greatest and worst leaders? How do you fit into this continuum of emotional intelligence? Do you share attributes with your great leader? Are there improvements you could make? Likewise, are there attributes you share with your worst leader? How might you shed them?

Emotional intelligence and self-awareness in particular have been shown to correlate with leadership effectiveness. People who demonstrate self-awareness possess an understanding of their own impact: their personality, experiences, culture, emotional expressions, and character.

The Importance of Trust

The foundation of your personal meta-leadership credibility is trust. Forming and maintaining trust-based relationships—across a wide spectrum of people, including those you don't know well—is particularly important when leading through ambiguous circumstances. Decisions and actions often must be taken without complete information or certainty, be it a volatile crisis or the launch of a new business initiative. Trust is crucial for leading through the cycles of complexity. It was central to the emergence of swarm intelligence among leaders during the Boston Marathon bombings response.

What is trust? It is predictability. When you trust someone, you know how they will react to new or unknown circumstances. It is a measure of assurance of someone's honesty and integrity. As you lead, the circumstances that confront you may be uncertain and even out of control. However, if you trust those around you, you have a solid platform upon which to assess what is happening and what should be done about it. Trusting relationships are marked by reciprocity: you do good for others and they do good for you. These are people you can surely count upon. They will be there for you through the toughest times. Just as you will be there for them.

Trusting relationships calm the brain's survival circuits and assist the process of wading through complexity. You are with people whose relationship with you and opinions you value and believe. Without trust, it is difficult to discern fact from fiction. A difficult situation becomes even more so, further deteriorating the chances of getting out of the basement.

Trustworthiness is a quality you earn. First, you establish confidence. You promise to do something, and then you do it. You provide information, and it is accurate. You encounter a problem, and you responsibly take care of it. Your actions and attitudes are reliable, even in the face of uncertain conditions. Only then do you achieve genuine trust. Trust is anticipatory. It is a reflection of integrity, faith, and safety. Without trust, leading is difficult, if not impossible.

Your followers evaluate whether or not to trust you. They assess what you do as a strategist, tactician, diplomat, and decision-maker—the person of the meta-leader—in the context of the situations at hand. Demonstrating your own integrity is the first and most basic step. Your followers are both calmed and subtly persuaded to follow and mimic when you present a model of composure, even-handedness, and reliability. What do you want people to know about your character? You provide information with every meeting, decision, and action. You also build trust when you show your willingness to listen and are receptive to feedback that your judgment may be askew. What is it about your great leader and your worst leader that signals trust or lack thereof?

You also learn to cultivate trust in your followers. Choose them carefully and invest in their leadership development. If you trust them and encourage them to act independently, you extend your reach. Then you can count on your followers, and they in turn can count on you.

What if trust is absent? Be vigilant toward people who lie to you, misrepresenting their credentials, information, or experience. In its most chronic form, the habitual fraudster operates without a moral compass, upending the very purposes that motivate your leadership. This person's lack of integrity damages yours. The methods and practices outlined in this book do not work in the absence of honesty and mutual respect. This profile may very well describe the person you chose as your worst leader.

Between your greatest and worst leaders, where do you fit on the trust continuum? However difficult, be honest with yourself. If you can't be honest with yourself, you certainly can't be honest with others. At its core, meta-leadership is a social phenomenon. The better you understand the contours of interpersonal dynamics—yours and those of others—the greater your success at building the trusted cohesion of effort that is central to meta-leadership practices.

People Follow You

Your relationships with other people are part of your meaning-making as a meta-leader. You care about other people, and they care about you. Their attachment to you signifies their attachment to the purposes, values, and objectives you pursue.

You experience a lot together. In the crucible moments, there is the elation of victories, the disappointment of defeats, the many descents to the basement, and the ascents back up and out. You and your followers may also experience meaningful interpersonal feelings of esteem, respect, and affection, as well as bitterness, jealousy, or disdain. Mirror neurons are in play: followers take spoken and unspoken cues from their leaders, and vice versa. The expression, reception, and understanding of those cues and feelings are critical to your meta-leadership practices and achievements.

How do you embed an appreciation for connection in your leading? Try this exercise for a day: Be fully present with everyone you meet, see, or come into contact with. Greet the security guard at work or the grocery checkout clerk by name. Thank them. Greet your colleagues, your family members, and friends in the same way: ask how they are feeling or what they are reading—and pay attention to the answers. Spend a day investing emotion in everyone you encounter. Treat no one as though they are invisible. Acknowledge and appreciate each person you encounter that day.

You will move beyond the transactional nature of each encounter to become fully aware of the personal interaction. See what you learn and note it in your meta-leadership journal. How do people react? How can you tell if you succeeded? Observe the impact on those who expected you to ignore or not acknowledge them. How do these interactions affect you? What do you learn about yourself? Beyond an exercise, how does this way of being fit into your meta-leadership practices?

You embody the values, motives, and purposes to which you rally your followers. You can't just *do* it. You must *be* it. In the words of the British novelist E. M. Forster, "Only connect!"

Muhtar Kent, former CEO of the Coca-Cola Company, demonstrated his ability to connect with people throughout his career, often displaying emotional intelligence when it mattered most.

He became the head of the company's operations in Turkey in his early thirties, charged with leading people who were significantly older and more experienced. "Listening and showing empathy were absolutely critical," he told us. "Our people were somewhat demoralized by the state of our business there at the time. Once people sensed that I understood *their* challenges and that I was there to support them, magical things started happening. We grew Turkey into one of the most important markets in the entire Coca-Cola system."

Kent faced a significant challenge shortly after assuming the CEO role in 2008. World financial markets went into free fall. His top priority was to ease the fears of employees, business partners, and shareholders about the long-term implications of the economic turmoil. With the company owning a limited number of bottling territories and holding minority investments in some of its franchise bottlers, the Coke system's internal business relationships can be complicated.

"One of the first things we did," Kent explained, "was bring our leadership team together with leaders from our bottling partners around the world and talk about the resilience and strength of our business. From those discussions, we began to create a shared vision for the next ten-plus years." Although much of this work could have been accomplished by teleconference, Kent understood that the face-to-face connection in a time of disruption was critical to keeping the enterprise focused and aligned for long-term success.

One of Kent's most difficult moments came in the aftermath of the 2011 Fukushima triple disaster in Japan—an earthquake followed by a tsunami and meltdown of nuclear facilities, with a resulting release of radioactive material. Japan is one of the company's largest markets. There was certain to be a drop in sales with production and distribution interrupted. Coca-Cola had employees and bottling partners who lost friends and family in the tragedy: "I felt it was imperative to get over there immediately and reassure everyone in our Japanese system that we were there for them. I was thinking about the personal struggles our people were going through. We were going to be there to help them get their lives and businesses back in order."

Kent knew the importance of being physically and emotionally present at a time of turmoil. Showing up demonstrates sincerity and builds trust. It makes it possible both to send and to receive the verbal as well as nonverbal signals through which people determine if they will follow you—and you will know if they are following.

Reflecting on connection, Kent said, "It is imperative to be real, authentic, and transparent. When people try too hard to impress or to be someone they are not, that always backfires. Leadership is less about authority and more about credibility and communication. A keen knowledge of the business and the job at hand are vital in that regard. When folks know you've walked a mile in their shoes and that you're not asking them to do anything you're not doing yourself, you build credibility. If the credibility is there, leadership will show."

We remain in contact with many graduates of our Harvard executive crisis leadership programs. We ask about their meta-leadership learnings and how they apply them. Many people cite the brain function and emotional intelligence lessons for how useful they are in regulating themselves and guiding others.

They also mention our advice, especially when leading through complex situations, to take chances and allow themselves to make mistakes—though preferably calibrated ones with small consequences. Leaders can take what they learn from this to recover and prevent a more catastrophic failure. Why is it so valuable to take chances and make mistakes?

Many high-achieving people have a spirited affinity for perfection. They want to get it right. They want to meet their own high standards, and they want to meet and exceed the expectations of others. In the real world, however, especially during a time of heightened turmoil and stress, achieving perfection is nearly impossible.

In crisis or change, there is no time for flawlessness. You make decisions and take actions based on incomplete and sometimes contradictory information. Cognitive biases and heuristics come into play. Accepting some measure of tolerable error reduces your own frustration and that of others.

Paradoxically, by doing so, you and others are more likely to succeed in your pursuits. You give people the confidence to put forward new ideas and try novel approaches. Creative problem-solving and innovation thrive as you take small steps to test what works and what doesn't. Then you are ready to recover and be flexible when all does not function as hoped. You get yourself and others out of the basement. You learn and improve.

The pursuit of the perfect actually increases risk. By liberating the cognitive bias toward perfection, you can let go of an impossible standard. Your thinking expands, your confidence increases, and you are able to better appreciate and respond to situations as they actually evolve. You will demonstrate a better understanding of what you can and cannot control as well as what is realistically possible and what is not. As your perspective broadens, your indecision eases and you become more productive and resourceful. You are more likely to adapt to changing circumstances and to be more resilient when all does not go as planned.

Many leaders become distracted by denying, hiding, and defending their mistakes. This is a waste of energy. Don't get stuck on one misstep: admitting you were wrong is simply acknowledging that you are smarter now than you were before. Trust yourself and others who merit trust. Accept mistakes, then refocus and get moving again. Live by this wisdom: learn to fail, or you will fail to learn.

The measure of meta-leadership is whether "people follow you." You are not leading things, like money or assets. The meta-view of the situation you face focuses on bringing together people with a problem to be solved or an opportunity to be harnessed.

Your impact on this situation depends on how you, as a person, engage and motivate the people who will move the stuff and make the desired outcomes happen. This is the gauge of your success or failure as a leader: in the situation, what do you accomplish?

Questions for Journaling

➤ If you tried the suggested connection exercise, what did you experience and learn?

➤ Keep a "basement" section in your journal where you reflect on your experiences there and what you observe of others in the basement. Are you becoming more adept at recognizing that you are in the basement? What is your trigger script for resetting your brain? How are you filling your workroom with useful routine patterns and tools? Are you recognizing and closing gaps as you ascend to higher-level thinking?

➤ Note when you perceive cognitive biases or heuristics at play in yourself and others. How do they shape your perceptions and actions? When and how do they help, and when do they hinder your problem-solving?

. . . .

SEVEN

DIMENSION TWO

Grasping the Situation

In the vocabulary of meta-leadership, there are two sides to "the situation": what is happening, and what to do about it. When you apply the meta-perspective, you see and act according to the complexity of your leadership situation, including all the many people, entities, and considerations that affect what is happening and whose participation is essential to a successful response. You benefit from Cone-in-the-Cube thinking: knowing that neither you nor anyone else has the full picture, you integrate different perspectives to reveal the otherwise unseen. With this awareness, you continuously drive a deliberative process to acquire knowledge, advancing from unknowns to knowns.

Your followership extends beyond your direct command; hence the importance of influence beyond authority and order beyond control. In a thorny situation, it is trust and confidence that earn you the mantel of meta-leader ("people follow you").

Remember, everything discussed in the prior chapter on the person of the meta-leader clarifies your awareness and action in the complexity of the situation. (And the situation, in turn, informs the connectivity discussed in later chapters.)

Consider the different situations you face and those you see others facing. The generic framework we provide applies to a range of situations—from everyday problems to full-blown crises. The goal here is to perceive more accurately and act more effectively.

The situation is the context in which you lead. It can appear stable and routine until the unexpected upsets your rhythm and distorts your perceptions. The situation could be anything from a great opportunity to an explosive crisis. It could be bad or good, big or small, personal or systemic. The situation signals the approach of a turning point, compelling a response. Freeze and you risk being overwhelmed by the situation. Do you incrementally adjust or fundamentally transform your response? Sometimes a wait-and-see approach is appropriate, though sometimes that approach could be a symptom of denial or avoidance.

The situation also includes you; you are a part of it. What you do or don't do is watched by people who look to you to lead.

An adverse situation—a crisis or a compelling need to change—most challenges your meta-leadership capabilities. You assess and understand what is happening, predict how it will unfold, make decisions, and take action. This is particularly critical when the stakes and pressure are high. Timing is critical, the risk is great, and there could be much to lose. The longer it takes to grasp the situation and act, the more losses accrue. Will you pivot into panic or into productive action?

We'll begin with a simple question that has a complex answer: what *is* the situation? Your analysis of it may be clouded by distortions and distractions—some blisteringly loud, some deceptively silent. Emotions may run hot. You and others may be going to the basement. Different people see the situation from distinct perspectives. Cognitive biases mask emerging realities. It is challenging—particularly in the beginning—to separate fact from perception. What is *really* happening?

Often, one bad situation spawns additional situations as those involved react in unexpected ways. Suddenly, you no longer have one situation. You have several. You seek out some situations, positioning yourself for the opportunity to lead. Others come to you as circumstances arise. Whether good or bad, your grit is measured by your navigation of this complexity: how nimbly and skillfully you recognize the situation, assess the risks, decide on a course, and maneuver through it.

Ethan Zohn holds no position in a major corporation. Typically encountered in athletic gear or a loose-fitting shirt and jeans, he is no one's stereotypical power broker. And yet he has mobilized people around the world for causes he holds dear. And while Zohn did not study meta-leadership, he is someone who naturally embodies its traits and sensibilities.

Zohn's passion is soccer. He played goalkeeper in college at Vassar and later professionally with the Hawaii Tsunami, the Cape Cod Crusaders, and Highlanders FC in Bulawayo, Zimbabwe.

In 2001, Zohn, then twenty-seven years old, secured a spot on the popular US television show *Survivor: Africa*. He endured through one daunting *Survivor* challenge after another and eventually won the competition.

"I proved that you can win this game without lying and cheating and stabbing people in the back," he later said. Zohn left Africa with a million-dollar jackpot and the celebrity that comes with a nationally televised triumph.

During filming in Kenya, he won a reward challenge along with the opportunity to play soccer with local young people. He got to know some of the people and was struck by how rampant HIV was among the population. Many people had been born with the ravaging disease and had little understanding of what they could do to stay healthy.

Zohn, who holds deep beliefs about social justice, found himself with a situation—and it was an exceptional one. His personal commitment to doing good (*Meta-Leadership Dimension One*) came together with an unexpected situation (*Dimension Two*) rich with opportunity. He decided to devote his newfound fame, his freshly won prize money, and his passion for soccer to working with and educating young people in Africa. His mission: to prevent the further spread of HIV and AIDS.

A year after winning the *Survivor: Africa* competition, Zohn cofounded Grassroot Soccer (www.grassrootsoccer.org). The group went to Zimbabwe to rally support for their new endeavor. In 2003, they introduced an interactive and soccer-themed HIV prevention curriculum. Its slogan: "Grassroot Soccer uses the power of soccer to educate, inspire, and mobilize communities to stop the spread of HIV."

Zohn and his cofounders started with a simple idea: "We combined the passion of soccer with education and the passion to save lives." To promote health, they teach young people about safe sex and HIV prevention methods through soccer-based activities. Their spark and imagination embraced an opportunity and leveraged it for all it could become. From its humble beginnings, Grassroot Soccer grew, securing funding from the Bill and Melinda Gates Foundation and eventually touching the lives of millions of young people in Africa. Other organizations, funders, and celebrities eagerly signed on to the cause.

Zohn and his cofounders learned to become the leaders that the situation demanded. Some focused on building infrastructure so that the organization could most effectively use donated money and volunteers, including more and more professional soccer players.

Zohn himself had become a celebrity, albeit a reluctant one. Though fundamentally shy, he was willing and determined to take to the field of play and make a difference. He learned to seize his fame and make it work for the enterprise. He attended events, embraced media opportunities, and became the public face of Grassroot Soccer. It was magnetic meta-leadership influence in the absence of authority.

In understanding how leaders respond to a new situation, remember: this crusade was never part of Ethan Zohn's life plan. An unexpected situation—the bounty from *Survivor: Africa*—opened up an opportunity, and he chose to take it. His abundant capacity for hope drew others to the cause. Zohn was able to make the most of his situation—his sudden wealth and celebrity—only because he came to it with expansive self-awareness and acute perception. Understanding that the *real* struggle for survival in Africa was not the game portrayed on television, he saw that he could help.

The opportunity of Zohn's situation—sudden access to resources he could use to tackle a pressing social issue—was a positive one. Most people understandably fear the opposite: the crisis, when lives, property, reputations, or livelihoods are suddenly at stake.

The Meta-Leadership Pivot

The most difficult situations are characterized by sudden, adverse, and complex change. Remember a time when a crisis happened to you. Step one was to get out of the basement. Step two was to discern the situation. These are always the first two steps in any crisis situation.

The crisis could be a mega-disaster. During the late summer and fall of 2017, the US hurricane season delivered one devastating hit after another: Harvey, Irma, Jose, Maria. People caught in the storms were overwhelmed, and responders were inundated. Crises happen when they happen. They don't follow your timetable.

The crisis can be organizational, such as news that a major bank opens accounts without customer consent, or a global auto manufacturer falsifies emissions data, or a medical breakthrough is actually a sham, or personal data has been improperly released. Perhaps it's research impropriety at an academic institution. These slow-burn crises have been building for years and might have been prevented had leaders acted earlier.

Or the situation could be personal. The crisis could be a fatal diagnosis, the death of a loved one, or the loss of a job. Eric worked with a company whose CEO collapsed and died at the gym. It was a personal crisis for the family and his colleagues as well as an organizational crisis for the company.

These situations have a common feature: the need for a pivot with the change in conditions and opportunities. A basketball player pivots by keeping one foot at its point of contact with the floor while stepping or swinging with the other foot. The player, the ball, and the action turn. As a meta-leader, you also turn intentionally.

The first impediment to the leadership pivot is the descent into the basement. Just when you need that higher-level brain power, it shuts down. Activate your trigger script and ascend purposefully to your workroom. Grab your tools—your practiced procedures and behaviors. Then give others jobs to bring them up with you.

Your first meta-leadership charge is to ask questions: What is happening? Who is involved? What is known and what is unknown? What might happen next? Be systematic in assembling that information. If you can, write it down on a whiteboard or flip chart. Organize what you are learning. This first snapshot readies you for what comes next. In the basketball analogy, this is your foot on the ground.

Next, working with people around you, start making decisions. Don't expect to know everything right away or try to make every decision perfect. Situations are dynamic. If lives are on the line, move fast. Then prioritize the rest of your decisions and methodically work through them. Keep observing what is happening and then adjust. Make sure you stay fluid and adaptable. In basketball, this adaptability is your other foot swinging around and changing your direction.

It's okay to not be fully rational. People are emotional beings. In routine situations, you have the luxury of time and calm for debate, logic, and careful analysis. In crisis and turbulent change, you have to assess quickly, draw on your knowledge and experience, and act.

As you become more fully cognizant of your own ingrained responses and those of others, you can better predict how you and different people respond to the same situation. Some will panic. Others will be cool and resolute. Still others will deny or fail to grasp what is happening. As a meta-leader, you anticipate this array of responses. It is part of the complexity of your situation. Draw upon your emotional intelligence to inform, not distort, your perception of this complexity.

Situations involve people, who are social creatures. You have one view of events; others have different perspectives along with varying definitions of both consequences and opportunities. Well beyond the Cone-in-the-Cube, the many people assessing the situation become invested in championing their divergent perspectives. Where one perceives potential benefit, another sees danger. Conflicts emerge. You may find yourself caught in the middle of a fiery standoff. When the circumstances are contentious, such battles further distort the situation. Not only must you deal with what is happening. You are challenged to cope with and balance the array of strong opinions and emotions.

Whether the situation is good or dreadful, risk escalates when you fail to accurately discern the situation and its surrounding social context. As a meta-leader, you remain open to the unexpected.

Most situations do not fully or quickly reveal themselves. You know that something is happening. At the outset you have only limited information about its scope and scale. Facts unfold incrementally amid a cacophony of rumors and false reports. With each new bit of information and evidence, your understanding of the situation and its direction changes and may clarify. Fixating on one point in time and ignoring incoming information, however, can cause you to lose touch and fall behind the situation's evolution.

Lenny Marcus was on-site to study the leadership of the 2005 Hurricane Katrina tragedy in New Orleans. Officials assumed that the looming hurricane crisis would be a "wind event." Once the storm passed, they determined that the wind caused significant though not catastrophic damage. However, the hurricane simultaneously unleashed a storm surge that overwhelmed levees protecting the city, flooding large sections, stranding thousands, and killing nearly 1,500 people. The real disaster in New Orleans was a "water event"—a situation requiring a fundamentally different response than a wind event. The response was flawed in part because as new information arrived, officials failed to adjust their understanding as rapidly as the situation evolved. This miscalculation was their situational blindness.

This is a common problem. In the most comprehensive research on corporate failures ever undertaken, Sydney Finkelstein and his team at Dartmouth College found that in every case, the causes of failure were there to be perceived in advance—but were not seen. Trouble could have been avoided or minimized had executives perceived all that was happening and looked beyond their rigid framing of what was relevant and what was not. Limitations on what leaders choose to see are built into economic models, business strategies, and assumptions about everything from security threats to competitors' strengths and weaknesses. Our colleague, Harvard Business School professor Max Bazerman, alerts leaders to counter this situational phenomenon in his book *The Power of Noticing*. Pay attention to the clues around you.

To the extent that your assumptions help you focus, they are useful. However, when you fail to occasionally check that your framing matches the ever-changing situation at hand, that focus can be disastrously myopic. Finkelstein identified a "seriously inaccurate perception of reality" as a consistent blind spot for otherwise smart, capable executives. Continually distinguish between what you *think* and what you *know*.

Nokia was an early innovative world leader in mobile telephone handsets. That is, until Apple introduced the iPhone in 2007. This device upended the market, starting the smartphone frenzy. Nokia went from being a successful engineering pacesetter to selling primarily low-end phones in developing markets. Between 2007 and 2012, its total market value dropped by 75 percent.

Did this dramatic plummet simply reflect the genius of Apple engineers and designers? Ironically, Nokia had developed a touchscreen smartphone seven years before the iPhone arrived on the market. The firm's managers, however, chose not to bring those products to market and instead focused on what were then highly profitable basic handsets. They failed to pivot, falling prey to a common change barrier: the belief that current success is a predictor of future performance. Today's moneymakers—and their impact on share price—create powerful blinders that obscure both emerging threats and opportunities. Nokia's rival, Motorola, similarly faltered when it was slow to pivot from analog to digital handsets.

Nokia struggled for years to catch up. Finally, in 2013, its device and service businesses were acquired by Microsoft.

When you fail to integrate new information and adjust your situational understanding, your analysis and subsequent actions become dangerously misguided.

To counter this hazard, assume that you will not *fully* comprehend a situation until it is over. Even then, there may be unanswered questions. These should spur further questions and keep you curious. Flex your imagination.

Learn as much as possible about what is happening. Seek data that is accurate and verifiable. Probe for what is missing. Most important, listen to others. Let them see that you are working to understand their perspectives and contributions.

Know that information will come at you in scattershot fashion, and some will be incorrect. Note anomalies. Determine what is more important and less so. Keep fitting pieces into the puzzle looking for patterns to emerge. Be careful about getting overwhelmed. And don't force-fit information into your preconceived notions. Beware of your cognitive biases and those of others.

The POP-DOC Loop

A situation with so much going on can be overwhelming. You're being pulled in many directions, and everything seems urgent.

The key to overcoming the chaos is to systematically decode patterns, anticipate decisions, and plan actions. If you stay disciplined, continuously driving to the known, you will foster more accurate situational awareness, which will allow you to test different strategies and tactics, even in crisis mode. To help provide structure and foster cohesion, we've developed a tool that we call the POP-DOC Loop: Perceive, Orient, Predict; Decide, Operationalize, Communicate.

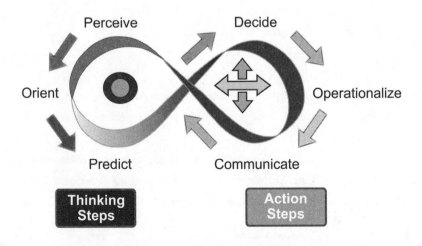

Here we've depicted the POP-DOC Loop as a figure-8 Möbius loop: a single, seamless progression of steps to guide your meta-leadership thinking and action. Start on the top of the left side of the figure-8 and move counter-clockwise: *Perceive* what is happening. *Orient* yourself to detect patterns and understand what they mean. Distinguish between what you *think* and what you *know*. Test for bias-driven blind spots. And then, based on the patterns and the probability of their recurrence, *predict* what is likely to happen next. These are the learning steps. They integrate the dimensions of the person and the situation.

As you cross over to the right side of the figure-8, now moving clockwise, you enter the action phases and shape connectivity: *Decide* on a course of action. *Operationalize* the necessary organizational resources. *Communicate* information out to and bring information in from relevant stakeholders. Then, to assess the impact of your decisions, operations, and communications, cycle back. Repeat the loop continuously, beginning with perceiving again—taking account of new information and changes you have instigated.

The POP-DOC Loop helps you grasp the true nature of complex problems, manage the consequences of your actions, and create sustainable solutions. POP-DOC discipline mitigates risk and increases your capacity to address multiple problems simultaneously.

The roots of POP-DOC are in the OODA Loop (Observe, Orient, Decide, Act) developed by Colonel John Boyd of the US Air Force during the Korean War. Boyd's OODA Loop helped explain why American fighter pilots were outperforming their adversaries. The faster they were able to go through an OODA Loop, the more effective they were. We build on Boyd's work and expand it to depict a useful guide and benchmark for meta-leaders. For you, we add "predict" and "communicate." Leadership, after all, is both anticipatory and social.

As a meta-leader, you use POP-DOC yourself, and to amplify its effectiveness you embed it in your organization and network. POP-DOC is a guide for creating the conditions for the active and intentional engagement of your followers and other stakeholders.

What is the significance of the Möbius loop structure? A Möbius is the only two-dimensional shape that must be rendered in three dimensions to be perceived. You can simulate one with a ribbon: make one twist and attach the

ends. On a complete cycle around a Möbius, you cover its full surface and return to your starting point without ever crossing an edge. This loop is a pathway for perpetually ordering, directing, and guiding your meta-leadership
practice in complex situations. The twist is what you do and accomplish as a
leader—the change you initiate. POP-DOC is a guide through complexity.
You understand and turn a situation, pivoting continually between thinking
and acting as you focus on your desired outcomes.

When Dr. Richard Besser was leading the CDC's response to the H1N1
influenza pandemic, he and his team were constantly called upon to inform
policymakers and the public about the future course of the outbreak. How
fast would it spread? How sick would people get? How many of the sick
would die? Which groups would be at greatest risk?

In the beginning, little was known for sure. The CDC had only the opinions of top scientists, not the data for complete scientific analysis. Policymakers and clinicians, however, could not wait for a perfect picture. Time
was of the essence. A decision was needed.

CDC leaders studied what little epidemiological data they had (perceiving) to assess the nature of the virus (orienting). With that, they predicted
that they could both minimize the spread of the disease and diminish the
social and economic impact that would result from mass sickness and fear.
Therefore, they encouraged people to engage in specific protective behaviors, such as coughing into one's elbow and frequent hand-washing. At the
outset, they ordered schools closed for two weeks (deciding) if even one case
was found among students. To operationalize the policy, they coordinated
with state and local officials. They held frequent press conferences and constantly updated the CDC website (communicating). Continuing around the
Möbius loop, they learned more, changed advisories, and executed policies
accordingly. That honesty and transparency reaped an uncommon 83 percent approval rating for the government's handling of the crisis.

The first phase in POP is perceive. Picture a wide-open zoom lens on a
camera. The more you see and the more information you gather, the better

informed you become. Look for solid, verifiable evidence to build as complete a picture as possible. Draw on all your senses to learn the circumstances
of the situation and the stakeholders involved. Speak and, more important,
listen to a range of individuals. Challenge yourself to be open-minded. Often
your most important clues are subtle, not the ones that shout out for attention. If you are in the basement, your perception will be limited, so engage
your trigger script to get out of the basement as soon as possible.

From that broader view, distill more data and narrow your perspective,
focusing on what you perceive to be most important. Zoom out again to
see the big picture unfolding. Ask "what if . . . " questions to expand your
thinking. Challenge assumptions and orthodoxies. It is your responsibility
as a meta-leader to be in the know. There is little forgiveness if the evidence
was available and you failed to notice and act on it. Venture out, reaching for
what others can't see. Be curious.

Information overload is a constant danger. Do not be afraid to stop gathering information or responding to concerns that prove irrelevant.

Phase two in the POP-DOC Loop is orient. During this analytic phase, you
are looking for patterns—the predictable stimulus-response sequences that
distinguish repetitive actions and behaviors. They help you discern order
amid chaos. Correctly identified patterns organize many data points into
logical arrangements of events and behaviors.

Search for patterns—both social and physical—that are legitimate, relevant, and useful in understanding the situation at hand. The social patterns
include lines of communication, decision-making norms, and relationships
among people and groups. The environmental and physical patterns include
the weather, chemical reactions, and animal migrations.

Draw on your prior experience and expertise to distinguish what is useful information and what is not. Fill in the gaps of information as best you
can. Don't try to paint every detail. Do not confuse assumptions with hard
data. Instead, work to grasp the big picture as it emerges. You will refine your
understanding as you perceive and add more critical information.

Patterns rarely occur in isolation. Understanding the relational effects as
different patterns converge in your situation is critical to your analysis. This

dynamism is complexity. As you accurately identify patterned reactions and the factors modifying those patterns, you discover overlapping phenomena that clarify what is happening. You collect clues that enable you to interrupt current patterns and, if change is called for, instigate new patterns.

As you work to understand patterns, keep in mind that correlation does not always equate to causation. The brain prizes coherence and can instantly stitch together visible data points into a picture that is plausible though not necessarily true. Paradoxically, the brain can fabricate patterns that bolster coherence in your perceptions. This is how optical illusions trick you. Your mind invents and accepts an explanation that makes superficial sense even though it is wrong.

CDC scientists, working to unravel the early mysteries of the H1N1 virus, applied incoming epidemiological data to discern how dangerous and spreadable it was. That information oriented them to a disease more akin to typical seasonal flu than to a massively fatal pandemic. The data revealed the patterns.

As you make your own sense of what is happening, you discover how others orient themselves based on what they perceive. What are the commonalities and differences among those providing and interpreting information? Why do they exist? Use this information to further refine your orientation to the situation.

Phase three of the POP-DOC Loop is predict. If you correctly identified and anticipated the progression of patterns, and if you expect those patterns to repeat themselves in the near future, you are ready to accurately anticipate what will—or what could—happen next.

At one point in the H1N1 outbreak, epidemiologists discovered that pregnant women were particularly susceptible to the disease. Scientists predicted that a disproportionate number of those women would succumb to the virus. That prediction informed subsequent decisions, operations, and communications that saved lives.

Prediction is a powerful tool as you lead. With the right information, the movements of people, the reactions of the press, and the responses of other leaders are all predictable. What you have seen before you may very well see again, shaped by all that is happening in your situation.

In a dynamic situation, you predict at the intersection of the past, the present, and the future: what was, what is, and what will be. For example, modelers use their sophisticated algorithms to look at history and current conditions to forecast future economic trends as well as the weather. A prediction mind-set, balanced by experience and information about the situation, helps to reduce uncertainty. You stay ahead of what is happening and guide those you lead to the appropriate decisions and actions.

The intent of POP-DOC is not to assume flawless powers of prophecy. Rather, accept that the accuracy of your predictions is not perfect. The purpose of Predict in the meta-leadership Möbius loop is to orient you to the future and instill discipline in your directive thinking and actions. The Möbius loop structure encourages you to decide and act without waiting for perfect information. You can revise and adapt the operational aspects of your endeavors as you learn more about the situation. Remember, the loop is continuous. If you don't get it right on this go-round, seek to improve on the next.

You may need to make multiple predictions. Assign each a probability for accuracy, though do so carefully. Precisely calculating probability does not come naturally to most people; typically, your results are closer to guesswork. Temper your intuition with facts and the available facts with intuition. Examine whatever data you have. Ask about base rates to determine if the deviations you perceive are small or large. Factor in the eventual regression of all patterns to a mean. In sports, for example, perceived hot and cold streaks tend to balance each other out in a way that reflects a player's or team's actual ability.

When accurate, trusted, and followed, prediction keeps you a step ahead of unfolding events. It requires and builds influence beyond authority. Some decisions and actions are yours to take. Others demand convincing other people—often leaders themselves—of the evidence of an emerging pattern and the choices and consequences that lie ahead.

Predicting accurately takes practice. Start today at your office or on your commute home. When you send your subordinates a sales update noting the gap between revenue booked and the monthly goal, you are predicting that the information will spur them to reach out to their accounts for new orders. When you choose the side-street route home, you predict that it will be faster than the highway. What is the big picture? What is your prediction? What information and experience are you using? What are the patterns? How often are you right?

A cautionary note on predicting: once you predict, you create a cognitive bias that affects how you perceive the situation going forward. You and others become invested in that prediction, seeking and giving preference to confirming evidence. Be as prepared for your prediction to be wrong as you are for it to be right. Over time you will increase your accuracy, though always be ready to admit an incorrect prediction. You may even need to completely reverse course.

Your predictive capabilities provide guidance as you transition to the next steps of POP-DOC. You are now ready to engage in multi-stakeholder problem-solving—the "people follow you" side of the process.

Phase four of POP-DOC is decide. If you do not advance to making a decision, you will fall victim to the POP trap—forever gathering and analyzing information without ever committing to a course of action. Paralysis by analysis. To move forward, you must decide.

First, there is the process of deciding. You are aware of the need for stakeholder buy-in and support if your decision is to be carried out. To achieve this, be transparent and certain about your intended decision-making process: Will you make the call yourself? Will you seek consensus among a core team? Will you take a vote, perhaps reserving veto power for yourself? You may even delegate the decision to someone whom you believe has appropriate perspective, such as a subject matter expert. You assess the situation as well as your own style, authority, and accountability and that of the others the decision will involve. Your intent is to arrive at the best outcome. Articulate your preferred decision-making process. It is better to deal with any dissonance over the process before you actually make the decision.

Next, when data are available and reliable, apply it. Algorithms, even simple ones, can outperform experts when causal factors are known. Companies such as Amazon and Netflix make decisions on product recommendations using automated predictive analytics. These conclusions, even more than customers' own choices, can be an accurate prediction of what customers will like. Health care organizations such as Kaiser Permanente, a large US integrated provider, rely on evidence-based protocols as the default choice for the treatment of many illnesses.

And then there are your "gut feelings." These actually derive from the rich reserve of data in your brain gleaned through life experience. Intuition is knowing without conscious reasoning or definitive evidence. The decision just feels right. Intuition is excellent for rendering decisions that are "good enough" in many situations, particularly if you have had sufficient practice with a particular type of decision. Experienced poker players cannot see every card, though by playing thousands of hands of cards they develop a sixth sense about whether to "hold 'em or fold 'em." This intuitive sense combines numerous data points, including the facial expressions and body language of others, that are more subjective than objective.

Experience-based intuition explains why a physician may choose to override the default protocol at Kaiser Permanente. She may feel that there is something distinct about a case that requires a different course of treatment. Having a default option requires her to articulate the reasons for deviating from it. This informs and improves the care of a specific patient as well as the data set on which the default is based.

Evidence and intuition serve to check and balance each other. They stretch across a continuum. If you have data and it does not feel right, ask more questions. Your gut may lead you in a direction that defies the facts at hand. Conversely, hard data may temper your first intuitive judgment. Considering your perspective, as well as that of others, can moderate your prediction bias. Your objective is to reach the best possible decision through the most appropriate process, and in a timely manner.

Phase five of POP-DOC is operationalize. Decisions do not become actions by themselves. Weight loss is a good example. Many people decide to get into better shape. Far fewer actually operationalize the choice by going to the gym and eating less. Making a decision and taking action on that decision use different circuits of the brain.

To operationalize is to take meaningful action, including activating others to do so. Your most visible and tangible meta-leadership activities materialize in this phase of POP-DOC. What you do here—or do not do—often determines the success or failure of what you ultimately hope to accomplish. Your operationalization is what others see and experience. It is when your impact becomes tangible.

Prompt operational progress by asking yourself and your team action-oriented questions: What must we do differently in order to carry out this decision? Who needs to be involved or informed? What resources are required? When do we act? How will we measure impact? These questions orient the brain toward *doing*. The answers propel the team forward. You identify stakeholders and the anticipated impact. You perceive interdependencies and relationships that may prove critical to implementing your decisions by allowing and encouraging you to delegate effectively.

There are many ways to go either right or wrong in the operationalize phase. Your best chance to get it right is to transition carefully through the four prior phases. Recall the significance of the Möbius loop structure: the steps are continual and sequential. Each step forward is dependent on your earlier POP-DOC efforts. You can progress either slowly and methodically or, in a crisis, you can traverse the loop in seconds.

How might you get it wrong? There are dreamers, chargers, and bean counters. *Dreamers* reach for a compelling vision, ignoring the pragmatic constraints and situation at hand. They get people excited about the desirable yet impossible to achieve. *Chargers* overlook the analytic phase of the POP-DOC Loop. They generate a lot of activity with little productivity. What they lead and do has limited connection to the problems or opportunities at hand. *Bean counters* tally what they have done, though it lacks direction and purpose. They precisely catalog actions with little awareness of their impact on or relationship to the situation. From their perch, the numbers themselves signal success.

There is a bit of dreamer, charger, and bean counter in every leader. Vision, action, and accountability are each essential to your effectiveness. The six steps of POP-DOC help you balance and temper your impulses and more accurately fit your actions and solutions to the contours of the situation at hand.

Phase six of POP-DOC is communicate. When we interview leaders and their teams after a crisis, the most frequently cited theme for critique and improvement is communication. Getting everyone the information they need to know when they need to know it is difficult, particularly when an operation involves many people as well as multiple agencies and organizations.

Communication is multidirectional: out and in. It includes both information out from leaders to followers and information in from the situation and followers to leaders. Master communication and it will be a powerful force for you; stumble and it can quickly become a daunting force working against you.

Visualize two types of communication: waves and flows.

Waves follow a regular schedule and rhythm. Think of a daily noon press conference or an end-of-day briefing during a crisis. It may be a weekly blog post by a CEO working to catalyze change in the organization. During a crisis, establish the rhythm of regular updates for key stakeholders at set times every day: 10:00 a.m. and 6:00 p.m., for example. Prime expectations and establish control of the communication parameters. Prepare carefully and forge a narrative of unity of effort to get people together on both message and means. This is how CDC leaders communicated with a worried public during the H1N1 crisis. The briefings were regular, and they were strategic.

Flows, by contrast, are constant. Think of the continuous activity on social media or the fluctuations in stock prices. You cannot control the flow; you must swim in it. Information that truly cannot wait for regularly scheduled updates needs to make its way through the system. Debunk rumors. Provide critical updates that enable you and your followers to make nimble adaptations to your strategy and tactics. If you have established and engaged in effective waves, you'll avoid being overwhelmed by information coming in and requests for news. You better manage the flow. For this reason, CDC leaders also accepted frequent requests for media interviews during the H1N1 crisis. In so doing, they maintained the information flow, mitigating the possibility of rumors and misinformation.

In volatile situations, information can emerge slowly while decisions and announcements are expected quickly. It is best to be forthright about what is known and what is not. Have your announcements conform with risk communication best practice: *This is what we know and what we are doing about it. This is what we don't know and what we are doing to learn more. This is what you—the audience—should do.* This was the CDC communication theme throughout the crisis. If you get it right, the people receiving your announcement will be calmed and feel directed. And in keeping with the meta-leadership definition, *people follow you.*

Organizations have prewritten holding statements ready to issue to the media, including social media, when crisis hits. There are many variants. "Acme holdings has just learned that [X] has occurred. Our priority now is the well-being of our employees. As we learn more, we will provide information to family members and the public." These at-the-ready communication statements are helpful when little is known and many are in the basement.

The POP-DOC Loop heightens intentionality as you take action in the high-stakes situations in which your meta-leadership comes alive. People above, below, and alongside you pay particular attention when you act—your decisions, behaviors, communications, initiatives, and more—and when you propel them into action mode too. Your meta-leadership has its impact in the actions you take. It is also in how you take action and how you express what you're doing.

POP-DOC is not merely a tool for crisis leadership. It can become part of your everyday analysis and action. Use it to guide business decisions, military strategy, or personal dilemmas. As you embed it, you become more intentionally thoughtful and balanced in your thinking and actions. Use it routinely and it will be ready when it matters most.

Meta-leading is fraught with risk. At one end of the spectrum, you could act impulsively. A miscalculation generates a new set of problems that can cascade out of control, with unfortunate outcomes. At the other end of the spectrum, you could hesitate to take action or make a decision out of concern that it might not go as planned. Such indecision creates its own consequences and implications, often adding to your troubles. Both extremes are basement behaviors.

Apply the POP-DOC Loop as a tool and continuous process to find just the right measure and balance. Test an idea by launching it modestly at first, then assessing the impact. You can perceive, orient, and predict the next steps based on your experience. If you achieve the intended effects, take it up a notch, implementing on a wider scale and with greater certitude. If not, recalibrate. Take small iterations through a number of loops before fully committing. Each cycle deepens your understanding and impact.

Engage others and involve them in your actions. Gather supporters, respond to concerns, and build larger constituencies, thus reducing the risks in moving forward. For followers, there is meaning, purpose, hope, and accomplishment in what you and the enterprise achieve. Together, you and your followers make a difference. This is why you are being followed. With each cycle through the POP-DOC Loop, you move closer to your overall meta-leadership purposes and intentions.

You may be wondering why we have yet to highlight the "how to" of a topic central to much of the discussion on leadership: vision. When our students discuss the great leader/lousy leader exercise, "having a vision" or being "visionary" are always on the "great leader" list.

It's hard to craft a compelling vision for where you are and where you want to go until you first get your bearings. The POP-DOC Loop is your tool for doing just that. As you systematically go through its steps, you grasp what was, what is, and what your direction will be. This is your vision. In POP, the process connects your vision to the strategy and tactics necessary to realize it in DOC. Beyond the inspiration itself, a vision untethered to the complexities of implementation breeds frustration.

Repetitively traversing the questions of the Möbius loop will connect POP and DOC into a feedback cycle that guides the evolution of your vision and actions. As you go through the figure-8, you continuously learn and refine to get closer to your goal. You adapt your vision to the realities in your situation, be it adjusting to market signals, responding to political shifts, or transforming your organization to better fulfill its mission.

In the Chapter 3 story of FEMA's transformation, Rich Serino and his boss, Administrator Craig Fugate, perceived disconnects throughout the disaster response system. Fugate had come from the state level, and Serino from a local agency; both now had federal-level responsibilities. Analyzing the patterns of gaps and overlaps, they predicted that a system that better integrated state, local, and federal agencies—along with private and nonprofit organizations—would improve outcomes and more effectively use resources. Their POP vision: a "whole of community" disaster response.

In their DOC actions, FEMA decided to call those other players "partners" and rather than supplant them, to operate in support of and in coordination with them. Inclusive communications emphasized the new approach. From the 2011 tornado in Joplin, Missouri, to Super Storm Sandy in 2012, to the hurricanes of 2017 and 2018 that came after Serino and Fugate left FEMA, that legacy iterated forward. The system was never perfect, yet FEMA, operating from vision to reality, continued to learn from its experiences.

Life's Pivots

In the years following *Survivor: Africa,* Ethan Zohn became a widely known and inspirational figure. Through media appearances and speaking engagements, as well as a large Web presence, he demonstrably changed lives through his charitable activities. Zohn made the most of a great situation.

Then, in 2009, he confronted a bad situation, an unexpected personal pivot. He was diagnosed with a rare type of cancer, CD20-positive Hodgkin's lymphoma. His situation was a medical one. But it was also a psychological situation, a public situation, a family situation, and an organizational situation for Grassroot Soccer.

Zohn faced a deeply personal, and possibly fatal, situation that was as bad as it could be. It was an existential crisis and the potential loss of everything. But, like every situation, it also had the potential to be transformative through greater self-understanding.

"After getting that call from the doctor, I immediately thought, *I'm going to die,*" Zohn told us. "And then I made a pact with myself to stay positive and fight like hell." After three initial months of intensive chemotherapy, the cancer returned. Zohn's life shifted into a cycle of bad news, more treatment, remission, hope, and then disappointment with the return of the disease. With each round, he underwent another and even more intensive intervention. During one of those bouts, he wrote on his blog: "The cancer is back.

It's entered my body. It's trying to destroy me. The stem cell transplant they gave me was like hitting the reset button on my body—the entire journey of cancer is like a triathlon." This was the POP side of his analysis: perceiving his situation, orienting to the patterns, and predicting that his attitude would affect his fate. And then he pivoted forward.

Zohn decided to become the person he needed to be to fight the disease. In November 2011, he told *People* magazine, "I don't want fear or cancer to define me, but it's always in the back of your mind." He went on to say, "Cancer isn't going to slow me down. I want people to know that you can still live a fulfilled life and move forward. I will get better, but it's going to take a while." This was the DOC side of his persona: he decided to fight, he put the plan into practice, and then he communicated his mission. In his many media appearances, he turned himself into another kind of hero, *Survivor: Cancer.* It was a choice that reflected his perception of the situation, what it meant for him, and for the many others who depended on him as well as the many more for whom he served as a role model. Though he did not ask for it, this new situation became for him another leadership opportunity.

Zohn was resilient. Resilience is the capacity to face anxiety and setback and then bounce forward to overcome it. Sometimes you become what you were before. In the best case, however, what you learn in the process transforms you into someone stronger and even more resilient.

"I think in the cancer world, the general perception is that there are winners and losers," Zohn told *People.* "[That] you either beat cancer and you win—or you don't and you die. But the reality of my situation is, I did everything in my power to beat cancer, and I did. But it came back. And that's okay, too . . . I'm not a failure. There are millions of people out there living with cancer and you can still have a fulfilled life. You can go to work, raise a family, and charge forward. That's what I'm doing here." He constantly honed his perception of his situation. He did not delude himself with false hope, nor did he resign himself to collapse.

Zohn told us, "Focusing on the plight of another human being helps you heal. There is scientific research that proves this. So I made a conscious choice to make the details of my life public. It helped me to help others. It was selfish and selfless at the same time. If I can effect change in the middle of my own crisis, that's a good thing."

With an accurate picture of the situation, he was able to fortify himself to fight and fight some more. He survives to this day.

Leaders often describe leadership as lonely, especially when the situation is bad. The worse the situation is, the lonelier it can feel. When the situation is really bad, you can be overcome with feelings of isolation.

Should you find yourself experiencing the profound loneliness of a bad situation, know that it can be also be an opportunity to discover your greatest personal resilience. That resilience is critical to the resilience of the larger operation—or in a very broad situation, the overall population. Your followers are far less likely to be resilient if you cannot find that quality within yourself.

This is the lesson of Ethan Zohn. Cultivating your resilience is critical to mastering the many situations you face. Life is not linear, it's complex. It is full of unexpected pivots. Should you simply dispense with planning because you know that you will face many situations, large and small, every day? Not at all. Remember, plans are directional, not deterministic. Context is dynamic. Be attuned to the world around you—and the world within yourself. Without this awareness, you will miss opportunities or needlessly succumb to setbacks.

Embrace a mind-set of striving to fully perceive, orient to, and understand the situations that surround you. Only then can you truly engage the enterprise of the people to whom you connect and who look to you for guidance and direction: those down, up, across, and beyond your organization. Connectivity—this is the topic we turn to in the next chapters.

Questions for Journaling

> Engage in practice runs with the POP-DOC Loop in routine situations such as during a staff meeting, a night out with friends, or a walk through airport security and check-in. What do you perceive? What do you later realize you failed to perceive? How accurate were your orientation and predictions? Were your decisions sound? How did you make things happen and communicate your intentions? How were your actions influenced by this exercise?

➤ Then apply POP-DOC to a crisis situation. It could be a personal crisis or a major organizational crisis. How comprehensive were your perceptions? Did your orientation reap useful patterns? And how accurate were your predictions? Turning to DOC, did your decisions achieve the intended effects? Were they operationalized as planned? And your communication efforts: did they work?

➤ Remember a time when you were called upon to pivot, in either your professional or personal life. What happened? What encouraged the pivot? What discouraged it? And did your pivot help or complicate your situation?

EIGHT

DIMENSION THREE

Building Connectivity

By now, we hope you fully understand that meta-leadership is not simply a tool set for when you lead. It is actually a systematic way of thinking and acting that informs both those grand meta-moments of crisis and change and the more routine decisions you have to make.

Ultimately, this is a story about you, both singular and plural. You are always ready to pivot quickly. And when you do, others must be ready to pivot with you.

Meta-leadership connectivity is a social exercise for cultivating, nurturing, and building person-to-person value directed toward linked objectives. Leveraging those relationships accomplishes more together than anyone could do on their own.

Why Connectivity?

When you lead on the meta-level, many people and entities become involved—whether it's bosses, employees, customers, bystanders, the media, or investors—and they all have some connection or stake in what happens.

One option is that everyone is in it for themselves. Each person goes off on their own, in separate, competitive, and disorganized ways. Chaos erupts, organizational silos become rigid, and resistance to change increases. The disjointed jumble adds to the disarray and magnifies gaps and overlaps. There is no coordination, collaboration, or cohesion and few checks and balances. The resulting mayhem only exacerbates the chaos and disorder.

A different option is to properly deploy the third dimension of meta-leadership—connectivity—so that all stakeholders become invested in a shared purpose. They come together, sharing what they know, what they are doing, and what they hope to achieve. There is order and unity of mission, and people engage one another with mutual cooperation. Everyone has a job to do and helps others succeed in theirs. There is mutual respect and good behavior. People trust both one another and the process that brought them together. The resulting goodwill bolsters productivity and fortifies the investment in the collective effort and accomplishment.

Assembling that connectivity of effort—or being a part of it—is your role as meta-leader.

We established the National Preparedness Leadership Initiative in the wake of the 9/11 attacks. This effort began our exploration of crisis leadership as a way for the country to better prepare for and respond to massive disasters. One common complaint at the time was the pervasive "silo mentality." Organizations and sectors whose joint work was intended to make the nation safer were operating in isolation from one another. Federal agencies were not collaborating. Within agencies, departments and offices acted separately. The federal government did not adequately cooperate with its state and local counterparts. And the private and nonprofit sectors were often kept out of the loop. Information, assets, experience, and relationships were not optimally connected. After 9/11, this disconnectivity quickly came to be seen as a national vulnerability.

To remedy that vulnerability, the Department of Homeland Security (DHS) was established in 2002 to better coordinate activities by combining twenty-two separate federal agencies into a single entity. However, it takes more than a bureaucratic structural change to accomplish that mission. Forging the actual connectivity was a meta-leadership responsibility. Six years later, DHS secretary Michael Chertoff noted, in addressing the NPLI at Harvard, "I am the first cabinet-level secretary whose job description is meta-leadership."

We rephrased the question: rather than dismantling silos, how could the silos be better connected and, through that connectivity, be even stronger? The idea caught on. In organizations, silos do in fact have important functions. Specialized knowledge and skills are found there. For example, if your boat capsizes, you want the Coast Guard to come get you. Likewise, the cardiac intensive care unit is where you want to be with a heart problem. A robust finance department is necessary to handle the intricacies of revenue, expenses, taxes, and regulatory compliance. Strong silos foster proficiency in complex work environments. They also offer a reassuring modicum of familiarity and comfort, especially during periods of high stress or crisis.

So silos themselves aren't the problem: it's poor communication and anemic connections between them. Silos reward inwardly focused behavior and can be highly resistant to transparency and collaboration with other silos. As a meta-leader, you appreciate the silo when it creates value while building momentum for even greater success through broader engagement. Connecting and empowering silos is what meta-leaders aspire to achieve in leading across and beyond. Influence is your essential tool.

Through our work at the NPLI, connectivity—between leaders and among organizations in different sectors—became a strategy for reducing the vulnerabilities aggravated by silo thinking and behavior. For example, from 2007 to 2012, we presented Meta-Leadership Summits for Preparedness, cosponsored by the CDC, the CDC Foundation, and the Robert Wood Johnson Foundation. These events brought together government agencies and private-sector businesses, and community organizations in thirty-two communities across the country. As summit participants embraced collaboration, new opportunities were revealed.

The benefits of connectivity became particularly apparent in large-scale operations, whether responding to a hurricane or terrorist event. No single leader can know how, or have the resources, to mount an all-encompassing response. There is not enough money, expertise, or capability in one place for that. Connectivity emerged for us as a central strategy when we realized that, when you grasp the big picture and how the pieces connect, new reservoirs of capacity and capability emerge.

We also saw that overcoming silo-based antagonism by crafting opportunities—including recognition and reward—encourages shared solutions. These incentives amplify the central narrative of your meta-leadership objective. Complement the typical incentive structure for in-silo performance with acknowledgment of cross-silo achievement and the value derives from it. Whether facing a problem or opportunity, you elevate what can be achieved when you replace traditional rivalries and conflicts with the gains of a shared enterprise.

As the meta-leadership model matured, we extended this connectivity premise to the everyday work of business organizations, government agencies, and nonprofits. Hence, connectivity became a practice to enhance the functioning of each individual, department, or office as part of a larger whole. This is a fundamental premise of meta-leadership.

Walter "Budge" Upton is the chief executive officer of Upton and Partners, a Boston-based real estate development and project management business. The firm oversees planning and construction of large public buildings.

Upton won the contract to serve as director of project development and construction for the ambitious expansion of the Art of the Americas wing at the Boston's renowned Museum of Fine Arts. The most significant enlargement of the prestigious museum in a century, it was a plum assignment. The dramatic 200,000-square-foot new wing connecting to the existing structure had to be built without closing the museum or moving any more of its priceless collection than absolutely necessary. Construction would be a high-wire act of engineering and logistics, as the design was ambitious, the budget firm, and the deadline set in stone.

One other detail: Upton was actually the fourth project manager to be given the job in the first eighteen months of the expansion.

Four designees started work in the role, and three had been dismissed. As Upton took over, he knew from the start that he faced an arduous challenge. "The project was public and very visible. It involved a high-powered board and museum director, a world-renowned architect whose principal offices were across the ocean in London, and one of the world's foremost collections of art. The work crews ranged from Italian artisans to union steel workers. It had a high profile physically, politically, and financially."

The project was also a significant meta-leadership undertaking. Upton had enormous responsibility and limited final authority: his leverage had to be earned through astute influence. He had to lead up to donors, who contributed vast sums to construct the project, as well as to the museum directors. He was confident that associates on his team—to whom he was leading down—were with him, though he would have to support them in weathering the anticipated storms of dissent in coordinating a complex and already conflict-prone operation. He led across to the architects, construction companies, and suppliers working on the building, some of whom were not directly under contract to the museum.

Upton appreciated that his project management and construction qualifications got him the job. It was his meta-leadership skills, however, that would make the difference between success and failure. He would have to lead—get people following him—in all directions simultaneously.

"You have to manage the psychology as much as the logistics," he told us. Early on, he created an expansive organizational chart that included his team plus the major donors, the museum board and management, public officials, and everyone else whose support he would ultimately need.

"I wanted to be able to see all of the stakeholders," he explained. Describing how he connected in the situation, he told us that he "walked the job" every day. "If you are seen, particularly by those from other organizations, people assume you know what's going on. I also had to learn to be a better listener. Every job is different, and so you have to learn all the time. You have to be tolerant in resolving the 'people' problems. And you have to learn to build confidence in your own problem-solving. When it is time for you to make a decision, you must. And you also occasionally have to eat a little crow along the way to keep things moving. You don't want to be right all of the time."

He learned critical meta-leadership lessons along the way: "Make the levels of authority clear so that you know where the lines are drawn as events unfold," Upton said. "You want to know who has authority, how much you have, and how much your superior has. When dealing with subcontractors, you don't have full authority, so you have to be careful about the contract: the scope, cost, and the schedule. You have to meet the people and go to their shop—look out for their attitude as well as their competency."

Critical in his leading up—to a powerful project executive committee of six influential trustees—was establishing a clear process to let them know what was going on. They met at least every two weeks during the project.

"If you sit on a problem, you're gone," Upton said. "Create a safe environment for airing all problems and then for reaching decisions."

There was also a large "anonymous" donor—whose identity was a well-known secret—with his own agenda. When it came time to choose a general contractor, Upton knew who was best for the job; however, he wanted the decision to be theirs—the trustees' and the anonymous donor's—as long as it was the right decision. The contractor he recommended—who was eventually selected—had never been sued by a project owner. This was a key attribute that spoke to relationships as well as the quality of work. Upton intentionally sought a general contractor with a history that demonstrated an orientation toward partnerships rather than adversarial relationships—in other words, a good connector. It would be good for the project and make his own meta-leadership easier as well.

Numerous problems arose that required Upton's diplomacy in leading across, among them the issue of the exterior stone selection for the building, a topic of extensive debate. Junkets were flown all over the world to look at different stone. Ten mock-ups were built, and opinions about them were diverse and passionate. The architect's preferred option—and the most expensive— was to reactivate a closed Italian quarry in order to extract its black marble. Concerns were expressed that, while it looked impressive in some lights, it could appear ominous and forbidding in others. The architect's team insisted, however, on presenting their recommendation to the trustees.

Upton did not want to get in the middle of this fight, even though he had an obvious stake in the outcome. He scheduled a meeting for the architect's team to pitch their preference to the trustees, orchestrating the discussion to ensure that the right people were in the audience. Upton knew that it was up to the trustees to make the decision. He also knew the option he wanted to go with himself in order to keep work on budget and on schedule.

Advocating for it directly, however, would have pitted him against the architects, with negative ramifications for the rest of the project. He had confidence that the trustees shared his concern about finances and timing, even as they respected the architect's vision and expertise. He trusted them to be prudent when they weighed all of the relevant factors.

After the presentation by the architect's team, the board decided to use gray marble from nearby Deer Isle, Maine. It was aesthetically pleasing, could be purchased at a reasonable price, and delivery was not an issue. It was a small yet significant victory and an important test of Upton's stewardship of the project.

The project architect remained resolute throughout. There was a dispute over whether to include light louvers planned for the top-floor gallery. The architectural team insisted on them. The anonymous donor's team said, "Over our dead bodies." Upton knew that indecision would seriously delay the work. He also discerned that taking the louvers out of the plan would be a significant change, costing about $1 million. The donor's representative did not want the louvers and even more, they did not want to spend the money to change the plans. This gave Upton the chance to establish himself as a decision-maker: the light louvers would remain. From the architect, Upton earned respect as a champion of the design. From the donor, he got credit as a guardian of the budget. He looked good to both while also managing to keep the project on track.

Upton offered political advice for meta-leaders: look for and connect with allies who understand the politics, especially if you don't. "I cultivated allies who understood what was going on. Without them, I would have been flying politically blind. As a result, I was able to protect myself. Often, you need those allies along with a lot of information to make a judgment, which may, from the outside, appear arbitrary. As leader, you have to provide direction to the many people involved and then accept the consequences. Be honest about your own strengths and weaknesses, and build your team to compensate for what you lack. Ultimately, in a job like this, you have to be accountable.

"As a leader, you want to model balanced decision-making behavior. Acknowledge to the stakeholders what has to happen. Put it on the table. Also acknowledge that all decisions will not be right and that sometimes the worst case can be no decision."

The museum's Art of the Americas wing, with fifty-three new galleries and more than five thousand works of art, opened on November 20, 2010, to rave reviews. Upton and his team made it all the way to successful project completion.

Map-Gap-Gives-Gets

Your meta-leadership ventures may not be as public or ambitious as Budge Upton's. Nevertheless, his story is instructive. He forged the necessary connectivity of effort to get the project done. He was a presence for everyone involved in a mammoth and complex venture. He engaged them and the situation, and in the process he learned, taught, and gained influence. Upton was able to guide decision-making in directions he saw as beneficial to the project, though he often did so with hands-off ingenuity. He managed as he led and led as he managed. Understanding key relationships and how one person can affect others, he leveraged that knowledge and those connections to build momentum where his attention and endorsement were needed. He clearly perceived the obstacles.

Recognizing the sometime divergent motivations of the many stakeholders involved, Upton was able to forge mutually acceptable—or at least mutually tolerable—solutions to guide the project over foreboding hurdles. Most important, in his coordinating role, he recognized the connectivity between one set of activities and other activities, and between one group of people and other groups. He was also aware of the impact of each decision and action on the whole enterprise. It was that sensitivity and understanding—the essence of the meta-leadership mind-set—that kept him on the project and kept the project on track.

To help other leaders achieve similar results, we developed "Map-Gap-Gives-Gets," a tool for building connectivity. The *map* shows the contours of the situation—what is happening or needs to happen. Upton's detailed project plan combined with an expansive organizational chart that included all stakeholders to create a map of the terrain he would traverse.

In being seen on the job and regularly meeting with key constituents, Upton was able to spot *gaps*—differences between what was supposed to be happening and the reality on the ground. He did not have the authority to command people to meet his every demand. Instead, in closing the gaps to resolve the conflicts over the exterior marble and the gallery louvers, Upton astutely laid out the consequences in terms that the stakeholders could appreciate. He specified the *gives*—tangible elements, such as money, as well as less tangible elements, such as aesthetics. This opened them to exploring what each was willing to give and *get*—the transaction—in order to move the project forward ("I'll give on the louvers I dislike because I'll get to avoid a million-dollar addition to the budget").

Map-Gap-Gives-Gets is a tool that uses four simple words to frame complex and critical calculations. Applying influence beyond authority, you persuade others to join together. Whether renovating a prestigious museum or preparing for a major crisis, you connect and leverage the wide-ranging capacity of organizations and people. When you lead an emerging integrated health system, you better and more efficiently meet patient health needs *and* you control costs by connecting different departments, specialties, and services. If your business is assembling a complex global supply chain, you connect with suppliers *and* with others who affect the flow of goods, including governments, nongovernmental organizations, shippers, trade organizations, and local communities.

Shortly after Coast Guard Commandant Admiral Thad Allen was asked by DHS Secretary Janet Napolitano to serve as national incident commander for the Deepwater Horizon oil spill in the Gulf of Mexico, he called upon Rear Admiral Peter Neffenger to be his deputy.

We observed Neffenger as he assumed his post in New Orleans on May 7, 2010. As we arrived, Neffenger was being prepared to conduct his first daily briefing to report on what was happening both at sea and on shore.

The first appointment was the 10 a.m. "governors call." This exercise in connectivity would become a daily ritual throughout the response. Leaders of the directly affected states met via teleconference with the array of federal agency leads and White House staff assigned to lead the emergency response. Neffenger reported each day on what the Coast Guard knew and what was being done in the field. That first day, he was told that four governors would be on the call, and he prepared accordingly. Roll call was taken. The governors of three states responded "present."

For forty minutes, Neffenger presented information on the situation and answered questions. He outlined what was known about the oil leakage far out in the Gulf, the resources and assets being assembled in each state to get ahead of the spill, and the efforts to limit damage to shore areas. Given the wide scope of the emergency and the limited supplies to contain the oil, it was necessarily a Map-Gap-Gives-Gets exercise.

Suddenly, a loud voice bellowed aggressively through the speaker: "I knew it. You're doing it again!" There was an uncomfortable silence. Finally, Neffenger spoke: "Excuse me, who is speaking?" Presidential senior advisor Valerie Jarrett, on the call to represent the White House, recognized the agitated voice on the line and welcomed a fourth governor to the call. Going into a tirade, he was furious that efforts were being discussed for each of the states—but not his. Once again, silence. Neffenger spoke slowly, "I apologize, sir, had I known that you were on the phone, I would have spoken about your state." The governor hit back: he and his staff had been listening silently to see what would happen. It was just like Katrina, he said—other states were getting attention and support while his was ignored. This governor was identifying a gap that affected his state and he was geared for a fight.

The governor began dictating demands for resources, including boom—the ribbonlike oil-containment countermeasure deployed close to shore. These demands were his gets. Neffenger did his best to outline what he knew of the current response efforts in the governor's state though noted that the initial efforts were concentrated on states in more immediate danger. Enraged, the governor demanded that Neffenger call him for a one-on-one conversation. Neffenger consented and the conference call ended.

There was a long moment of silence in the command center. Neffenger looked drained.

"Admiral," Lenny then said. "You are in the basement."

"You're right," Neffenger agreed. "I am completely in the basement." And so was the governor.

Admiral Neffenger's experience offers a useful frame of reference—a map— for situations in which multiple stakeholders are affected in distinct ways. Each of the four states faced different risks. Their governors focused narrowly, protective of their jurisdictions and constituents (their gaps and their gets). Neffenger, however, looked broadly at the overall requirements and allocated resources in the Gulf-wide response. What could he give to whom, accounting for the limited resources?

In Washington, the Map-Gap-Gives-Gets equation was much different. Officials were as concerned with the politics and optics of the situation— how it appeared to voters and the media—as they were with the technical details of the oil spill response. Thus, they turned to political advisors as well as subject matter experts in their deliberations about the oil spill. The Obama administration did not want this event to be "Obama's Katrina"—an outcome that would tarnish the new administration and have both short- and long-term implications for their political future.

Local officials had a pragmatic, on-the-ground view. During the oil spill response, Billy Nungesser, the president of Plaquemines Parish in Louisiana, gave daily interviews to CNN's Anderson Cooper, each night accusing the federal government of dereliction of duties (a nationally broadcast and embarrassing gap). When the Coast Guard eventually dispatched a liaison officer to work with him and respond to his concerns (a "give"), Nungesser shared his newfound satisfaction with Cooper. No longer newsworthy, the daily interviews ended. His silence was a get for beleaguered federal officials.

Later, Neffenger recounted that the telephone duel with the governor completely changed his perception of his leadership role in the situation. He arrived in New Orleans ready to address an oil spill in the Gulf. Instead, his first days there revealed that the spill itself was just one of many situations requiring his attention. Neffenger had to perceive and understand each of the discrete events—including the politics—both separately and as part of a larger narrative. The essence of Neffenger's meta-leadership challenge was attending to these many interrelated situations, and when he could, influencing events toward a positive outcome.

The Situation Connectivity Map

In your own situations, you may face a CEO, not a governor. Your parish presidents may be department heads. The dynamics, however, are the same: Who plays which role in expanding the range of situations? How can you expect them to behave? What are their perceived risks and potential rewards? What motivates them? What are their basement tendencies, and how will you lead them up and out? The more deeply you consider these factors from the outset, the less surprised or distracted you are as the situations unfold. Drive the POP-DOC Loop to understand each situation. Use the Cone-in-the-Cube to discern different perspectives. Apply the Map-Gap-Gives-Gets exercise to build connectivity exchanges. Use the resulting answers to champion a compelling vision that inspires unified effort.

In driving connectivity, it's your challenge to understand how different stakeholders align, differ, and compete. The more accurate your information, the more effectively you will assign limited resources. The better you are at interpreting different motivations and interests, the more judiciously you will guide yourself and others to the best possible outcomes.

Reflecting on Admiral Neffenger's experience in the Deepwater Horizon event, we developed the Situation Connectivity Map to help leaders navigate complexity. It is a tool for visualizing multiple sub-situations, ascertaining the stakeholders in each one, and discerning connections among them. An oil spill in the Gulf was not one situation. It was many situations: political, environmental, economic, health, and cultural, to name but a few. As a meta-leader, your job is to see and work the full map of stakeholders and build the connectivity necessary to meet the situation at hand.

To create your Situation Connectivity Map, draw a circle for the main incident in the center and surround it with sub-situations, as illustrated in the figure. Add stakeholders for each situation. Look for connections, alliances, and conflicts (Map-Gap-Gives-Gets). Assume a wide meta-perspective as you add to your map until you capture the range of key themes, pressure points, evolving problems, and possible solutions.

Once you've created your map, briefly set it aside. When you return to it freshened, you probably will find that there is more to add. After doing this revealing exercise several times, you will find yourself tracing connections with a mental map in real time. It will become second nature.

The goal for you and others is to perceive patterns central to sense-making, which will help you forecast what might come next. Apply the POP-DOC Loop. If your perceptions are correct, you will get in front of the situation, even with incomplete information. If you lag behind, the situation will overtake you. As a meta-leader, you are forward-looking. Anticipate and direct activities to keep yourself and your followers a step ahead.

In that effort, it is critical not just to recognize patterns that are familiar to you. Actively attend to discovering and becoming familiar with new ones. Assemble fresh patterns by undertaking new experiences, acquiring new skills, and engaging a variety of people. If the crisis is happening someplace else, eventually go there physically to see it for yourself.

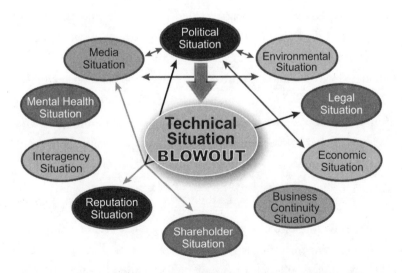

Deepwater Horizon Oil Spill

Every Crisis Has Multiple Interdependent Situations

As you think about the gives and gets, consider the basis of your connections: are they grounded in organizational agreements, personal relationships, mutual interest, shared values, contracts, or some combination of these? Evaluate their structure: are they formally enshrined, or are they simply informal understandings? Assess their quality: are you connected to the right people, organizations, and resources at the right time and in ways that allow you to work together toward desired outcomes that you share? Gauge the robustness and resilience of the connectivity: will it endure through personnel changes or marketplace shifts?

These are not either-or questions: connectivity's colors are shaded along a spectrum, reflecting stronger and weaker linkages. In your network, both organizational and personal, who are your stronger relationships, and who are your weaker and less reliable connections?

Connectivity goes beyond relationships alone. It is also a transactional process of giving and getting—a marketplace of sorts intended to create value. What do you hope to gain through your connectivity, and what are you willing to give in order to achieve it? Your connections may offer both tangibles (money, space, equipment, data) and intangibles (recognition, endorsement, introductions to other possible connections). In discovering what you can offer and what you hope to gain—the potential gives and gets—you both learn about and inform others. What are the expected transactional priorities, intentions, and outcomes? The rapport you build and the connectivity you shape motivates the quest for new value: the benefits that flow from a more deeply engaged enterprise.

There is a flip side to these questions. You cannot be connected with everyone. The more value you bring to the table, the more people will want to be connected to you. Allowing for too many connections creates the very distractions that can get you off track. Spreading yourself too thin, you lose your mission and do not take care of yourself.

Be strategic about those with whom you connect—and those with whom you do not. Think in terms of networks. Your connections with other organizations might not be direct—with its burden of responsibility—but indirect, through intermediaries, networks of connections, or professional associations. Be clear about your priorities, as well as those of others, and decide and act accordingly. Your Situation Connectivity Map can be a useful tool in constructing that strategic network.

Connectivity in Practice

Connectivity is first a personal and social process of subtle cues and communication. Much is found in Dimension One, the person. Your individual qualities and tendencies signal your attitudes about connectivity, which often are embedded in your emotional intelligence. If you are a natural connector, others will perceive this, and those who also are connectors will respond to you with interest. If, on the other hand, you find yourself challenged by or resistant to connection—perhaps you are introverted—others will detect your behavior and be less likely to engage. You transmit cues as you note those of others. Be intentional.

Another factor is the situation, Dimension Two of meta-leadership. Connectivity is contextual. What is happening? What will motivate action? Who else is affected? How do they perceive the situation? How will the situation affect important relationships? Every situation is seen differently by stakeholders, who can either drive or impede success.

You have a wide range of choices in building connectivity. Determine who your actual or potential friends and helpers are, craft positive linkages with them, and nurture those relationships.

Be alert to those who could disrupt or defeat your efforts—the "forces against" you. However, don't cut yourself off from your adversaries completely. Talk with them and you may learn important and significant information. Remember the words of the Chinese military strategist Sun Tzu: "Keep your friends close and your enemies closer."

"Competitor" is a relative term in a world in which individuals and organizations are combatants on one front and collaborators on another. Connectivity varies. For example, the footwear makers Nike and Adidas are fierce rivals in the retail marketplace. Yet they actively share information through the Fair Factories Clearinghouse to ensure that the factories manufacturing their products adhere to high ethical standards. Because the same subcontractors often serve both firms, each factory benefits from coordinated standard-setting, reporting, and performance auditing.

One important aspect of connectivity is forging strategic partnerships. Carefully assess the connectivity you have and the connectivity you need in order to accomplish your priorities. Survey your marketplace. If your competitors are building strategic alliances that erode your value or market share, consider what your counteractions might be. Isolating yourself from potential allies marginalizes you and your organization. Link and leverage where you find strategic advantage to your purposes as well as those of others.

Connectivity potential is all around you. If there are friendships, alliances, favors owed, or shared history among bosses or subordinates that can be useful in your relationship with other stakeholders, leverage them. If you have the full support of your boss, that's an advantage you can deploy to spur action or reinforce urgency. These assets bring added relevance and significance to your endeavors.

Getting this right is essential to your success. Building collaboration and fostering connectivity are core meta-leadership competencies. The meta-leader consistently matches and rematches objective to strategy and situation. As circumstances change, today's competitor may be tomorrow's enthusiastic ally. Be flexible and adaptive.

There is value to connectivity. It can sometimes be measured in dollars, and at other times it can be measured in goodwill and community benefit. The Schlumberger HSE for Youth program is an example. It illustrates Map-Gap-Gives-Gets connectivity in action.

Schlumberger is a global energy services company. Operating in eighty-five countries, the company employs more than 100,000 people representing 140 nationalities. Recognizing its importance to both employee well-being and its corporate reputation, Schlumberger prioritizes its health, safety, and environment (HSE) function. While many companies view HSE as a matter of compliance, Schlumberger views superior HSE performance—in everything from field operations to trip monitoring and cyber security practices—as a disciplined mind-set that differentiates it in the marketplace.

Since 2014, we have worked with HSE executives to embed meta-leadership in the company's crisis management capabilities. A common vocabulary, tool set, and training experience foster connectivity and coherence across the enterprise. Relationships build as skills are absorbed, all contributing to corporate HSE connectivity of effort and making Schlumberger managers better able to lead through adversity, from natural disasters to geopolitical disruptions in whatever region they are operating.

In our work with the company, we met an emerging leader who shared her story of thinking broadly about connectivity. Muriel Barnier joined Schlumberger as an intern. In that role, she helped develop HSE for Youth as a way to share Schlumberger's commitment to HSE with the communities where it operates. Now a full-time employee, she is passionate about the program and its impact. "As an organization, we have deep expertise in HSE," she noted, "and we felt that knowledge could be useful to people beyond our employees in their everyday lives." The HSE for Youth trainings, delivered around the world to both children of employees and non-employees, educates on relevant HSE topics, such as driving safety, HIV/AIDS, malaria protection, safe cyber security practices, and personal security. Each year, HSE for Youth reaches approximately five thousand children through as many as two hundred workshops.

HSE for Youth fosters connectivity among a range of stakeholders: local governments, communities, employees, and corporate management. In Russia, although the program had to be approved by the government, officials enthusiastically granted that approval after seeing a pilot program in action. The goodwill generated by the program has a halo effect that benefits the business. "HSE for Youth lets us demonstrate our core values as a company, engage with key constituencies in ways that demonstrate our expertise, energize our employees, and make people safer," Barnier said. "That's a win for everyone."

The most important benefit, however, is the impact on the ground. Barnier told us about a driving safety program in Abu Dhabi, presented specifically for the children of Schlumberger employees. School buses in the emirate have seat belts, though children rarely wore them. Kids, it seems, like to defy authority no matter where they are from. After participating in the HSE for Youth program, one girl convinced her friends that it was cool to wear seat belts. A few weeks later, her bus was in an accident. "It could have been catastrophic," Barnier said. "Instead, because they were wearing seat belts, there were no serious injuries."

Schlumberger created additional connectivity by using volunteer employees and employee spouses as trainers in the programs. The inclusion of spouses "creates a special bond and respect between them and Schlumberger," Barnier said, "as does delivering HSE for Youth workshops to their kids, their kids' friends, and the community at large."

Attentive to the larger, meta-view of HSE education and training, and having learned from what has worked with children, Barnier continues to explore ways to improve the company's HSE offerings. One change is the transformation of the adult HSE training for employees from instructor-led, PowerPoint-heavy sessions to interactive workshops with more engaging discovery exercises and virtual reality components.

What's next? Barnier wants to give "ownership to the kids." She envisions a youth leadership program through which young people will develop and design projects to bring HSE to their communities.

HSE for Youth is more than a "feel good" gesture by a big corporation interested in public relations. In fact, Schlumberger is rather quiet about this initiative. They identified critical stakeholders in their business, considered how they could and should be connected, and took tangible, meaningful steps to share the benefits. Executives appreciate the social capital deriving from the meta-leadership connectivity with community constituents. This was their Map-Gap-Give-Get exercise. HSE for Youth is simply one component of those efforts.

Mutual Success

As a meta-leader, you understand that your success is interdependent with the success of others, from subordinates and your boss to your peers and an array of external stakeholders. You judge your results by whether you succeed and also by how many others succeed along with you.

Work today is increasingly team-based and collaborative. It is more complex, interdependent, and dynamic. Information flow is more open and democratic. With these changes, organizations have become flatter and more networked. Accountability is faster and more transparent. Employee engagement is increasingly measured and correlated with overall performance.

Workers in an organization come and go with increasing frequency. Circumstances shift more quickly. Teams form on the fly.

Given this evolution, connectivity can pay significant dividends. Allowing others to thoroughly invest and share pride in what they accomplish together creates a more productive and resilient enterprise. Success rarely comes solely from the acts of one individual. Typically, it is the result of the well-calibrated endeavors of many people and organizations, connected and able to work together toward a common goal.

Leadership is dynamic. It is not simply a matter of choosing whether to be connected or to be detached from others. People and their situations shift based on circumstances, relationships, and objectives. Meta-leadership is about the constantly adaptive process of balancing your interests, the interests of your subordinates, the interests of those to whom you report, and the interests of other relevant stakeholders (see more on this in Chapter 11). You ask, "What are we each trying to achieve?" and when there is an intersecting answer to that question, "How might we strategically align what we do and how do we do it to best achieve those shared objectives?"

In the next two chapters, we delve into two distinct conditions for connectivity: first, in your boss-subordinate relationships that are affected by authority connections, and second, in relationships outside your direct hierarchy, in which formal authority is less relevant.

Questions for Journaling

➤ Across your many leadership activities, how does connectivity vary? What adjustments would you make? How would you actualize those changes?

➤ Take a problem or opportunity you've encountered and apply the Map-Gap-Gives-Gets exercise to it. What do you find?

➤ What might you do to improve your personal capacity to optimize connectivity? Are you a natural connector, or is this something for you to work on?

NINE

. . . .

CONNECTIVITY

Navigating Authority Dynamics

Societies—including nonhuman societies—are arranged in hierarchies. It's one way individuals make sense of their immediate social surroundings. Think workplace bureaucracies and troops of monkeys in the Amazon. Who sits where in relation to others may be determined by strength, age, knowledge, expertise, formal rank, coolness, or attractiveness. The criteria vary by species, culture, organization, group dynamics, and values, as well as from generation to generation. Ultimately, hierarchy helps people understand both relationships and productivity.

The bulk of the literature frames leadership within formal chains of command, as a top-down arrangement within the confines of the "four walls" of a single organization. The charge to those at the top of this arrangement's formal chain of command is to raise the productivity, compliance, and conformity of subordinates.

Although important, hierarchical leadership is but one facet of your connectivity development. Particularly in times of change and crisis, much of your leadership activity occurs outside formal chains of command and involves people beyond your authority. You lead also in situations defined more by informal influence than by ranked position and authority. Doing so requires skill and agility, especially when navigating diverse authority and power structures. Recognizing this bigger picture and how to work within it puts the "meta-" in meta-leadership.

As a guide, we break connectivity into four directions: leading down to your direct reports, over whom you have formal authority; leading up to your boss, who has formal authority over you; leading across to other internal stakeholders within your organizational structure; and, as discussed separately in the next chapter, leading beyond to people outside your organization. Aware of all four directions your leadership can take, you emphasize one over the other as the situation demands.

The contours of institutional authority are changing. Societies everywhere are experiencing a transformation of hierarchical relations, the relationship between work and production, and social expectations. Some of this change is generational—older versus younger—and some reflects digital enthusiasm versus analog loyalty. People are more apt now to work remotely or in a shared workspace, and overall, organizations are flatter. It takes an abundance of awareness to traverse these changes and be productive at the same time.

Observe this evolution through your meta-leadership lens. How people worked back then likely does not work as well today. Organizations certainly will be different tomorrow. Not every organization or function evolves in sync. In a tech company, a visionary founder, rich in the "new" skills that spur a high-growth enterprise, may retain the highest rank even though lacking the "old school" experience and expertise to steer the structure and discipline needed in a large company. Ultimately, it is important to get the right person in the right job—someone with all the relationships needed to guide a company's work and evolution in a productive manner.

Despite changes in how we work, many organizational relationships are still governed by lines of formal authority, ordered communication, and prescribed decision-making structures down, up, and across the institution. Even alternative organizational forms, such as decentralized, self-organizing holacracies, have agreements that delineate who does what. Informal networks and processes also emerge in every organization. Whether the relationships through which you lead are formal or informal, hierarchies arise among the people involved. These hierarchies are revealed by who has more influence, who is more respected, and who has access to important resources. As you observe different people and the effect they have on relationships and decision-making, look for opportunities to forge connectivity and unity of effort that leverages who you are and what you do, together. The answers are dynamic because, as you engage others, the circumstances of your connectivity can change.

Within your organization, whether large or small, authority is embedded in job titles and encoded in the laws, policies, protocols, organizational charts, contracts, and culture that govern what you can and cannot do. There are times you more actively exercise those prerogatives, taking charge, issuing orders, and being the commander. There are also times to more thoroughly encourage the opinions of your followers and engage them in extensive deliberations.

As a meta-leader, you apply the Cone-in-the-Cube metaphor to elicit, integrate, and ultimately connect different perspectives. Each choice, in whatever direction, is geared toward generating productive processes and a positive outcome. You continuously balance obedience and persuasion, speed and inclusiveness, decrees and guidance, authority and influence. In the end you are answerable for the decisions and results that derive from your efforts to better link and leverage work and relationships.

There are checks and balances, such as delineated decision-making authority and rules that ensure consistency and avoid mischief, putting limits on what any one person can do alone. Large organizations are divided into departments, professional groups, offices, or bureaus, each with separate functions that contribute to the operation of the whole. These divisions demarcate who knows what, who can do what, and how decisions are made. One lesson of the #MeToo movement is that, in many organizations, these check-and-balance systems have not worked to ensure employee safety and personal discretion. Male bosses—and to a lesser extent female bosses—have used organizational authority to hide (and in some cases sanction) sexual harassment. It takes tremendous courage, tenacity, and leadership to speak truth to power and, in doing so, elevate accountability, responsibility, and personal security.

The mistake by many executives is to see a report or disclosure of sexual harassment as the crisis. It is not. The harassment itself is the crisis, especially for the person involved. Start by looking through that peephole in the cube. Everything else simply cascades from the original incident. Resolving the first crisis promptly with fairness, firmness, empathy, and transparency makes it possible to deal with the subsequent concerns more effectively. Otherwise, you will create a downward spiral of negative consequences.

Societies are in the midst of the evolution from an industrial to a digital age, with many organizations operating with a mix of the two orientations. The new economy is based on the constant flow of knowledge, goods, services, and funds over digital networks. Consequently, organizations—and the challenges of leading within a chain of command—are shifting. Processes are becoming more dynamic and value chains more complex. Today's leader is more often a visionary and a sense-maker who connects and collaborates with others to perceive a bigger picture, make things happen, and recalibrate operations in response to fluctuating conditions. Think meta-leader.

Today organizations continue to become ever more complex. Research by David Krackhardt and Jeffrey R. Hanson shows that much work in an organization is accomplished through undocumented shadow networks that people use to circumvent formal channels. Customers, and even competitors, are involved in multiple aspects of your operations. Markets and the news move in milliseconds. Innovation and agility are prized. Outsourcing and strategic alliances are common.

As a leader, you rely on people and entities you don't fully control to do work whose complex technology you may not fully comprehend. You assess when to deploy a tightly controlled, linear process and when to rely on emergent self-organization. You learn to become comfortable with independent decision-making by your subordinates. You hope for the same from your boss.

Part of your job is to focus on enabling others to solve problems. As a present-day meta-leader, you take a more nuanced view of authority and you exercise it more nimbly. And here again we see that influence, even within formal organizational structures, is more robust than authority for solving multifaceted challenges.

Leading Down

"Leading down" through a chain of command describes your role as boss. If you founded your business or enterprise, you are the boss because you got the operation off the ground. Most bosses, however, are given the job by someone else.

As your leadership career advances, you are likely to find that with each promotion, more and more people are calling you the boss. Eventually, your direct reports supervise their own subordinates. Your administrative span swells as your responsibilities and the scope of your work expand. You may ultimately lead hundreds or even thousands of people further down in the hierarchy. Your expanding responsibility offers you the opportunity to realize significant impact. Your workforce becomes a force multiplier for what you hope to accomplish.

There are many different types of bosses: great ones, lousy ones, and every kind in between. There are laissez-faire bosses and taskmasters. Some bosses are concerned only about the next promotion, and others do little more than play defense in the hope of retaining their current position.

As boss, you develop a style and a strategy for leading subordinates based on your personality, training, experience, lessons learned from previous bosses, and instructions given from above: the CEO, the board of directors, and the larger milieu in which you operate. Ultimately, however, you choose the type of boss you will become through the decisions you make over time.

People follow you. In an ideal world, you handpick your team to ensure that they possess the skills and attitudes that make your leadership job gratifying. They grasp organizational priorities, are committed to the mission, offer new ideas and abundant energy, and embrace even the thankless though necessary jobs along the way. Few bosses, however, have such a perfect array of subordinates. In any existing organization, you inherit at least part of your team as well as the legacy culture. You play the hand you are dealt.

One goal of your meta-leadership is encouraging connectivity as you lead down, building and developing your team to reach their full potential.

As a meta-leader, you ask: How can I link and leverage the work we are doing to make it most productive and fulfilling for my stakeholders? How can I help make each member of my team a success—given each individual's unique capabilities—and then make us a success together? How do I support my reports in their work, providing appropriate independence, intervening when necessary, and letting them make mistakes that are in the realm of the reasonable? How do I best reward their productivity and support them when things go wrong?

Your job is to demonstrate to your subordinates that you value and appreciate the work they do, both individually and collectively. In so doing, you encourage each of them to value and appreciate what they are doing together and the distinctive contributions of each member of the team. You all do more because there is greater satisfaction and success in getting it done together. You shape your team.

Eric McNulty has held numerous supervisory positions. One of those positions was leading an in-house creative services group within a much larger organization. Morale was low when he started in his position, thanks to unrelenting pressure to produce more in less time. Employees had to bill their hours to internal clients, who were in turn rewarded for keeping company costs low. Given the overhead of a large organization, the in-house rates were higher than those of the outside freelance alternatives against whom Eric's group had to compete. It was hard to win at this game.

The team received little recognition within the company. It was their clients who got the accolades, because the organization rewarded revenue and profit, not the collateral work that helped generate that income.

The unit's survival depended on producing high-quality work for its clients, and that objective required attracting and retaining talented designers. These designers were a small but critical component of the larger unit. When one of Eric's most creative and productive people threatened to resign after a frustrating client encounter, he went to the basement. If Eric couldn't craft a compelling vision that reframed the situation for his subordinates and satisfied their clients, they all would soon be looking for jobs.

Eric could have griped to his superiors and fought for more internal acknowledgment. He knew, however, that any such recognition would feel forced and wouldn't do much to bolster his team. In this case, there was a clear hierarchy within the company: revenue-generating business units were on top and support units were underneath them, a situation that was unlikely to change. Eric had to lead down with what resources and ideas he had because of his limited options for leading up. He took a two-pronged approach to improving the morale and motivation of his followers.

First, he carved out a small budget to enter the team's work in external design award competitions. His group would contend against outside freelancers, advertising agencies, and design firms. They entered only contests whose judging criteria included the results achieved. This made for a solid business case for entering these competitions.

There were plenty of benefits: his people and their work were judged against their peers, free of company politics, and when they won—as they did several times—the team felt triumphant. Winning was also good for the designers' careers; entering their work in these competitions showed that Eric cared about their next steps, whether in the company or elsewhere. In the meantime, their internal clients—their colleagues—could share in the glory. It won the team much-needed credibility that helped build relationships that went beyond billable hours and deadlines. As a result, they were seen differently within the organization.

The second part of his new approach was an unorthodox but intriguing attempt to shift the mind-set of the group and build the self-confidence of its members. Eric introduced the metaphor of the character actor—the performer who does consistently great work without getting top billing. The group talked about deriving satisfaction simply from a job well done. They discussed the importance of craft. They shared how gratifying it was to be highly regarded by one's collaborators. They began to develop confidence based on how good they knew they were, not on how many accolades they got in the company newsletter.

As the group explored this idea, the actor Brian Dennehy surfaced as someone they had all enjoyed in one role or another. Dennehy, it turned out, was taking a star turn as the lead in *Death of a Salesman* on Broadway. Eric decided to take the group from Boston to New York to see the production. He also wrote to Dennehy, explained the mission, and asked if he would meet the team after the performance. Remarkably, the actor agreed.

"It was a great day for the entire team," McNulty recalled. "I decided that the company would contribute the day off, but each person would pay for their own ticket to the show and their share of the van rental to New York. Dennehy was brilliant as Willy Loman in the play. Every person was moved by his performance. And then, to spend a few minutes backstage with him was a treat for everyone. He was exhausted from the show but shared fascinating insights about acting.

"It bonded us as a team and brought to life the idea that satisfaction comes first from within. It cemented the culture of the group as one where we would value each other's contributions. The excursion was also a bit of an outlaw adventure, as I did not get official sanction for the trip. It gave me 'boss credibility' as someone who would take a risk to support my people."

Entering his team's design work in competitions and taking them to see a Broadway show weren't just examples of leading down with authority. They also exemplified Eric's meta-leadership. He leveraged limited authority to help the team develop a new attitude toward what they were doing. As a result, they struck a new balance both with each other and with the company. Productivity rose along with the satisfaction that comes from being on a team of people—including the boss—who value and care for one another.

The most troubling predicament faced in leading down is the subordinate who is intentionally disruptive, inappropriate, ineffective, or acting without integrity. It happens. Ultimately, you as boss are responsible. You work within the framework of your organizational authority. There are procedures and contractual agreements to follow, including notifications, documentation, and grievance processes.

After a thorough and fair review, you decide that the reasonable choice is to terminate this individual's employment. Remember that you are judged by more than what occurs with just one employee alone. All your other employees are watching to see how you respond, as are your boss and colleagues. Have you been just and sensible? Or rash and volatile? Have you perceived the problems in a timely manner and with reasonable clarity? How have your actions with one employee affected your relations with others? Are they relieved to see the troublemaker go, or are they feeling more vulnerable and wondering if they may be the next to go? Remember, you demonstrate your character, values, and priorities in how you respond to this situation.

In the good times, you reveal much in how you conduct yourself with your reports. You also do so in bad times, when you need to pay even greater attention to your actions. Everything you do affects the morale and productivity of those who report up to you.

In leading down, you cast a shadow, setting the tone for subordinate behaviors, relationships, and outputs. People observe what you do and how you relate. Then, in both subtle and noteworthy ways, they mimic those behaviors.

Likewise, the policies, procedures, and protocols you establish are carried out by people down your chain. If they are clear, collaborative, and transparent, those qualities are replicated in how others carry them out and everyone is better able to work together. Activity aligns to stated objectives. If policies, procedures, and protocols are unclear, conflicted, or ambiguous, then the message extending out to your reports is equally so. For better or worse, this *shadow effect* cascades down through the organization.

The first step in creating a collaborative environment is setting a tone of collaboration, within your operation as well as with your leadership peers. The openness to working together proliferates, informing interactions as well as policies and protocols. As a meta-leader, you talk the talk and walk the walk. Connectivity becomes the expectation for intra- and interorganizational dealings. This expectation extends to relationships with your customer base. In Chapter 2, we cited the collaborative and supportive tone set by Southwest Airlines executives. That attitude cascades down to flight attendants and gate agents and pervades the passenger experience. Southwest's day-to-day work and problem-solving are defined by those behaviors and policies. No airline's performance is always perfect; however, Southwest maintains its collaborative attitude through good times and bad.

By contrast, when leaders set a tone of antagonism and distrust, that likewise is transmitted throughout the organization and beyond. Conflict

The Shadow Effect of Conflict

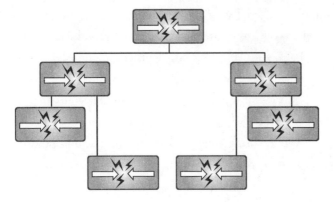

The Shadow Effect of Collaboration

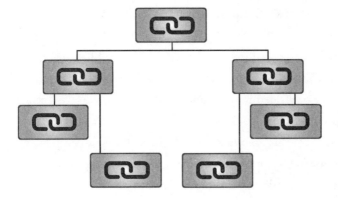

becomes the expectation for intra- and interorganizational competition. Political posturing and petty battles can erupt. The friction and discord reverberate in relationships with customers, suppliers, and communities. From your traveling experience, contrast Southwest Airlines with some other air carriers whose flight attendants are curt and gate agents are disinterested. Their bad attitudes did not typically start with them. Rather, they are extensions of a shadow spreading a tone of conflict and distrust from above.

As you lead down, you set the conditions for the continued employment and promotion of your subordinates. They want to please you, and they want your acceptance and endorsement. They replicate the behaviors, connections, and performance you model. So too do their subordinates. Be cognizant of the shadow you are casting, what it means for others, and how it affects what your enterprise is or is not doing.

Leading Up

On the flip side, you lead up to your boss. If you're a middle manager, your boss is likely to have a boss. If you are a top boss, you still have constituents to whom you are accountable: a board of directors, a customer base, an electorate. If you work in a matrix organization, you may have multiple bosses. Though you lead down to many people, you lead up to one or at most only a few. Therefore, those to whom you are accountable loom large in your career and your success. Bosses vary, and so does your relationship with each of them.

You lead up to your boss in many ways. You provide reports and briefings about work for which you are responsible. If you are a subject matter expert, you make recommendations on strategy and operational priorities. If meta-leadership is "People follow you," through this relationship, your boss may follow you at times, accepting your guidance and direction. When your boss is in the basement and you are the one to help him or her out, you have provided a potentially career-saving leading-up service.

Some bosses are terrific. Bringing contagious passion, motivation, and integrity to the job, these bosses are a delight to work for. They wake up every morning committed to figuring out ways to help make you and your endeavors a success. They are fair, supportive, and encouraging. They provide helpful guidance and make clear the connection between your contributions and the larger mission. A good boss values what you do and wants to hear from you. Unfortunately, this breed of boss is often elusive. And for the most part, you do not get to choose your boss. You adjust to the person who holds the position.

Why do you want connectivity when leading up? The more your boss is a champion for what you hope to accomplish and understands your contribution to the overall objectives of the organization, the better able you are to leverage capacities beyond your specific sphere of authority. Your boss helps make you a success, and you in turn help make your boss a success. The overall enterprise benefits if all are working toward similarly defined success.

The relationship is defined in part by the responsibility and reporting relationship between you and your boss. You do not have authority over your boss; he or she has it over you. However, you can find ways to positively influence that relationship to encourage productive cohesion of effort.

What if you are troubled by something your boss is doing? It could be priorities, behaviors, decisions, or outcomes. Whatever the cause, this is your "truth to power" moment.

You may feel compelled to express a contrary recommendation, voice an objection, or call your boss out on inappropriate activity. Or perhaps you choose not to. This is the most sensitive side of leading up. Your intent should be to open an exchange that strengthens your relationship with your boss, not a confrontation that ends it.

You are careful and thoughtfully diplomatic as you offer your boss contrary advice or criticism. Express your concerns, objections, and alternative opinions prudently, accurately, and respectfully. Consider how your actions and recommendations will alter the situation. Be open to hearing your boss's rationale. You may be unaware of all that your boss knows, such as other business considerations at play or distinctly personal factors. Watch body language. Work to perceive the situation as accurately as possible and help your boss do the same.

What if an important contractor is paying local officials for favorable treatment? What if the company is shipping substandard products from one market to another with lower regulatory standards? What if you are a governmental subject matter expert and the elected official to whom you lead up is acting irresponsibly during a crisis? What if you discover that your boss is having a romantic relationship with a direct report? These examples are based on actual cases. All such cases have consequences; when possible, you want to ensure that you don't own them.

When you recognize serious misbehavior, what is your obligation as a follower? If someone is breaking the law, you could be legally complicit if you are obediently compliant. "I was simply following orders" does not grant immunity from moral responsibility or legal prosecution. Honest and morally upright bosses will appreciate your forthrightness, if they respect your motives. Supporting broader purposes is quite different from simply trying to get your own way.

Challenging established power does not always lead to being fired. In fact, it might even be beneficial for your career. It's all about the approach. If you do it right, you can cultivate legitimacy as someone committed to the larger mission. You say much about yourself and your commitment when you demonstrate the courage to take what could be a risky stand. Your candor could save your boss and your organization from a costly error.

There are some bosses who expect you to keep your reservations to yourself, no matter the circumstances. For this boss, personal loyalty trumps organizational responsibility. If this is your boss, it is critical for you to understand the potential conflict in your predicament: you work for your boss and you have a job to do for the organization. Document your concerns, recommendations, and thinking even if this record goes no further than your files. You may later need a record of what you said and the reaction to it, especially in a situation with legal ramifications.

Deliberating on these issues requires reckoning with your values, your sense of fairness, and your core beliefs. It forces you to ponder what the situation means for you as a subordinate, as a moral being, and as a breadwinner. Speaking truth to power would be easier if your financial welfare and that of your family were not dependent on your job. You may feel compelled to shut up when your family's economic security is on the line. This is a powerful and sensitive reason to be concerned, though it cannot be an excuse for ducking necessary decisions, however difficult.

Confronting established power may well take you to the basement. Get yourself up and out. Carefully weigh the options and consequences. Remind yourself of why the truth is significant. Finding and drawing the line—balancing what you believe is important, your relationship with the person you must confront, and the impact on all of the stakeholders—is your responsibility as a meta-leader.

Take what appears to be the best course of action in the long run. Telling the truth as you see and believe it can feel uncomfortable in the short run. Assessing what you did and how you did it becomes far clearer in retrospect, when you can recollect whether you did the right thing given the situation and whether you had the intended effect.

Look first to yourself, Dimension One. Reflect on what sits right with your conscience. Still stuck? In an earlier chapter, we suggested flipping a coin as a way to uncover the pathway your unconscious mind would have you take. Flip the coin and pay attention to your emotional reaction as each option is revealed.

Now reverse the scenario. Reread the last few paragraphs with a boss mind-set. How would you want your subordinates to behave? This exercise may be uncomfortable and take you to the basement. However, if you want subordinates and external contractors who are forthright and transparent, if you prefer to deal with problems when they are in their infancy, and if you value knowing what is really going on, then you must be ready and willing to listen when others speak truth to power to you.

James "Jimmy" Dunne III is the senior managing principal of the investment bank Sandler O'Neill + Partners. You'll meet him in greater detail in the next chapter. He was clear in his discussions with us about his view on speaking truth to power: "I want bad news to find me fast. I make it widely known that bringing me bad news fast actually puts me in a good mood. It allows me more time to work on solving the problem. Screwing up once will rarely get you fired here, but covering up will every time. Hiding bad news only makes things worse." This attitude takes strength and courage. When "you're it," these are traits you muster and model for those who bring difficult truths into the conversation.

Marc Mathieu enjoys a vibrant career as a marketing strategist. He has worked for several major corporations, including the French food conglomerate Danone; the global beverage-maker Coca-Cola; Unilever, a British-Dutch consumer goods company; and most recently, Samsung, the electronics manufacturer. As an astute and experienced observer of authority and power, he has discerned how to work when you have them—and when you do not.

"In the next ten to twenty years," he told us, "corporations are going to have to let go of leadership from the top and embrace leadership from the bottom. Mission, vision, and direction come from the top. Energy, ideas, and initiative come from the bottom." He sees a power shift under way.

"There are two kinds of people: those managing for impact—they are willing to get fired—and those managing for input—they want to feel assured they have a job, so they offer their input only when it is sought and appreciated."

In one early position, Mathieu was advised that "here, you don't make life difficult for your bosses." This organization valued cautious input, not boldness. He survived and thrived there for twelve years by learning that in leading up, he had to accept that he did not get to pick his bosses. He understood that he needed to work *with* them, not against them.

Over time Mathieu came to believe that, for him, organizational impact was the only alternative. He was willing to go to the mat for his principles. That mind-set, accompanied by energy and drive, does not always blend well into established corporate power structures where bold ideas are suspect. He moved on.

Later in his career, when he was being considered for the corporate marketing role to revive the iconic Coca-Cola brand, he gave his prospective boss two pages of initial thoughts. He laid out ten fundamental beliefs he had about what was important in his work. Strategy and tactics change. Attitudes toward teamwork and the power of an iconic brand do not. Mathieu wanted to make sure that he and his boss were on the same page. If they were not, he didn't want the job. He was using his power as a desirable candidate and picking his boss. He believes that this is a conversation worth having before taking any new job or agreeing to work for a new boss. Are you clear that your core values about work are in sync with those of your boss?

Simply aligning with the boss, however, may not be enough when your work has impact across a global enterprise: "I was brought in to revitalize the brand icon in part because I am a 'mischievous revolutionary,' and I applied revolutionary principles to my work," Mathieu said. "However, I was not aware enough that revolutionary activities and attitudes alienate institutional power. For future work, I became much more conscious of engaging senior people—not just the boss—and not distancing them."

For inspiration, Mathieu looks to people who fought for ideals, not power, like Martin Luther King Jr. and Mahatma Gandhi. "Fighting for ideals galvanizes people and moves them," Mathieu said. "Fighting for power just serves the leader."

Mathieu may not fight for power; however, he clearly understands how to work with it. He developed the ability to remain true to himself and be a force for change, using leverage drawn from insightful leading up, perceptiveness about the marketplace, and a deepening commitment to his values.

Leading Across

The third direction of internal organizational connectivity is leading across to other silos and leaders—those who head other divisions, offices, or departments within your organization. These people are outside your chain of command though very much within the scope of your work. You don't control them and they don't control you. With them, you may share the same boss and governance structure, that affects all of you. These are compelling reasons to forge that leading across connectivity.

The best organizations amplify what they do by aligning "forces for" to work toward collaboration and productivity. However, when silos are arrayed for battles with one another—for budget, recognition, or authority—the successes of one silo become a "force against" for others. Internally ruthless organizations are less competitive externally because so much of their effort and potential is consumed by internecine rivalries.

Leading across is different from leading beyond because internal levers of authority within an organization can be exercised to mandate coordination of effort. A boss can order middle managers to meet and cooperate (though they have many subtle ways to resist). Even though there is the expectation that people within the same organization are on the same team, the question remains: what is the best way to encourage connectivity of effort between different organizational units? Tools for encouraging connectivity include executive decrees, rewards for collaboration, influence beyond authority, and simple enticements: free pizza offered at a meeting, for example, is a convenient lure to engagement. An informal get-together is a less threatening opening to collaborate that can evolve over time into a more formal cross-organizational endeavor.

Leading across is an intraorganizational Map-Gap-Gives-Gets exercise, as described previously. The meta-leader makes a compelling strategic case for cross-silo connectivity of effort, articulating persuasively the benefits and costs of both doing it and not doing it. In tangible terms, what can be leveraged by combining forces across your enterprise? When different divisions within your organization collaborate, knowledge, assets, and expertise can be shared for the benefit of the whole enterprise. You can point to gaps that create vulnerabilities or missed opportunities. For example, when related government, law enforcement, or intelligence agencies don't appropriately share critical information about the activities and whereabouts of malicious actors, attacks are likely to increase.

The more complex your organization, the more difficult it is to generate enterprise-wide connectivity of effort. Within a health care organization, efforts to encourage "population health" require that different caregivers, clinics, and outpatient units coordinate patient information and services. Compared with costly "fee for service" medical care, these "fee for quality" strategies promote healthy alternatives and lower overall health care costs. Getting the different silos of a health care organization to work together, however, requires changes in practices and reward structures. These efforts, spurred by external policy and reimbursement incentives, are often met with deeply engrained internal resistance.

In the corporate sector, aspiring leaders in global enterprises are required to transfer between different functions and regions so that, when they reach top corporate positions, they will better understand the full scope and scale of the company. They will have seen the company's numerous divisions that link and leverage strategies, operations, and supply chains.

Though integrated cross-silo efforts can be mandated down the command chain, they also require leaders at all levels to leverage the advantages of coordination of effort. Your leading-across objective is get the balance right. Just as there are many strategic advantages to building intraorganizational collaboration of effort, there are potential downsides. These can include endless time spent in committee meetings, a laundry list of sign-offs before anything can get done, or a loss of focus as you try to satisfy too many customers.

Think of leading across as an investment. Establish your expected return on time and effort. Seek balance as you gauge potential collaborators and competitors. Weigh advantages and risks. On one side of the scale is activity, and on the other is productivity. The question is not simply whether there should be connectivity or not. It is better to ask: how can connectivity be organized and oriented to maximize efficiencies (in this case, gaining the most productivity for the least activity)? You meta-lead other organizational stakeholders to focus on shared priorities and ways to leverage capacities that are best achieved through collaborative efforts. You expect to reap benefits out of connectivity. It is not a good in and of itself; rather it is an effort that is both led and managed.

The Role of Management in Leading Up, Down, and Across

How does day-to-day management fit into this equation of leading down, up, and across? To get the job done, order and accountability are required.

As boss, you are answerable for the activity and output of people who report to you, and you are answerable to your boss for the same. If you are part of a cross-organizational work group, you hold collective responsibility for what is produced. Authority and responsibility are housed in management positions and reporting.

There is much debate in the leadership field on the distinctions and overlaps between management and leadership. In practice, your job is to master both. Leadership and management are interdependent in ways that are important though puzzling. Here is a simple distinction: management is more about the *what* of your endeavors, and leadership is more about the *why*.

Meta-leaders establish and clarify purpose for the enterprise (the *why*). They imbue activities with meaning. They set big picture direction and objectives. They communicate the value that derives from the initiative. They help individual workers understand how their efforts contribute to organizational mission and its significant impact. Eliciting commitment beyond compliance and order beyond control, meta-leaders find ways to spur innovation to best adapt the enterprise to changing circumstances. These are the human factors.

Leadership without management is a prescription for disappointment. The management side of your meta-leadership is ultimately responsible for achievement. It is management that sets goals, solves problems, and produces outcomes valuable for people, the organization, and those the organization serves. Without substantial advancement toward tangible objectives, you are merely a dreamer, full of aspirational ideas that gain no traction. It is one thing to create a vision; it is another to manage its realization. Leaders cannot ignore the order and benchmarks established by the management reckoning of the equation.

Management without leadership likewise generates activity that accomplishes little beyond the routine. Managers are ultimately responsible for productivity—for an organization's smooth functioning, high output, and optimal quality. However, sustained peak performance is not possible when people are unmotivated and lack a sense of purpose in what they are doing. Subordinates who do not share a commitment to the larger mission and whose contributions are not valued do not invest themselves in their work. Managers cannot ignore these human factors and the engagement and commitment that derives from them.

How do you solve the leadership-management puzzle? Picture the skills and capabilities associated with them lying on a continuum, with management at one end and leadership at the other. Getting stuck at one pole or the other limits your reach and effectiveness. Instead, strive to move fluidly between the two poles, according to the problem or opportunity you face, the people involved, and the purposes and objectives that motivate you and others. In some circumstances, management skills will be dominant; at other times, leadership capabilities will be more critical.

We frame the challenges of both leading and managing as three zones: vision and mission, strategy and execution, and impact and assessment. Your *vision and mission* (your why) must be clear and compelling to your followers, your boss, and your allies. Your *strategy and execution* (your what) should be effective and efficient. Finally, your *impact and assessment* (your measures of success) should be tangible, relevant, and tracking continuous improvement over time.

Think of accomplishment as the outcome of productivity divided by activity. Your goal is to reach or exceed the intended level of productivity by ably expending reasonable energy, effort, and resources. For example, you create ten units of productivity with ten units of activity. Pretty good. What if you expend one hundred units of activity for that same productivity? Not so good.

An unclear mission, poorly conceived strategy, or lack of appropriate metrics leads to high activity with low productivity. Likewise if your mission

The Meta-Leadership Accomplishment Equation

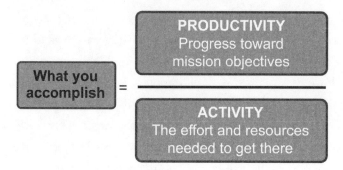

is championing a social cause or responding to a crisis: what effort does it take to achieve critical objectives? Excessive meetings, cumbersome reporting, and petty internal skirmishes escalate activity and contribute little to productivity. Your goal is to increase the productivity resulting from each unit of activity.

Avoid becoming stuck in one zone. Instead, seek value and connection across all three zones. Shift your attention between zones as needed, calibrating and recalibrating your decisions and actions to leverage resources and activity as you work to improve outcomes. A meaningful and important vision should result in significant and measurable impact. Driving the learning curve in all three zones boosts performance, improves feedback, and increases accountability. You both stimulate change and show progress that reflects achievement.

In times of crisis or significant change, uncertainty increases, individual and organizational status may be in question, and autonomy may be restricted. Sensing a loss of control, people go to the basement. This is a time when your leadership practices rise to the fore.

Research by David Rock and others shows that this social pain is processed by the brain in similar ways to physical pain. It's important to attend to it. Clarify why your activities are important and meaningful to your followers. Create a rallying narrative, and restore certainty through transparent

The Leadership/Management Continuum

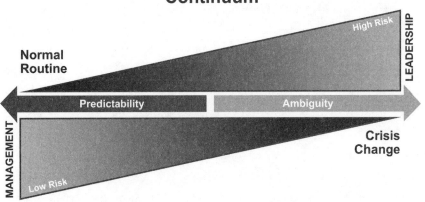

processes. Confidence in a process brings stability even when people disagree with its outcome. Reassure people of their status: *We can do this. You are important to the team.* Empower people to do their jobs. Demonstrated competence is a sure route out of the basement and back to productivity. Your goal is achieving both unity of effort and tangible results.

By contrast, in times of certainty—when the organization and its people are in a steady state—you manage internal systems to optimize performance. You "keep the trains running on time." These are moments when you are confident about the predictability in your external environment—the market, the political landscape, or customer preferences—as well as the stability of your internal procedures. The same actions and conditions repeat from day to day with little variance. In a dynamic world, such conditions are rare; when they do occur, recognize them for what they are. Get yourself out of the way and let people get their job done.

For meta-leaders, there is no either-or choice between management and leadership: you live at the intersection, and its balance is always shifting.

The figure illustrates how the balance between leadership and management changes in different contexts. As a meta-leader, you dissect and blend leadership and management in myriad possible permutations.

Routine situations typically require greater emphasis on management, so you draw more on those skills and resources. In crisis and change situations, with ambiguity, dynamism, and risk increasing, you shift on the continuum, applying the necessary leadership capacities and skills.

For example, when safety, security, or strict quality standards are the top concern, the more regimented thinking, processes, and protocols of your management tool box serve you well. When devising strategy, discerning the implications of shifting demographics, or charting the reorganization of your company, however, such fine-grained control stifles the necessary questioning, innovation, and creativity in your brain's executive circuits. These are times to draw predominantly on your leadership capabilities.

How do you both lead and manage at the same time? Choose to be an intentional designer of your relationships. At times you deploy the full measure of your authority. In other situations, you have or you use very little. Proactively set the expectations of those with whom you connect.

Meta-Leading Your Organizational Relationships

Many individuals believe that they "own" their position and its authority. They do not. In fact, occupying a spot in a hierarchy is far more like a time-share—a place you inhabit for a fixed period and then pass along to someone else. The position itself usually precedes you and is likely to still be there after you move on. Your job as meta-leader, in part, is to leave the place in better shape than you found it. Remember, when you leave, your authority stays behind.

Treat your position as though it were on loan. It must be sustainable in your absence. Your subordinates, boss, customers, and others should be better off for your having been in it. Build and encourage leadership capacity throughout your organization. Overcome fears that your followers might upstage you; instead, learn to invest in them and their accomplishments. If your unit cannot function without you, you are not doing your job. Find and prepare people who can eventually assume your responsibilities. Remember, you can't be promoted if there is no one to replace you.

In leading down, up, and across, authority resides in distinctive measures that can be taken in different interactions and relationships. "The boss gives the order while others obey" simply does not describe productive leadership situations.

Relying solely on your formal authority as boss and always deferring to the authority of your boss are both recipes for failure. As a boss, you have powers that come with the authority of your position. As a subordinate, you cede powers to your boss. There are certain decisions you cannot make. As a colleague leading across, you have authority that is often far more fluid. Understanding the dynamics of the authorities you possess and knowing how to leverage the authorities of others is essential to your success.

As you craft the transition between what *is* and what *can be,* your meta-leadership task—up, down, and across your organization—is to intentionally apply your authority in combination with your influence. Beyond your organization, your authority is limited, and so influence is your currency. We turn next to leading beyond authority.

Questions for Journaling

⫸ Marc Mathieu, Eric McNulty, and James Dunne work in different industries and face different contexts. Each proved himself adept at using his authority and working with the power and authority held by others. How can you achieve similar success? What tools should be ready in your workroom?

⫸ What are the problems you typically encounter? How will you know if you succeed?

⫸ How is authority allocated within your organization? How might it be better designed and practiced?

TEN

CONNECTIVITY

Leading Beyond to Recraft Relationships

It's a beautiful sunny Tuesday morning. Jimmy Dunne, one of three managing partners at the Wall Street investment banking firm Sandler O'Neill + Partners, is making the most of the weather on a Westchester golf course. He is playing to qualify for the US Mid-Amateur Championship.

The three partners who run the firm maintain a pragmatic balance. Herman Sandler is a polished gentleman and a mentor, a guide to employees, and an icon of stability for customers. Chris "Quack" Quackenbush is the sharp negotiator, in charge of investment banking for the firm. Quack and Jimmy have been best friends for nearly thirty years, ever since they met on the golf range as teenage caddies.

Dunne, a tough Irishman, is loud, brash, and known for being the enforcer within the firm. When someone has to be fired, the other partners come to him. Dunne, who is his own man, finds the arrangement convenient. He says what he thinks. And the arrangement works because he balances and is balanced by his two partners.

That Tuesday morning is September 11, 2001. At 9:03 a.m., United Airlines Flight 175 crashes into 2 World Trade Center, where the firm has its main offices on the 104th floor. Of the 171 employees, 83 partners and employees are already in the office; 66 will die, and 17 will survive. Among the dead are Herman Sandler and Chris Quackenbush.

Dunne first hears the news on the golf course. He experiences an unspeakable and overwhelming flood of loss. Quack was his closest friend. All the others, his friends and colleagues, are gone as well. The firm is now smoldering in the rubble.

As the shock of the losses sinks in, he has a decision to make: will Sandler O'Neill fall with the building, or will it come back to life?

For Dunne, the answer is obvious: Sandler O'Neill will endure. He ascends from the basement of his despair. He has to provide for the families who lost loved ones and support the employees who survived. When he eventually learns that Osama bin Laden was determined to destroy the American way of life by attacking Wall Street and the World Trade Center, Dunne gains a cause and an enemy to rally against. Bin Laden will not win this fight.

This is Dunne's "you're it" moment. To bring the firm back to life, he needs to be a different kind of boss, not the old Jimmy Dunne. Knowing he will have to adopt a new mind-set, he begins by saying, "I need to be more like Herman now. I need to be more like Chris now." These words become his refrain. He wants Sandler O'Neill to embody the best of its three leaders, to carry on their legacy in his leadership. He can't simply be the tough guy. His employees are too vulnerable for that. He has to be something else. Change, though difficult, is imperative. Dunne has to transform himself if he is going to transform the company.

"The more the pressure, the higher the heat, the better I'll perform," he later told us. "I get very calm under pressure. My colleagues say, 'If Jimmy is calm, the problem is big.' You are what you perceive yourself to be. Crises don't build character; they reveal it."

As he and the survivors at Sandler O'Neill pull themselves and the business together, Dunne differentiates what he calls his right-hand issues from his left-hand ones. The right hand is about the grieving families, the distraught and mourning employees, and their emotional trials and difficulties in moving forward. The left hand is about the business: finding new space, hiring new employees, taking care of clients.

Dunne is clear on one thing: the right hand will always take precedence. He and the firm do what is necessary to help people get through, providing salaries, bonuses, and health care for survivors of the employees who died. Dunne finds that taking care of the right-hand issues puts the left-hand issues into a context that makes them surmountable. The remaining staff rallies.

Dunne has to do more, however, than rally his people. He must regain the trust of his customers and other Wall Street firms. That is his live-or-die mission as leader of the company. An epic narrative of compassion, collaboration, and resilience unfolds. The firm wins the goodwill of other Wall Street firms, which lend them space and people so that they can get back on their feet. Companies, even competitors, send them business.

Jimmy Dunne emerged as one of the icons of post-9/11 resilience in part because he became a multidimensional meta-leader. He showed his emotions and he encouraged others to do the same. He attended dozens of funerals for his lost colleagues. He supported his employees and helped them as they took steps toward recovery and productivity. Being supportive was part of the healing, his own as well as the company's. Even though Dunne hated wearing suits, they became his steady wardrobe; in fact, he dressed impeccably, just as Herman Sandler had. Without his two partners, he alone had to balance all three dimensions of meta-leadership: He became "the person." He remained hopeful while embracing the harsh realities of "the situation." And he brought people together, serving as a role model for building "connectivity." He was "it," and people followed him.

Just two months after the 9/11 attacks, Sandler O'Neill was again profitable.

On September 6, 2006, the following appeared in the *New York Times*: "No one will ever accuse Jimmy Dunne of being the perfect boss. 'He's not always the most patient listener, and he can be brutally blunt,' said the firm's former co-chief operating officer, Michael Lacovara. 'And I think he believes he can do anybody's job as well as they can do it themselves.' Mr. Lacovara added, 'If on September 12, 2001, he hadn't felt that way, we wouldn't be here today.' Mr. Dunne turned out to be the exact right person to lead Sandler O'Neill out of the abyss."

Jimmy Dunne transformed himself so that he could transform his company. This is what it means to become a meta-leader. It is an all-in effort designed to create an all-in outcome. It is leading every day so that you're ready when it matters most.

Dunne's story encompasses much of what is critical about connectivity across your personal and professional network. You draw upon this network daily, leading beyond to people over whom you have no direct authority or context for command.

Dunne honed his ability to recraft a range of relationships. He earned confidence and trust by demonstrating his commitment, reliability, and integrity. He built productive connections with those to whom he was accountable. And as evidenced by the actions of his employees, customers, suppliers, and even competitors, he was adept at fashioning strong bonds with both those over whom he had formal authority and those over whom he had no authority at all. He didn't order that trust and respect; he earned it. When a negative situation arose, he was able to draw on the wealth of support that bolstered his own resilience and that of the company. Despite daunting challenges, that connectivity enabled him to keep himself, and his organization, focused on the core mission.

Leading Beyond in Practice

In leading beyond, you sketch the big picture to make sense of a wide range of factors, including people, objectives, organizations, resources, and ideals outside your own organization. It describes what everyone can do together—as an enterprise of entities—that cannot be accomplished separately. All involved believe in you, what you stand for, and what you aspire to—the value of the enterprise.

What motivates all these people? And how do you satisfy and balance the variety of their ambitions? They are persuaded to join because the combined mission is inclusive. The extent to which you extend influence beyond your authority is your measure of "people follow you." As a meta-leader, your authenticity is your currency. You advance through the confidence people have in you—singular—and the trust that you—plural—together can do IT.

You become the meta-leader needed in the moment. In leading beyond, Dunne rallied the full range of stakeholders. Without all of them, the company probably would not have survived. It was Dunne's suddenly found multidimensional "us" perspective that enabled him to accomplish so much, for so many, in so short a period of time. He calculated that balance and got it right.

How do you transform your outlook into that of a multidimensional meta-leader? It is a choice you make.

Viewed from the meta-perspective, what you do is part of a larger whole. Your actions have an impact on you, the situation, your subordinates, your boss, your organization, and your customers, suppliers, and community, as well as society at large. For you and for your diverse, connected stakeholders, your endeavors have meaning. As a meta-leader, you grasp this complex system, your role in it, and why it matters. You animate the picture, giving it life in a way that engages you and conveys it to others. Doing so is your way of saying to those others, "You're it," gaining their buy-in to this recrafted value and purpose.

You describe this bigger picture in the narrative you shape and share. Show others the greater impact of what you are all doing together, whether it's "saving lives," "creating hope," "beating the sales goal," "protecting the environment," or "preserving our culture." Imbue activities with direction and achievement. You hope your boss will encourage and derive satisfaction from your motivation, energy, and the connectivity you forge. Your subordinates will better grasp why the production goal, the service introduction, or the crisis preparedness mission objective is so important. External stakeholders will gravitate toward your shared purpose and progress.

Your job is not simply completing a task. Rather, it is producing value and accomplishing desired results. This is what it means to get people to go "the extra mile." The innovative thinking, abundant effort, and determination that result in extraordinary achievement spring from such efforts. Other stakeholders, both internal ones and those beyond your direct authority or control, experience that you fully appreciate their contributions. This way of leading—inspiring a connected network of people to move in a coordinated direction—is more productive than any threat or financial incentive alone.

While the big picture provides context, nothing speaks louder than concrete action and tangible progress. Even small steps along the way can be significant. Measure and mark the evolution and note the milestones you encounter. Celebrate successes and credit the triumphs to the whole—to what you are able to do together. Mark your progress—for example, with an illustrated office thermometer charting headway or a widely distributed blog providing updates. Posting pictures of people at work on the internet energizes the organization's social network. Acknowledge and reward people for their contributions. Forward movement is compelling and reinforces the collective belief in what can be achieved together. Think, act, and achieve expansively.

There is also a real attraction for people to being part of something bigger: the excitement and sense of belonging to a group of like-minded people working toward an aspirational mission and accomplishing goals together. This is the emotional and intuitive side of fostering change and progress. It's an immeasurable: the belief system the leader nurtures and followers share.

The Learning Organization

As meta-leader, you create the conditions in which all this productivity and exploration happens. Peter Senge calls this a "learning organization." New and creative ideas are promoted, considered, and challenged. Mistakes are learning opportunities and problems are challenges to overcome. When followers are allowed, even encouraged, to fail within acceptable parameters, they are more likely to take the risks that achieve remarkable results. Your responses to performance and outcomes provide followers with signals about what is acceptable and what is not.

Be the role model for the type of follower you hope to cultivate. Nurture a culture in which it is safe to challenge assumptions, confront orthodoxies, and test new options. A generative process in which your followers further inspire resourcefulness will be contagious for the followers to whom you lead down, up, across, and beyond. Your meta-leadership amplifies your vision, goals, and methods beyond your organization and out to your wider enterprise of activity.

None of this implies that, as a meta-leader, you are a pushover. You can be both tough and open at the same time. Be clear about expectations, hold standards high, demand accountability, and be rigorous in your assessments. Match toughness with fairness, transparency, appropriate rewards, and an understanding of stakeholder impact. That combination will garner exceptional motivation, loyalty, and effort.

Meta-leading takes more than mere intelligence and optimism. It also requires courage and energy as you often navigate uncharted territory. Success is not guaranteed. For some, this is a terrifying prospect. As meta-leader, this is a vast and exciting puzzle to solve. At times, it evolves from a crisis. Sometimes, it is a wild new idea. Recognize the "you're it" moment when it happens and navigate accordingly.

In our interviews with and observations of meta-leadership practitioners, we are curious about how they achieve their insights and maintain their drive. We find two consistent attributes. Meta-leaders are eager learners, studying the people they lead, the work they direct, and the larger world in which they operate. And they are equally enthusiastic teachers and mentors, imparting their experience with generosity and a firm commitment to the people and tasks at hand. They inhabit the three dimensions of meta-leadership in their quest to understand themselves, the situation in which they lead, and the many people who are part of getting the job done, including those beyond their direct scope of authority.

One person who began as our student and is now a colleague, Rich Serino, is an exemplar. You met Rich in an earlier chapter, as the FEMA deputy administrator leading the federal response to Super Storm Sandy. Serino lives the thinking and practices of meta-leadership. He has the capacity to lift himself up and out of the basement and encourages followers to do the same. By actively listening, he perceives and understands situations systematically, shaping the involvement of followers. He leads up to his bosses the way he wants followers to lead up to him. And he pursues cross-organizational coordination of effort in ways that are replicated by others.

During Serino's tenure as FEMA deputy administrator, a major flood hit North Dakota. The damage was extensive. Rich was dispatched to the area as the senior federal official. On the trip out, advisors warned him that North Dakotans don't like FEMA and the federal government. They share an inborn Midwestern antipathy to Washington, and he was told to expect a hostile reception. Once on scene, he was helicoptered over the devastation. Making the case for federal funds to support the recovery, the North Dakota National Guard adjutant general (TAG) pointed out the damage: "That school is gone. That bridge is out. That neighborhood is devastated. No one died. No one was injured. That library is gone." He went on until they returned to the base emergency operations center. Serino walked into a room of angry-looking local political, emergency, and business leaders. This was his leading-beyond moment. Everyone was fixed on Serino, and ready to attack.

"Before I say anything else, I just want to say thank you. I just was taken out by the TAG and I saw all the devastation. And as he pointed out what happened, he told me, 'No one died and no one was injured.' That was because of you. What you did. You saved lives. You made a difference. So, thank you. Yes, money will come here to North Dakota to help in the recovery. And we'll bicker about how much. But for right now, thank you for all you've done."

The room was silent. The hostility subsided as everyone realized they were together on the same side of the disaster. Leading beyond: recrafted connectivity.

Bringing the Swarm Together

Connectivity is when people, organizations, and systems work together with congruence and synchrony. In addition to all the tools we give you to develop the meta-leadership mind-set, there is an innate quality—embedded in human nature—that generates and nurtures this connectivity.

In the first chapter, we described swarm meta-leadership. In the face of unknown risk and immediate urgency, Boston Marathon bombing response leaders rallied a web of connectivity, aligning organizations, communities, and individuals. That web provided protection, knowledge, and support. Its robustness fostered the resilience the city needed. Yes, there were already official agreements, systems, and drills in place that defined how collaboration was supposed to work. However, the complex and cross-jurisdictional crisis scenario faced in the moment tested existing parameters and assumptions. The impact of the compelling human solidarity that emerged exceeded what the formally established response network could have achieved alone. You can make that swarm meta-leadership part of your connectivity-building, even in noncrisis, everyday situations.

As with basement responses, instinctual human behaviors are prompted by deeply embedded neural connections. Relationships are shaped by these instinctive stimuli combined with learned behaviors. Parenting patterns and family and tribal affinities are hardwired into human nature. The learned behaviors are the "how to." A baby cries on a plane. Most people ignore the noise or are silently annoyed by it—people have learned socially appropriate responses. By contrast, the parents go into a tizzy of activity. Instincts prompt them to nurture and protect.

Connectivity is instinctive. We naturally engage others in solving problems, pursuing opportunities, and building solutions. Despite cultural nuances and differences, humans are fundamentally social beings. Those social impulses impel connection. Think of the genuine connectivity and caring seen—at times—in warm family gatherings, supportive faith-based organizations, in-harmony musical groups, winning sports teams, high-functioning work groups, and bonded neighborhoods. Ilana Lerman described that connectivity in her work for social justice.

Humans also engage in conflict. Flip each of the above examples and you find humans at their combative worst. In the quest for survival, one group coalesces to defeat the threatening other. Your brain instinctually calculates risks and rewards, deciding who to work with and who to fight. Friend or enemy. Survival depends on both individual and collective, innate and learned, calculations of the collaborate/compete equation.

Since we first developed the five principles of swarm meta-leadership, we have taught them to diverse audiences and observed their application for upgrading inclusive connectivity in businesses, professional groups, and communities in both crisis and routine operations. You will mold these principles to fit situations through which you lead. There are many variants on swarm meta-leadership that emerge within organizations as well as beyond them.

Here we present the principles in their most challenging form: for leading beyond to people outside your organization or authority structure.

How can you apply the five principles of swarm leadership practices to both your everyday scenarios and a crisis scenario? In the following pages, we answer this question by detailing the application of each principle.

Unity of Effort

Every swarm has a shared purpose. As a meta-leader, the narrative you craft rallies followers to your mission. That narrative is your vision, compelling purpose, or solution to a complex problem: your words are the glue that holds people together. In a few succinct words, your message must be meaningful and motivating to those you hope will follow.

In genuine ways, you model and live that unity of effort. People then believe in you, and they join the cause, purpose, or organization. When Rich Serino told North Dakotans, "You saved lives. You made a difference. So, thank you," he demonstrated appreciation, which opened the door to mutual respect that turned antagonism into agreement.

Unity of effort can formulate around a social mission, a business objective, the pursuit of victory, or beliefs. The measure of your message is in its motivation. Do others care about where you lead them? Do they believe it can be accomplished and that you can lead them there? Is the purpose worth their time and effort? The greater the pull of your purpose and message, the more others adhere to its cause. Ethan Zohn created this unity of effort for HIV prevention in Africa through his Grassroot Soccer initiative. Bottom line: will "people follow you"?

Generosity of Spirit and Action

How is commitment to the collective effort expressed? If people are on board with you, they contribute their time, energy, money, resources, smarts, and goodwill—all necessary ingredients for whatever you hope to accomplish.

In keeping with the Map-Gap-Gives-Gets discussion, the meta-leader expects followers to anticipate a return. It might be intangible: the gratification of being part of your efforts, the satisfaction of making a difference, or the camaraderie in your swarm. Or the return might be tangible: money, opportunity, resources, recognition, or reciprocal contributions to their own efforts—your time and effort in exchange for theirs.

Therefore, for everything you "get" from those in your swarm, there is a "give" from you to them. People like to be part of solving a problem. They take pride in their collective accomplishment. You demonstrate appreciation in your comments, actions, and recognition.

Meta-leaders rally people to make a difference. Following 9/11, Jimmy Dunne coalesced a swarm to fight back and rebuild Sandler O'Neill. The organization needed that generosity of spirit to jump-start the business. Dunne demonstrated generosity with so many people and inspired others to be generous with him and his cause. He also brought them into the battle against Osama Bin-Laden as together they fought for survivors, family members, and a better future. He gave many people their "you're it" moment.

Stay in Your Lane and Help Others Succeed in Theirs

Large, complex organizations apportion work, expertise, and responsibility into specialized units: departments, offices, professions. Everyone has a job whose function is one part of overall production. With that job come perks, including a budget, recognition, and opportunities for promotion.

It is not uncommon for competitive people or professional groups to expand their scope of responsibility. Some health care clinicians, for example, claim that they can do what has been the sole province of others, such as when work traditionally done by doctors is shifted to nurses. The conflict that often ensues is about revenues, prestige, and control. Doctors defend their territory by claiming that they hold the "real" competence or concern for patient well-being. Interactions turn adversarial as information, knowledge, and know-how are withheld and resources are hoarded. The attitude becomes: "be the winner, or else you're the loser."

Overcoming the territorial instinct, the meta-leader points to the potential gains reaped by working together. In leading down, you work to make your subordinates a success. So too in leading beyond: you craft networks of linked professionals who, in their unique mission or responsibility space, can also serve to make each other a success. In the health care example, the question could be: how can we draw even more patients and revenue into our system? We work, market, and collaborate together as a "center of excellence" to achieve the absolute best and most efficient clinical results. The "center of excellence" structure delineates the lanes in which the swarm's participants undertake their individual and team tasks—an arrangement that motivates the required gives and gets to achieve their collective mission.

Your meta-leadership role is to highlight the big-picture benefits of mutual success and focus on the requisite collaboration and cooperation. Monitor the gives and gets to ensure that everyone has a unique job to do that does not infringe on others. Keep everyone satisfied. If someone feels screwed and pulls out, your efforts could go for nothing. Emphasize appropriate sharing of what is known, done, and possessed for the combined good. In formalized situations, such sharing requires intellectual property agreements, nondisclosure clauses, and contractual arrangements. This is all part of creating a network of expanded contributions and expanded benefits. Uplift the mission: it is rousing to be an "honored member" of a "center of excellence."

These principles are particularly vital in the midst of crisis. Applying Map-Gap-Gives-Gets, Barry Dorn, back at Fort Dix, faced a mass casualty crisis. Map: He knew what he faced and what he needed. Gap: "I did not have enough of anything." Get: Medical supplies, blood, clinicians, support staff. Give: You are part of a lifesaving mission. Get: Everyone lived. Mission accomplished. Barry instantaneously mobilized a system to care for the wounded, effectively rallying support from organizations well beyond his base.

When we observe leaders practicing the principle of "stay in your lane and help others succeed in theirs," we find seamless effort—both individually and together—among the leaders, agencies, and people involved in the network. They accomplish their responsibilities knowing that other leaders and organizations are doing the same. People do not intrude into the work of others. They assist one another to succeed, knowing that the scope of responsibility for each differs.

In large complex endeavors—such as a political campaign, social movement, or organizational transformation—there is much to be done and a lot to be coordinated. Working together, leaders get the gears of a complex system to connect, achieving more than any one group or organization could do alone.

No Ego—No Blame

In most parts of the world, aviation is impeccably safe. That's because aviation leaders long ago adopted a system allowing and encouraging pilots and others to self-report errors and safety problems. As long as there is no intentional negligence, people are protected by a no-blame culture of correction that extends from pilots to airlines, regulators, and mechanics. The accumulated information is incorporated into policies and practices that improve the design of aircraft and communication protocols, embedding the culture of safety. That assurance sure feels good when you are in the air. Health care and other industries are adopting the same mind-set.

Getting beyond blame requires a shift in thinking and culture. Getting beyond ego requires a shift in behavior and attitude. Leadership, with all its attention and perks, does attract people with aggrandized self-esteem. They mistake the collected efforts of many people for their own and expect solo credit. They are jealous of attention given to others. They are "me"-centric. Everyone has an ego—after all, it serves certain purposes—though when overgrown, the inflated ego defies surgical extraction.

The attitude shift is from solo to shared credit. The behavior change lies in acknowledging, appreciating, and celebrating the combined efforts of the whole cast of involved characters. The shared enterprise—the swarm—accomplishes more than what anyone could do alone. This changed behavior requires seasoned emotional intelligence, abundant self-confidence, and profound maturity—attributes found in the person of the meta-leader.

In large, complex endeavors, we find that when "no ego—no blame" is practiced, no one organization or individual snatches the credit for the mutual successes. And though there are always moderate mistakes and failures along the way, no one points distracting fingers of blame.

In keeping with the "shadow effect"—as explained in Chapter 9—this tone cascades from top leaders down through their operations. A genuinely collaborative tenor emerges among leaders at all levels of parallel organizations.

We observed "no ego—no blame" in practice during the Boston Marathon bombings response. Leaders from different agencies and elected officials shared the podium, shared the credit, and established the character of the response. They demonstrated a rare level of emotional intelligence in their work together. There was a mutual understanding that with no ego and no blame, infighting among agencies was less likely to erupt as a problem or a distraction. Leaders do not always behave well when situations are tense and emotion-filled. That week, self-awareness and self-regulation made a difference. And those attributes permeated the community. It was the backbone of the "Boston Strong" narrative.

A Foundation of Trusting Relationships

Situations carry unknowns, mystery, and risk. In an unpredictable situation, you can't be sure what the outcome will be, whether good or bad. You hope for the best and prepare for the worst.

Though the situation is puzzling, you trust other people with whom you lead: people who follow you and people you follow. Trusting them, you predict how they will react in difficult circumstances. Confidently, you count on them. They have your back and you have theirs. However unpredictable the situation, knowing that the people with you, reassuringly, are predictable is the foundation of your meta-leadership through the difficulties of complexity, change, and crisis.

When Budge Upton was brought on as project manager to oversee construction of the wing at the Boston Museum of Fine Arts (Chapter 9), he was faced with sharp differences of opinion, difficult decisions, and countless financial, timing, and design risks and uncertainties. Despite the ambiguities and critical consequences, Upton's job was to get everyone involved connected and amicably working together. Recounting the story, he reflected on the relationship-building, trust, and confidence that formed the bedrock upon which differences were resolved.

A foundation of trusting relationships is particularly important in crisis leadership scenarios. A mega-crisis quickly overwhelms existing capacities within a single jurisdiction or organization, and so leaders from different agencies, areas, and specialties are brought in. It is often heard, "Don't wait for a crisis to exchange business cards." Know other leaders and build trust before the crisis hits. Drills, professional conferences, and even retirement receptions all play a role in getting to know the people on whom you may need to depend in a crisis.

When it matters most, that foundation of well-established and trusting relationships provides a measure of safety in unsafe times. "I can count on you. You can count on me." Leaders demonstrate maturity, emotional intelligence and a shared commitment to the mission at hand. Those relationships, in shaping your swarm, become the basis for the connectivity and unity of mission you build.

The five principles of swarm leadership are a road map for bringing diverse people together. In 2017, we shared these principles with American Red Cross leaders as they responded to a series of disasters, including hurricanes and wildfires. Brad Kieserman, vice president of disaster operations, shared with us, "We're baking swarm and 'how can I make you a success' into what we're doing every hour. Our team is embracing it."

What happens when the opposite side of swarm leadership emerges—when groups are working against one another?

From Swarm to Suspicion

The swarm can have a dark side: humans are innately tribal and can become scared, defensive, and loyal only to tribe mates. In the face of perceived threat, you naturally protect your tribe: your profession, family, work organization, gender, religion, cultural group, beliefs, or team. No matter how noble your goals may be, tribal affiliations—and loyalty to them—can prompt conflicts and wars, both offensive and defensive. Edward O. Wilson, who spent his career studying sociobiology, including swarm phenomena, warns: "We have created a Star Wars civilization, with Stone Age emotions. We thrash about" and are "a danger to ourselves and the rest of life."

Tribal suspicion builds antagonism, contest, and competition. It may derive from beliefs of superiority over others combined with the conquest impulse. The higher the stakes, the fiercer the fight. Leaders create the ideological basis for conflict and rally people behind it.

Looking at your own leadership experience and practice, what fights and battles have you witnessed? What was the rallying cry? How was the fight waged? How did others react?

Tribal suspicion leadership emerges when swarm principles are reversed:

Swarm Principles and Behaviors	Suspicion Principles and Behaviors
Unity of mission	Competing missions
Generosity of spirit and action	Selfish focus on individual's benefit
Staying in lanes to help others succeed	Extending authority and turf, setting others up to fail
No ego—no blame	Self-promotion: All ego—blame others
A foundation of relationships	An environment of distrust and scheming

What has been your experience with leaders prone to suspicion behaviors? Think about your observations and readings of certain world events and leaders to understand the manifestations of tribal suspicion leadership.

How are swarm and suspicion connected? On all sides of a complex problem, there are "forces for," "forces against," and "forces on the fence" (see Chapter 3). People can be brought together, and people can be divided. Suspicion leaders apply swarm principles to promote an us-versus-them perspective, offering only a shared, defensive huddle of safety and security against a common foe.

Within the in-group, people swarm to battle the out-group. Suspicion and fear of the other side energize the in-group/out-group dynamic. Too often today, political discourse, intraorganizational hostility, and cultural differences reflect such divides.

In practice, swarm and suspicion leadership can be arrayed across a continuum. It is rare to see either practiced in its purest, most extreme form. Even your enemies have a measure of kindness. And the good guys too have their mean streaks. Assess where leaders put themselves on this continuum, observing the mix of their motives, practices, and results. And remember: both the good guys and the bad guys have innate tribal characteristics. Terrorists swarm too. It takes swarms to defeat them. In the Boston Marathon bombings response and in Jimmy Dunne's response to the 9/11 decimation of his company, good people swarmed against bad guys, the terrorists.

Leading Beyond to Shape a Swarm

Kellie Bentz, of Airbnb, is a compelling meta-leader in the world of private-sector emergency management. She leads a team that helps meet the needs of survivors and response workers in crisis, utilizing the organization's extensive, decentralized network of hosts. They provide support in a range of incidents, including terror attacks and natural disasters.

We first met Bentz when she attended our NPLI executive crisis leadership program at Harvard. At the time, she was director of disaster services programs at the Points of Light organization. Before joining Airbnb, she worked in the crisis management team at Target Corporation. "I first became engaged in this field," she explained, "when I was in New Orleans working on a recovery project after Hurricane Katrina. I'd never been to New Orleans or to a disaster before, but was asked to start a volunteer project by Hands On Network, organizing spontaneous volunteers to get things done."

Her path from there has hardly been linear. "I've gone from hyperlocal in New Orleans to having a global span of activities across 191 countries at Airbnb. I never could have predicted it." She shared that her role progressed from individual contributor to team-builder as her career evolved. "I've leveraged an understanding of structure and an appreciation for the energy of an entrepreneurial setting." In other words, Bentz assembles swarms.

Bentz's personal journey and that of Airbnb are both stories of connectivity. Personally, Bentz used her professional network of NPLI alumni and others for peer support. "One of the challenges when you are the only one in the 'crisis management bubble' in an organization, that is not primarily focused on disaster or crisis, is that you often get 'crazy' ideas from people who want to do good things but don't understand the implications. You begin to question yourself—am I being too cautious? When you connect with others in your domain, even in other organizations, you get reassured that you are competent and are raising the right issues." She added, "I've had a bit of imposter syndrome along the way. Now, with more experience and connections, I fully know why I am in the room and I am confident that I know what I am doing.

"Articulating what I do and the need to explain to people who don't fully understand the space is a challenge up, down, across, and beyond," Bentz said. "My most effective tactics are to listen and continually educate people. I used to react a lot. Now I focus on reframing, taking a step back, and responding more thoughtfully. This helps me turn good intentions into good outcomes."

Airbnb's entire business is based on connectivity. Its platform brings together hosts and guests for short-term housing rentals across 80,000 cities in 191 countries. "Airbnb is hyperfocused on our community of hosts and guests," Bentz said. "That's how we got into disaster response." She explained that the company was contacted by a host in the New York area after Super Storm Sandy in 2012. At the time, the lowest price to list one's space was US$10.00 per night. The host wanted to list for free. The company agreed that it was an idea worth supporting. Bentz explained that a team of engineers worked around the clock to program and install the change. It became the company's "disaster tool" and has since evolved based on field experience.

After this initial effort, Airbnb created "Open Homes," an initiative that allows hosts to offer free rooms, both proactively and reactively. "It started as a great grassroots idea. We then built the platform and policies to make it sustainable," Bentz said.

Open Homes is just one part of Airbnb's global disaster response and relief program. Bentz described it as a blend of crisis management and corporate social responsibility. "We look to use our assets to help the greatest number of people," she said. Airbnb monitors the news and weather to provide 24/7 notification of major events to hosts and guests. This fills an important gap: in previous crises, government officials have often had difficulty reaching the traveling public. Bentz and her team facilitate cross-functional coordination across the company. For example, they create event reports for customer service agents as they support people in the community. The team also creates preparedness and response messaging, which is particularly helpful with advance-notice events such as hurricanes, Bentz said. Across the enterprise, Bentz and her team serve as subject matter experts on crisis response, supporting Airbnb's various functions and helping employees get involved in response efforts where they are able.

As Airbnb's crisis response efforts grow, an increasing portion of Bentz's work involves leading beyond to recraft relationships outside the company. She explained that Airbnb provides travel credit to response and relief workers in the organizations with which they partner, such as All Hands and Hearts as well as Team Rubicon. This helps solve a vexing challenge: finding housing for both survivors and relief workers in the aftermath of a major event. Airbnb enables a "housing surge" that helps communities rebound and be resilient in the face of adversity.

"What's exciting for me is that we are finding new ways to build connectivity across the public, private, and nonprofit sectors," Bentz said. "We are building capability and boosting capacity. I am glad that I learned about leading with influence beyond authority. That's most of what I do every day."

As a meta-leader, you are a connector. There is much for you to leverage in forging connection: authority down, up, and across your organization, as well as interests, motivations, and exchanges beyond your enterprise. It is a wide panorama of people, silos, stuff, and experience. You see the bigger meta-picture and discern ways to reconceive it so that it matters to many people. You make it happen: "you're it."

As you craft connectivity amid all this opportunity, you encounter an abundance of conflict and diplomacy. As a meta-leader, you negotiate the differences, build solutions, and resolve the conflicts. Embedding the necessary analysis and skills into your meta-leadership thinking and practices is the topic of our next chapter.

Questions for Journaling

➤ Thinking beyond the borders of your organization—to the enterprise of people who are part of broader endeavors—is critical to meta-leadership. What has been your experience in this larger realm? What have you seen other leaders do in recrafting these relationships? List what works and what does not.

➤ Whether in your family, workplace, team, or faith-based organization, what have been your swarm leadership experiences? What
bound people together? What behaviors or challenges got in the way
of a swarm?

➤ What have been your suspicion leadership experiences? What was
done to elevate those suspicions, and how did those actions affect
followers? What divided people? Was anything done to temper those
suspicions?

ELEVEN

THE WALK IN THE WOODS

Negotiating Differences and Resolving Conflict to Build Collaboration

Meta-leaders coordinate a wide cast of characters into cohesive effort. This is no easy feat. It requires understanding motives, finding common themes, building organization and communication, and finally, securing outcomes that justify investments. All that sounds good. Problem is, with so many people around the same table, there is going to be a lot to disagree about. It is a complex process.

Though onerous, conflict is a wall you surmount in your meta-leadership practice. When unresolved, conflict festers and distracts. These are not only differences that involve other people. Often you, the meta-leader, are at the center of the squabbling. Your visibility makes you a convenient target. You tussle over philosophical, strategic, or tactical questions. The conflict is a burden constraining you and obstructing progress toward larger purposes. The struggles assume a life of their own. Your credibility and influence are affected, perhaps negatively, even when you win the battles.

Often the very purpose of your meta-leadership is convening divergent stakeholders, overcoming points of conflict, and galvanizing connectivity to reap the resulting advantages. When this is the case, your thrust is conflict resolution. It's not always pleasant. It is a necessary part of the job. If that is what you face, what can you do to handle differences constructively?

To aid your meta-leadership practice, we developed a practical negotiation method for your problem-solving tool box. Applicable to just about every aspect of managing conflict, this method can be used to facilitate complex negotiations, build cross-silo teamwork, and resolve conflict. As a personal discipline, the method can privately guide you through one-on-one negotiations with subordinates, bosses, peers, or even family members.

The framework is called the "Walk in the Woods." The Walk is based on the principles of interest-based negotiation. Through the negotiation process, this collaborative approach helps parties discover and develop mutually beneficial solutions. It contrasts with positional bargaining, which is oppositional and pursues win-lose outcomes.

The Walk assists stakeholders in (1) identifying their key interests; (2) understanding each distinct viewpoint; (3) finding imaginative, successful solutions; and (4) clarifying the give-and-get exchanges necessary for a mutually beneficial and acceptable outcome.

The Walk in the Woods is named for the 1982 saga of two Cold War nuclear arms reduction negotiators. Delegations from the United States and the Soviet Union were meeting outside Geneva, Switzerland. Paul Nitze led the US delegation and Yuli Kvitsinsky led the Soviet delegation. Facing a desperate impasse, the two sides called a break. As the story is told, Nitze and Kvitsinsky bumped into one another outside the pastoral retreat center and together agreed to take a walk—as it were given the location—in the woods. The conversation opened with discussion of the impasse and its complexities. It continued to stories about their backgrounds, careers, and families and eventually reached the topic of their mutual desire to overcome the impasse.

As the walk progressed, the two distinguished men shared their concerns and objectives, some of which were divergent. Yet they also came to realize that their positions on other issues were actually quite similar. They eventually achieved an understanding for what the escalating arms race meant for their countries, the world, and the future. They realized that it was in both national interests to reach an agreement. With that, they explored steps to realize significant mutual force reduction, noteworthy given Nitze's reputation as a hardliner on the Soviets. Concluding their walk, they settled on options and solutions to break the impasse, which they brought back to their delegations at the conference center. Though their agreement was subsequently rejected by Moscow and Washington, the discussions were immortalized in a Broadway play and came to exemplify the advantages of personal bargaining and interest-based negotiation.

By design, our Walk enhances the transparency and efficiency of the negotiation process and ultimately the buy-in and satisfaction of stakeholders. This method systematically expands the range of interests and objectives incorporated into agreements and solutions. When caught in conflict, this structured, four-part progression for renegotiating working relationships is a guide for those with a stake in both the process and its outcome.

The Walk serves as a detour from the normal course of discussion. In typical problem-solving, parties rush to argue the relative merits of their preferred solution: "My plan is better than yours." "My demand is more legitimate (stronger) than yours." The conversation becomes polarized. This heightens adversarial sensitivities and tendencies.

This detour is analogous to the walk taken in Geneva. It starts the negotiation process differently. The first step is for the group to define the problem and understand how it is perceived differently by each of the parties involved, a process similar to the "Cone-in-the-Cube" discussed earlier. This wider perspective ensures that each participant feels heard. It opens them to hearing others. The intent is to deescalate tensions. The focus turns more to solving the puzzle and not winning the battle.

The Walk is a transparent process for understanding problems from multiple perspectives and then—based on the reframing that results—finding responsive solutions as a joint enterprise. The process itself readies participants to discover fresh perspectives. As important, it reduces debate over solutions that ignore the fundamental interests of those around the table.

The Walk in the Woods has four distinct and sequential steps to guide stakeholders from the problem toward solutions: (1) self-interests, (2) enlarged interests, (3) enlightened interests, and (4) aligned interests. Each step entails a specific negotiation activity and outcome that motivates and prepares negotiators for the action required in the next step. At each step, it is useful to record what is being said on a whiteboard in order to capture the array of interests and ideas put forward. Before going into depth, we next provide an overview of the logic.

The Walk in the Woods

The Walk starts with stating *self-interests*. Each party describes the problem with a focus on their own interests—what they hope to accomplish, what they believe is fair, and their concerns, motives, principles, fears, and values. Participants are encouraged to listen to one another actively and genuinely.

Next is the *enlarged interests* step, during which people look first for points of agreement among the self-interests each has expressed. Then they turn to the points of disagreement. Most often, because principles and values

The Walk in the Woods

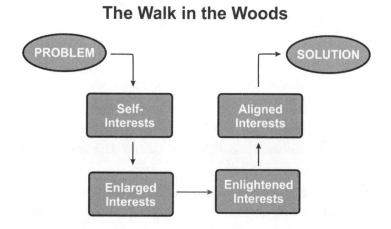

align, agreements outnumber disagreements. This realization reframes the discussion, stimulating the search for solutions that resolve differences.

During the *enlightened interests* step, the parties are encouraged to think creatively, inventing new ideas and possibilities to resolve their disagreements. We often find that many of these new ideas had not occurred to anyone prior to the Walk. The group assembles a list and then distinguishes between feasible options and those with less potential.

The *aligned interests* are the focus of the final step of the Walk, which is devoted to solution-building, bargaining, and gives and gets. The parties come to an agreement that reflects overall shared interests and motives, thereby generating buy-in for the negotiated outcome. They build it so that all will have an investment in its success. Not every point is resolved, though the positive experience of realizing common interests and coming to terms on some disagreements generates momentum and prepares the ground for future work together. Resolved conflict breeds the potential for further collaboration.

If you are leading or facilitating a Walk in the Woods, your most important tool is the question. At each step, questions prompt the discussion, and the responses encourage further questions, all in the interest of discovering common ground and solutions for complex problems.

The Walk in the Woods in Practice

We have facilitated hundreds of Walks with a wide variety of groups. These negotiations are generally governed by a nondisclosure agreement, so with the following case, the descriptive details are changed to preserve the identities of the individuals and organizations involved. The issues and outcomes, however, are real. We place you in the role of facilitator.

Two technology companies, T-Pro and OmniTech, are in the process of a merger. Each has a good reputation and is financially successful. The merger was initiated with hope that the combined entity would be more competitive against larger rivals and therefore able to remain independent while under the same umbrella. Both T-Pro and OmniTech fear being acquired by one of those mega-firms. That fear, and the business crisis it would have created, prompted the merger.

While the respective boards have reached an overall agreement, they decided to let the corresponding business units work out their integration within the general guidelines of the master deal. Encouraging people to determine their own fate is considered more productive than dictating a solution from above. We were asked to help with the integration of the two research and development (R&D) groups. Their expected collaboration was a major incentive for the merger.

When facing disagreement, your first meta-leadership task is getting the right people to the negotiating table: stakeholders who believe they have a say in the matter or who will be affected by its outcome. In this case, each group is composed of six people, and all are invited to the Walk. T-Pro's R&D unit is headed by Bill, a respected veteran who has been an innovator since the days of mainframe computers. OmniTech's team is led by Wendy, a whiz recruited right out of university. Bill believes in tight process parameters to keep projects on track. Wendy is a freewheeling rebel whose shop operates with minimal structure. The two leaders are fiercely competitive and have been known to spar aggressively on panels at industry events.

With the parties assembled, the Walk begins. As the facilitator, you open with a welcome and review of what prompted the meeting (the situation) and lay out what it is hoped will be achieved.

You explain that the purpose of this Walk is to build confidence and ultimately trust between the parties. The hope is that they will learn to see one another as something other than an enemy to defeat. You ask, "Do you see a cost to not resolving your issues?" There is general agreement that there is indeed a cost, and that it is best to minimize or eliminate it. You move on to a brief overview of the specific steps coming up: how they work and lead from one to the next (see the brief description provided earlier). You make certain that everyone understands that whatever agreement emerges from the process will be developed by the stakeholders themselves. If successful, the groups will begin to identify the possibilities and advantages of working together, simultaneously uncovering both motive and incentive for resolving differences.

From the outset, you establish and model the appropriate tone: serious, yet cordial and considerate. To encourage expression of interests, you explain that the Walk is a safe zone of mutual respect and recognition. What people hear and learn is often more important than what they say. Attacks must be avoided. The intent is to inform others at the table in a way that generates understanding and even empathy.

Step 1: Self-Interests

Going from person to person around the table, you ask, "What is your view of the issues being negotiated?" You might also ask, "What do you hope to achieve through this conversation?" Opening statements of three to five minutes are about right. Discourage long, tedious speeches.

A range of issues and interests are raised in the opening phase of this Walk. From the outset, one thing is abundantly clear: each team wants its leader to take charge of the combined unit. Bill and Wendy are symbolic of their distinct cultures.

There are also compensation issues. OmniTech's engineers and coders receive incentives based on sales once their innovations go to market. T-Pro's people receive bonuses based on meeting cost and delivery targets for selected projects as well as on patents secured. Each team advocates strongly that their physical space should be the home for the combined unit, even though the companies' campuses are less than two miles apart in architecturally similar buildings.

There are also differences over how work is assigned. At T-Pro, individuals are assigned to projects based on their experience and expertise. At OmniTech, Wendy believes in letting people choose their projects with the idea that the best ideas will naturally attract the best talent. The issues seem intractable. The sides are far apart.

You should not be surprised to find wide gaps like these on the issues. If there were agreement from the get-go, there would be no need for a Walk. However, through respectful sharing of different perspectives, cracks begin appearing in the defensive walls of each group. You can tell through softening tones and more relaxed body language that the parties are beginning to recognize and appreciate both their commonalities and their legitimate differences. Even though they may not agree with one another, they are talking and beginning to see the logic behind their diverging points of view. The Cone-in-the-Cube analogy discussed here earlier starts to look to them like an appropriate image for the observations and insights deriving from this first step. You might even show the image to make this point more concrete. The participants begin to better appreciate the many perspectives on the problems they face.

Step 2: Enlarged Interests

When the Walk began, it was difficult to imagine that there would be important points of concurrence, and perhaps even many of them. Now is the time to uncover that possibility. You move the conversation to the second step—the enlarged interests phase. "Now that everyone around the table has articulated their interests, let's look for the points of agreement and the points of disagreement." There is momentary silence. You write "Agreements" and "Disagreements" in two columns on a whiteboard at the front of the room.

Finally one of the participants speaks up. "Is there *anything* we agree on? I don't see it."

You prompt them. "Quality?" Both teams offer that they value high quality. You write "Quality" on the whiteboard under "Agreements," and you continue jotting as more points emerge.

"What else? How about product releases?" They share that they work hard for product releases with few bugs. Each team prizes breakthrough innovation and finds it gratifying to leap ahead of a larger, more established competitor. Both appreciate commercial success, even though only Omni-Tech's team is directly rewarded for it. Each team also acknowledges that the merger is happening whether they like it or not. They have three options: find a way to get along, look forward to a tension-filled existence, or leave to find new jobs.

It turns out, however, that they already agree on a lot. While disagreements remain, they look quite different in light of these profound points of consensus. Individuals from one side are echoing and amplifying what those on the other side are also saying. The initial basis for common ground is being formed.

This exercise in finding agreement reframes the parties' understanding of what they are negotiating. They started the Walk with "unidimensional/me for me" and "two-dimensional/me against you" mind-sets, a contest in which everyone is out for themselves. In the enlarged interests step, this mind-set is transformed into a more encompassing, multidimensional "us together" view of what they face. Achieving this view is the intention of reframing.

Once the parties are exposed to the interests of others around the table, the newly acquired information reshapes their understanding of both the process and the possible outcome of their negotiation. They recognize that many of their interests and motivations overlap. With that realization, they discover the possibility of finding agreement that can advance their shared motives, values, and interests, prompting a new understanding of what they are negotiating about. This reframing opens the possibility that the Walk will lead to unanticipated opportunities.

Points of agreement almost always outnumber points of disagreement, and that is the case here. You write the issues in contention on the whiteboard: location, leadership, and incentive structure. Though significant, those disagreements look quite different—less important and more resolvable—when seen in the light of the newly minted and enlarged points of agreement. The reframing process is complete when the parties discover a fresh perspective on the shared problem and a renewed energy and hope for finding a resolution.

Once this reframing is achieved, all sides are encouraged to explore shared solutions rather than simply scheme to overcome the other party. It is a breakthrough moment, and the change in the negotiating tone propels the parties into the next step Here they build on the shared perspectives and new confidence they are establishing together.

Step 3: Enlightened Interests

Moving now to the creative step of the Walk, the tone of conversation is significantly changing. Meta-leadership and interest-based negotiation, at their best, are methods for finding and taking advantage of opportunities by exploring new options and discovering innovative solutions. Imaginative thinking requires concerted effort. Why?

People accumulate a mound of "baggage" as their lives and careers progress: biases, sour experiences, resistance to change, competitive impulses, and downright stubbornness. Time constraints and pressures compel the path of least resistance and acceptance of less desirable outcomes. Organizational incentive structures often reward selfishness over collaboration. All these factors obstruct imaginative problem-solving and obscure creative possibilities. Innovation requires abandoning habitual blinders.

Just as listing points of agreement and disagreement was a useful exercise during the enlarged interests step, an exercise to encourage creative problem-solving, and practice mini-deal-making, is at the heart of the enlightened interests step.

You go up to the whiteboard where the "Agreements" and "Disagreements" are preserved for all to see. You lay the ground rules for the enlightened interests: this is a "No-Commitment Zone" for creativity. No one should fear that he or she is expected to do something just because it is raised in this step of the Walk. You instruct the parties to brainstorm, encouraging as many creative ideas as possible. You ask questions that open with phrases such as, "What if you tried . . . ?," "Imagine that . . . ," and "Would you be willing to consider . . . ?" There is to be no commentary, editing, judging, or disagreement about what is being said. You seek to uncover no-holds-barred ingenuity.

Perhaps because of the inherent creativity and ingenuity in a group of product developers, the brainstorming is robust. This crowd enjoys problem-solving. You record their new ideas on the whiteboard to be referenced during the subsequent analytical process.

It becomes clear that while the two groups are competitive, they also admire each other. Some of Wendy's people long for a bit more structure, while some of Bill's want more time in the sandbox to experiment.

One of Bill's engineers proposes a two-stage system in which projects can be developed to a certain point in a loosely structured way and then be moved into a more formal process once they have gelled a bit. People will be able to volunteer 25 percent of their time to work on phase 1 projects, and then be assigned to subsequent projects for the balance of their time. If phase 1 works as planned and the best talent brings the best ideas forward, being assigned won't feel like conscription. Heads nod around the table.

A proposed bonus structure drawing on both of the current models emerges: 50 percent to be based on commercial success, 25 percent on delivery and budget targets, and 25 percent on patents secured. They agree that this structure balances short- and long-term measures and aligns their work with the overall objectives outlined in the master merger agreement.

Building on this positive momentum and nascent trust—and still in the no-commitment zone of the enlightened interests step—Wendy takes a leap. "How much longer do you want to do this, Bill?" she asks. He pauses to consider her question. "Two or three years, I suppose," he replies. "I would like to do some teaching before I retire, perhaps in some part of the world that really needs to develop technical expertise."

"If that's the case, I think that you should head the unit," Wendy offers. "I've got a lot to learn from your experience."

"And I've always believed in hiring a number two who is at least as smart as I am, so I'd be happy to put you in that spot and groom you to take over," he says. "I have a feeling I have a few things to learn from you too."

There is a palpable excitement in the room. With differences yielding to possibilities, people see a bright future together. One of Bill's people then puts forward an out-of-the-box solution to the space dilemma: a refurbished brick factory building has recently come on the market not far from the two campuses. Why not start their new corporate life together in completely different and newly designed space?

After completing the brainstorming list, you facilitate a group process in which every point is individually discussed and assigned a number: 1, 2, or 3. If everyone agrees on a point or believes it is feasible, it gets a 1. If there is clear disagreement, it gets a 3. And if there is ambiguity about whether agreement or disagreement predominates, the idea is assigned a 2. After discussing all ideas, you do one last review of those that received a 2, asking whether what was learned could modify and thereby nudge any of them up into the 1 grouping or down to the 3 category. Or perhaps a proposed solution that received a 2 could be modified or traded for something else in order to turn it into a 1. Parties are open to unconstrained dialogue because they are in the no-commitment zone.

Points assigned a 1 are the *deal-makers,* and those given a 3 are the *deal-breakers.* It is important to know what is newly possible, and it is just as important to know what is impossible. The points that garnered a 1 will be carried into the next step of the Walk as substantive bargaining gets under way.

Step 4: Aligned Interests

The momentum sparked during the enlightened interests step is carried into the final step of the Walk, the aligned interests. In the first three steps of the Walk, the groups discovered the map of possibilities and the gaps to be closed. That process serves as a prelude to the bargaining—the actual getting and giving. In this fourth step, the agreed-to ideas from the enlightened interests phase are honed. The consensus proposals will be presented to senior management. With an air of collegiality, greater specificity is added.

To align their priorities, the "gets"—what each party wants to gain in the process—are described, defined, and ranked by each side. They each decide which gets are "must haves," "nice to haves," or "don't needs." The lists for each side are different, as is common in complex negotiations. In similar fashion, each side articulates what they are eager, willing, and unwilling to "give" in order to achieve an agreement. Wendy is willing to let Bill head the unit. What does she want in return?

The discussion during this step encourages the parties to adapt their lists as long as the ultimate dividend—the agreement—satisfies a desirable combination of interests. Some items at the top of their lists drop into secondary positions as it becomes clear that flexibility is necessary for a deal to be reached.

You are cognizant that the arrangement reached here must meet several tests if it is to be upheld for the long run. It must be acceptable to each of the constituents. It must make conspicuously clear what each stakeholder has to gain (the gets) and what each stakeholder has put on the table (the gives). Wendy, Bill, and their teams then will have to lead up together, convincing their bosses that their plan will be beneficial for the newly merged enterprise. Each side evaluates the deal in terms of whether, on balance, it meets the test of fairness. If it does, there will be buy-in, ownership, and championing of the agreement that would never have developed if the arrangement had been imposed from the outside and not generated from within. With development and buy-in from within, the proposed solution is more likely to stand the test of time.

When the T-Pro and OmniTech groups launched their Walk, each had a divergent notion of "success." The objective of the Walk was to achieve mutual success, not simply have one side "win." Through the Walk, horizons were expanded to include multidimensional solutions that neither group had imagined at the outset. They redefined shared success together.

The agreements crafted through this Walk in the Woods were finalized as a proposal memo for the CEO and senior management team: It outlined the reporting structure, proposed compensation, and the facilities and workflow arrangements. The report also briefly described the process: the different initial perspectives, the agreements and disagreements, the fresh ideas accepted and rejected, and the alignment and exchanges that led to the agreement.

A few days later, the proposals were accepted with minor modifications.

The format and process of the Walk in the Woods reframed a toxic situation into a win that the parties could share. Similar to the arm-wrestling exercise in Chapter 3, the negotiators shifted from an adversarial push against one another to a mind-set oriented toward their joint situation. The outcome satisfied the merging companies, the R&D teams, and the individuals involved. And it is still working well.

Using the Walk in the Woods in Your Meta-Leadership

Here are some situations in which the Walk can be applied:

1. *During meetings:* Especially when controversial, complex, or strategic questions are under consideration, the method ensures that everyone is heard, common themes are identified, and outcomes carry the support of key stakeholders. The Walk is a constructive framework for retreats, strategic planning sessions, staff meetings, and venues that convene diverse constituencies. It is a useful guide in your leading down.

2. *When caught in high-stakes, emotional, divisive conflict:* The Walk provides a process for systematically delineating the issues and seeking resolution of a conflict. If you have a direct stake in the conflict or

its outcome, have someone else lead the Walk, such as an impartial facilitator or mediator recruited from outside your immediate circle.

3. *To prevent conflict from escalating:* The Walk can become part of your group's vocabulary, thinking, and culture. At the earliest sign of a problem, someone suggests, "Let's take a Walk on that." This is a gentle way of suggesting that there is a problem requiring attention and a reminder that it can be addressed without blaming, raising voices, or allowing issues to fester to the point of confrontation. This technique can be helpful in leading across with other departments and offices.

4. *In preparing a negotiation:* If you or your group are readying for an important meeting, especially a difficult one, you can anticipate what will happen by pondering each step of the Walk. You can do this even if the Walk is not being used to structure the meeting. If you foresee an unavoidably adversarial confrontation, the discipline of going on a Walk beforehand can help you anticipate others' interests and thereby outsmart them. The Walk becomes a tool for building situational awareness and developing calculated options.

5. *To represent your constituency at a meeting and then report back to your boss:* The steps of the Walk are a useful way to structure the narrative of a report or briefing. This structure will represent both sides—their interests, points of agreement and disagreement, new ideas proposed, and ideas accepted. Merely reporting the outcome without an account of the process tells only a portion of the story. You will get better questions, discussion, and ultimately buy-in for what was decided by including the full account. The Walk is part of your leading-up repertoire of tools.

6. *Anytime you are driven to the basement:* When someone or something sends you to the basement, prompt yourself to get up and out by going to your tool box with one word: "Walk." Do not comment or react in the basement. The most important tool of the Walk is the question. Pose one that seems most relevant: Why? What? Who? Take what you learn and use it methodically to chart your next moves. In personal terms, the Walk is a discipline for exercising your emotional intelligence and getting yourself and others out of the basement.

You have seen how the Walk works in a large, facilitated session. Here is an example from our health care negotiation practice. Again, the details have been changed slightly to protect confidentiality, though the issues and outcomes are real.

An elderly woman passed away. Following her death, the woman's daughter learned that her mother suffered from advanced cancer and that it had not been treated aggressively. She filed a complaint against her mother's longtime doctor and threatened legal action against the hospital. She was persuaded by the hospital to enter into mediation. The Walk in the Woods was used to facilitate the discussion between the daughter and her mother's physician.

In the self-interests step, the daughter stated that she wanted justice for her mother's suffering and the pain that it was now causing her. The doctor stated that he wanted to provide the best care for his patients. It was here that the physician revealed that it was the mother's decision to forgo aggressive treatment for the cancer. The daughter had been unaware of her mother's choice.

In the enlarged interests step, it became clear that both the daughter and the doctor were interested in quality care and respect for the wishes of patients. The daughter related that her mother had spoken highly of the doctor on many occasions. The daughter's anger was in part now redirected at her mother for not sharing the cancer diagnosis with her. The doctor disclosed that treating the cancer would have put her mother in a great deal of discomfort without a guarantee that the outcome would be favorable. He also admitted that he could have been more insistent that his patient reveal her diagnosis to her family. He said that perhaps he had not been empathetic enough with the daughter when discussing the mother's death. A great deal of tension was released during this step of the Walk.

In the enlightened interests step, they discussed how the doctor could have been more comforting to the daughter. For example, he might have offered to speak with her at the time of diagnosis in case her mother was uncomfortable doing so. The daughter still wanted to take some action, though now preferred not to resort to a legal battle.

In the aligned interests step, they agreed that the doctor would make a significant donation to a cancer research charity in the mother's name—there was a bit of back-and-forth on the exact amount—and attend a patient communication workshop. They also agreed that if he took these two steps within three months, the daughter would not file a formal complaint with the medical board or file a lawsuit.

The Walk process offered an opportunity for each of these individuals to express themselves and hear one another. It deescalated the confrontation and opened the door to a novel solution. In the end, they both left satisfied. It was a cordial conclusion to a contentious situation.

Pragmatic Tips for Leading a Walk in the Woods

The best way to learn the Walk is to use it. First, apply the model as a personal technique to chart problem-solving and negotiation. As you become more familiar with its premises and practices, use it to facilitate meetings or to resolve more complex conflict scenarios.

The specific objectives, methods, and intended outcomes for each step of the Walk lay the groundwork for what comes next. It is useful to begin each step with a brief review of what is to be discussed, why it needs to be talked about, and what the step hopes to achieve. It is helpful to conclude each step with a synopsis of what has been discussed and resolved and the ways in which it leads to the next step.

Be flexible when leading a Walk. Though the process is described here as a neat, linear, step-by-step method, in practice it does not always progress in a straight line. Go with the flow, and go back to earlier steps as needed. The method is a guide and should not be applied so rigidly that it constrains fluid and valuable discourse.

It may be difficult to cajole some of the key players to the table. Take subgroups on strategic and small pre-Walk Walks that prepare them for the full spectrum of issues that will eventually be addressed. One Walk can certainly lead to another. As with all you do in your meta-leadership, these are iterative processes toward ambitious objectives.

The most important dividend of the Walk in the Woods is buy-in. Because the participants formulate their solution, they are motivated to see it succeed, even if is not what they anticipated at the outset. In the first self-interests step, they recognize both the opportunities open to them and the constraints they face. During the enlarged interests step, they build the connectivity necessary to forge a solution together. With this shift, they develop options during the enlightened interests step that would not have otherwise surfaced. The give-and-get negotiation process of the aligned interests step provides a balanced, pragmatic, and workable solution across the array of interests they face together. It is a solution they craft and own—hence the buy-in to its success. This buy-in is what encourages the parties to implement the agreement in good faith.

Participants probably would not accomplish this same buy-in through an adversarial process. By contrast, the Walk reduces hyperbole and posturing and replaces grandstanding with candor and flexibility. The parties redirect their collective energies toward generating gains that would otherwise elude them. It is a simple formula: more gain equals less pain.

The Walk in the Woods is your meta-leadership guide for facilitating decision-making and fostering common purpose. In the end, it is the ownership of process and product that is most critical to the success of the experience, both for the stakeholders who will benefit and for you, the facilitator who has led them through the steps.

The steps of the Walk align and integrate with the phases of the POP-DOC Loop described in Chapter 4: the self-interests and enlarged interests steps are the learning phases in which you perceive the positions of the various parties, orient them toward common challenges and opportunities, and predict where they may be willing to come together. The enlightened interests and aligned interests steps are the action phases in which the group makes decisions based on the options they have generated and then lays out the plans for operationalizing and communicating their new agreements. Use these tools together as you navigate high-stakes conflicts.

Meta-leadership is distilled from real-life experience. Specifically, the dimensions derive from what it takes to succeed in the high-stakes, high-pressure environment of crisis. In our next chapter, we take another Walk: this time through crises that challenge you and your meta-leadership.

Questions for Journaling

➤ Try using the Walk in the Woods at work and at home. Be conscious of the four steps and how you employ them. How do they shape your thinking and actions? What questions did you ask to guide the process? What is the reaction of the other parties as you guide them through the Walk? How does the process affect the outcome?

➤ Have you been through a negotiation or problem that could have benefited from the Walk structure? Compare what actually happened to what could have happened.

➤ You may find that some of these practices and principles are already integral to your problem-solving approaches. How does what you are learning fit into what you have already been doing?

· · · · · · · · · · · · · · · · ·

TWELVE

WHEN IT MATTERS MOST

Mastering the Pivots

During crisis or organizational transformation, meta-leadership requires readiness and an ability to shift behavior and direction. You pivot.

Crises arise in many shapes and sizes, and each one wreaks its own havoc. There are big crises with extensive loss of life and major property damage. There are market failures when whole companies disappear. Smaller though significant personal crises mark life's passages: the death of a loved one, illness, divorce, or job loss. There are crises with advance notice, such as hurricanes and snowstorms, and crises that provide little or no notice, such as a terrorist attack or an industrial accident. All crises require a proper response, and when that response falls short, the result can be disaster upon disaster.

When crisis hits, each step you take involves a pivot. You pivot from your normal everyday reality to the basement, where the situation is unclear and panic sets in. Then you gather information and pivot to your trigger script of learned and intentional actions to reset your brain. Finally, you work the POP-DOC Loop. With each pivot, you systematically advance from unconscious and unaware to conscious and aware, from unintended and innate to intended and learned. This is the process for mastering crisis meta-leadership.

As you systematically traverse these pivots, your thinking, actions, and direction are transformed. You are in a different mode. Alertness heightens. Attention focuses. You move yourself and others beyond the basement. You see both the big meta-picture and the critical priorities for immediate action.

Because such thinking and actions become your routine for tackling day-to-day problems and mini-crises, your pivots during a major crisis are practiced and known. This is among the most valuable assets of adopting the meta-leadership mind-set.

You can't know for sure the moment when crisis will hit. When you are a leader in that instant, suddenly "you're it." People turn to you. What do you do next?

Preparing to Pivot

Resilience is the theme of crisis response in Israel. It pervades the nation's planning and procedures during terrorist attacks, war, and earthquakes. For a small country in a hostile region, resilience assumes existential import: this is the "why" of what Israel does. The country systematically pivots in times of war. Response systems instantly pivot in the face of terrorist attacks. Pivoting is woven into the personality of its people and culture.

We met Professor Kobi Peleg on our many investigatory visits to Israel to study the country's preparedness and response, leadership and resilience. Prof. Peleg established the Israel National Center for Trauma and Emergency Medicine Research at Gertner Institute and co-established the Master's Program for Emergency and Disaster Management at Tel-Aviv University. He contributes groundbreaking research on emergency disaster and terror-related mass casualty incidents. He has joined Israeli international human-itarian assistance missions to Armenia, Rwanda, Indonesia, and Haiti and was dispatched as a United Nations specialist to assist disaster response coordination in the Philippines and Nepal.

"The intent of terrorists is to convince the population that they cannot trust authorities and to instill panic and anxiety. Therefore, everything we do

is designed to reduce the fear of the population." For this reason, Israeli officials do their best to quickly restore routine after a terrorist attack.

Standard operating procedures are used to reestablish order, and each
contributes to the pivot process. Following a mass casualty event, survivors
are evacuated from the scene as fast as possible in a practice called "scoop and
run." Out of concern for secondary devices, responders have learned not to
linger. "This also helps save the injured because they will get better care in
the hospital than on-site," Peleg explained.

Following quick investigatory work, glass fitters, carpenters, and weld-
ers restore the damaged area to its original condition. Ample psychosocial
support is provided to the injured and victims' next of kin to aid in their
recovery and well-being, both short- and long-term. Typically, in the spirit
of "life goes on," the terrorist attack site soon returns to its prior level of foot
traffic and activity. The rapid return to normal—the systematic pivot from
crisis to routine—restores a sense of calm in the area and assists in long-term
recovery, for both individuals and society as a whole.

"Experience also plays a role in resilience," Peleg pointed out. "If something happens repeatedly, the population becomes accustomed to it and to
some extent learn to cope with it through normalizing the phenomenon.
For example, we studied fluctuations in the Israeli stock market following
terrorist attacks. Early on, in periods of frequent attacks, the market would
significantly decline for several days after those attacks. With time, though,
as the population became more accustomed to the news and believed in society's resilience, the dips would be much less significant and the market would
jump back much quicker."

Israel has had significant experience exercising its methods for enhancing
resilience. We asked Peleg whether the country has recently gained any new
insights. "We came to an interesting observation while assisting after the devastating 2015 Nepal earthquake," he replied. "Countries around the world,
including Israel, dispatched search-and-rescue teams. There were 2,248 international rescuers on 76 teams. We realized that, with all that, only 16
people, by our count, were rescued from the rubble alive. In looking at other
earthquakes, we discovered that the number of people rescued alive from under the rubble was very limited. With further investigation, we found articles
stating that most of those people were saved by family members, neighbors,

and volunteers, not by professional responders. We shared this lesson with our civil defense system, the Home Front Command. Earthquakes are also a danger in Israel. So, we taught 75,000 Israeli high school students easy-to-learn light search-and-rescue methods—for example, how to use a car's jack to lift up debris to save someone trapped under the rubble. We conducted surveys before and after the training intervention. We were encouraged to find a higher level of perceived competency and resilience after the training. They were confident that they would know how to effectively respond in an emergency. If you provide people knowledge and skills, you increase their own as well as their community's resilience. When they feel helpless or don't know what to do, their resilience declines." Here Peleg was describing the pivot from helpless to helpful.

"The same is true in helping an injured person," he added. "If you come upon an injury with massive bleeding and know how to stop the bleeding, you will provide the basic care and feel good about it afterwards. Otherwise, you panic and feel guilty and ashamed afterwards, especially if the person dies."

Peleg emphasized a similar sort of know-how in coordinating the work of response agencies. "We prepare our plans, conduct training, and drill together across the many organizations involved in the response. If you are training together, you know the people from other organizations and they are speaking the same professional language. It is difficult to say no to someone you know. It is easier to say no to someone you don't know. Together, this allows us to anticipate what is needed. Even before I open my mouth, you know what I need from you and you are already there providing it.

"Leadership plays a pivotal role in resilience," Peleg continued. "Leaders first must trust themselves. They must prepare themselves to be resilient because other people are watching. It could be people in their organization, their colleagues, or the whole country. If leaders are not resilient, they will bring down the resilience of others."

Practicing the Pivot

How do you insert all the lessons here into your crisis leadership toolbox? First, practice.

You daily face miniature crises.

Heading out to that critical meeting, you discover that your keys are missing. A trivial yet instructive set of pivots ensue. "Oh no! Got to be on time." Basement pivot. Deep breath. Methodically, you pivot to retrace your steps from last night's return home, and then remember that, distracted, you inadvertently left your keys in the door. Move on: you won't do that again.

Here's another: you receive a nasty and accusatory email from a colleague. Basement pivot: anger and the temptation to blast a fiery "reply all" retort. Instead, recognizing an amygdala hijack, you intentionally pivot out of the basement, calming yourself by slowly counting to ten, your trigger script. You take a moment to acknowledge your outrage and then pivot to your toolbox, thinking, "no email." Instead, you organize your thoughts in a handwritten response. Now composed, you pivot to problem-solving, imagining a methodical Walk in the Woods. What was she thinking? What are you thinking? What are the differences? Where's the agreement? And the disagreement? Do you have any new ideas? Is there potential for alignment? Give it time so that you can better figure out how to repair the relationship.

You open the morning paper and find yourself and your organization on the front page. There is the "What the . . . ?" pivot. Where did this come from? You go to the basement and blow off steam. Pivot. "One step at a time." In the toolbox pivot, you traverse the POP-DOC Loop, convene your team, and get the full story. The situation begins to make some sense. What can you do to deescalate the problem? You forge a strategy, both responsive and proactive. You can do it and once you do, you'll recover and move forward.

When you pivot to your higher practice and analytic capabilities, you get smarter than your brain.

What happens when you don't pivot intentionally? You never do find those keys, and you blow a major contract by being absent from the meeting. You lash out at your colleague in a "reply all" email, embarrassing yourself and alienating others. And your fiery public response to the newspaper article adds damaging quotes to the story. You're famous now for all the wrong reasons.

Going through this drill for relatively minor threats helps you when everything is on the line in a real crisis. Calculating how to get above and beyond the peril isn't easy, and it's impossible when you're stuck in the

Pivots in Crisis & Change

	Conscious	
You admit in you're in the basement You gain personal awareness You gain situational awareness **2**		You're aware and intentional You traverse the POP-DOC Loop You're active and directed **4**
You go to the basement You're hijacked by your amygdala You're passive and undirected **1**		You activate your trigger tcript You go to your tool box You help others in the basement **3**
Instinctive		Learned

basement. Reflect afterwards on what you did, how well you handled the situation, and what you can improve upon. Study yourself and embed the lessons learned for next time.

Assess also what happens when you fail to discipline yourself. When you, the leader, are in free-fall descent, the anxieties of your followers intensify. How do the reactions of others inform your self-reflections? How do you get a grip?

As you lead others toward productive response, your collective capacity to assess and move expands. People follow you. If you move up, they follow, confident that you will rally toward a better situation. Order beyond control.

Your leadership pivot can also be personal, expressed in ways that guide and inspire others.

Every year, during our NPLI executive crisis leadership program, participants hear from key leaders who were responsible during a recent crisis that shook the country, such as a hurricane, a mass casualty attack, or a pandemic. With great care and sensitivity, we changed course in June 2018, when we invited someone who survived a crisis to join us. How might leadership be differently expressed and realized by a survivor?

Four months earlier, at the Marjory Stoneman Douglas High School in Parkland, Florida, Eden Hebron was in English class when Nikolas Cruz killed fourteen students and three staff members. In her classroom, eight people were shot, three of whom died, including her best friend. It was Eden, accompanied by her mother, Dr. Nicole Cook, who joined us in our classroom at Harvard.

It took enormous courage for a fifteen-year-old to address a Harvard lecture hall filled with senior crisis leaders. Like many of the young people and parents who lived through the Parkland shootings, Eden and Nicole are on a mission. For some survivors, that mission is gun control. For others, it is political change. For Eden and Nicole, it is change of the response and resilience system. They found the right audience in Cambridge.

Eden began: "It was February 14, and I was in room 1216. The entire shooting lasted six or seven minutes. First, there were shots in the hallway, and then it seemed like, right at that moment, the first person in our classroom was shot. I went behind a table across from the door. The shooter never entered any classrooms. All the shootings were from the hallway through the doors. I ended up behind a table. I was never trained on what to do when there's an active shooter. I thought this was fake at first, then I saw everyone run—run behind a wall or desk. I went straight to the closest place, behind a table and ended up by myself. The closest person to me, she was shot since she was hiding across from the door. Behind the table, the teacher had a bin to hold papers. The shooter came twice to my room, so I took the bin and put it in front of me. The table had a tablecloth, and I didn't want the shooter to see my feet or my face. I don't know why, but in that moment, that's what I thought would help me be the most protected in such a dangerous situation." Hidden from view, Eden survived the attack, physically unharmed. Her room was splattered with blood, glass, and anguish. "Three people in my class were killed," she told the audience.

After sharing what happened, Eden turned our attention to her mission. "There were so many systematic failures of law enforcement in Parkland. Our student resource officer [Scott Peterson] who had a gun could respond, but he didn't. And it didn't seem like the school or law enforcement had a well thought out protocol or plan to attack or respond. It took so long for them to get in that building. People were killed on the third floor in the final moments of the shooting. If we had officers that knew how to take care of a shooter properly, all six students could have been saved. There were many systematic failures that need to be fixed. Maybe we can't prevent shootings, but we could prevent the number of victims from going up.

"And because they didn't have an effective response, when the police officers finally arrived in our classroom, they came in shouting at us. We thought he [the gunman] was back a third time. We didn't know it was law enforcement. And if they had said anything like, 'You're safe now, here's where we are, here's where the shooter is,' it would've made it better. Instead, they busted the glass and broke their hands through the door. There was no sensitivity, and for us, we had no trust in them, that they would keep us safe. That was something the students needed in that moment. We didn't know—all we saw was a gun. And all they said was, 'Get up and run.'

"I always had so much trust in police, but in that moment, we didn't feel safe. And in that moment, the shooter was still out there. They evacuated all the students before they caught the shooter. We had no information when they sent us out into the hallways. And now I know, after reading through all the coverage and other shooting incidents, that there are effective protocols for shootings. When we think of Newtown [the December 2014 shooting at the Sandy Hook Elementary School in Connecticut], and how long it's been since that happened, by this point our school's [officials and law enforcement officers] should be more educated and told what to do and this is how to do it."

Then Eden's mother spoke: "We've got millions of students out there today who have been in a classroom in this scenario or have seen it through a video. You have millions of students who are going to be adults who have almost zero trust in what's going on right now with law enforcement or being prepared for mass shootings. I can't imagine how many high school students are trying to learn right now while still suffering from PTSD [post-traumatic stress disorder]. But nothing systematic has taken place to help treat this kind of trauma—many services that have been brought in are from private citizens. And among those, there is little focused on mental illness and continuity of care. There's no screening in the school for PTSD or following kids over time. From a security standpoint, very little has been done to build that trust back. And now students are expected to learn and take AP [Advanced Placement] exams? When I think of all these students being scared for their lives instead of being focused on learning, it's tragic. We could lose a generation."

Eden raised her call to action. "This is real, and it can be your child if we don't do something about this. I pray that no other kid has to see what I saw, one of my best friends getting shot in front of me. We felt all that pain and felt all the things that we don't want anyone else to feel. But this can happen to them if we don't do something now."

We asked Eden and Nicole what they wanted to see changed. Eden called for better protocols, training, and preparation of law enforcement officials to mitigate active shooters. She also advocated preparation for students so that they know what to do and expect in an active shooting incident. She added, "Anyone with signs of mental illness or violent or aggressive behavior can't get their hands on any firearm—that needs to be regulated. There are many kids who have violent behavior and don't see consequences and aren't treated as if they can be harmful in the future. Kids need to suffer consequences if they display violent behavior." Nicole wants to see systemic reform to provide prompt post-trauma care to survivors and family members. Together, they have joined efforts to push gun safety legislation at the state and federal levels.

Eden and Nicole are taking their message to crisis response professionals, people who can translate the Marjory Stoneman Douglas High School experience into tangible change. Participants in our Harvard classroom vowed to apply these lessons in changing protocols for their agencies and to bring the call for system change to professional audiences.

Out of crisis, good can emerge. It was clear to us that Eden's resilience is in part powered by her commitment to seeking real change. She wrote us afterwards: "I honestly feel so much better and satisfied when I make an impact on someone or something. And I got that feeling as I left Boston." This is a noble and courageous meta-leadership mission for an articulate and mature fifteen-year-old.

The Emotions of Crisis Meta-Leadership

Vulnerability. Fear. Helplessness. These are the disquieting emotions you feel during a crisis. Recall a time when you felt those sensations. They can motivate and activate. They serve as "forces for" when they bring people together to seek security, protection, and safety from the hazards of the situation. These emotions also rally people to fight real and perceived threats—the emotional "forces against." A crisis shapes a "to do" list.

Arranged on a continuum, these forces range from swarm to suspicion. Are other people ally or enemy? Shield or assault? Defenders or destroyers? Lines are drawn and affinities established. It is a calculation of who wins and who loses.

During the Boston Marathon bombings response, the crisis leaders, their organizations, and the community-at-large jointly swarmed. That coming together—the swarm strength of the motto "Boston Strong!"—provided people with a comforting sense of security, protection, and identity. It was all of Boston together against the bad guys—the perpetrators of the horrific attack.

Just as the basement is the innate fear response of an individual, swarm and suspicion are the collective inborn responses of groups of people. Within the in-group—those who share an affinity, such as family, nationality, political bent, or work—people swarm. The swarm within the in-group provides reassurance, safe haven, and the fortification of togetherness. People rally against the menacing out-group, threatening others they've identified as a moral, cultural, identity, or physical menace.

As the meta-leader, you coalesce followers in ways consistent with swarm instincts and principles: unity of effort, generosity, staying in lanes, no ego—no blame, and trust.

The Boston Marathon bombings response had a clear lineup of good guys and bad guys. Not all crises have those clear distinctions. During the Hurricane Katrina response in 2005, government agencies, which miscalculated the disaster and were slow or hostile in their actions, failed to pivot and thus became the bad guys. Likewise, in the Deepwater Horizon oil spill, the bad guys were both the responsible party—BP, the company that oversaw the drilling operation—and the government agencies that oversaw the response. One of the more difficult leadership puzzles was aligning government leaders so that together they could provide the best possible coordinated response. Leaders worked to shift from suspicion to swarm. Recall also the earlier story of parish president Billy Nungesser during that incident. Once the Coast

Guard responded to his requests, he was transformed from a force against to a force for.

Jump-Starting a Crisis Response

A crisis and its response attract attention. There is fascination with crisis. Often, there are conflict, consequences, and departures from the norm. The news media cover crises because they're new, emotional, interesting, and usually happening live. As a crisis meta-leader, your pivots take you to the epicenter of this storm of attention.

By definition, a crisis demands that you do a lot. If you lead an emergency response organization, your followers include both professionals and volunteers. The professionals are accustomed to crisis response structures, such as the Incident Command System (ICS), that can exclude those volunteers. Through your meta-leadership, you complement and amplify the benefits of ICS by motivating heightened connectivity of effort between those with formal responsibilities as well as those with informal roles. We saw this in abundance in the Boston Marathon bombing response (Chapter 1) and the Super Storm Sandy response (Chapter 2).

Focus activity to form a determined, productive group of people working together to alleviate the crisis. People are eager to follow and pivot with you: many are in the basement, awaiting your direction and instructions. Reassure, comfort, and invigorate them. This is the power of your meta-leadership. It is why people have trust and confidence in you and what you ask of them.

Whether you lead just a few people, an organization, or, as in the Boston Marathon bombings, a whole city, it is up to you to embolden people with the strength of their togetherness and the good they can accomplish together. "You're it"—both you personally and the collection of other leaders who follow you and whom you follow.

Earlier in the book, you met Coast Guard admiral Peter Neffenger, the deputy incident commander during the 2010 Deepwater Horizon oil spill. Five years after the spill, President Barack Obama asked him to assume leadership of the Transportation Security Administration (TSA). In June 2015, just before Neffenger was sworn in, news leaked that in a test by the Department of Homeland Security Inspector General, 95 percent of the mock explosives and weapons carried by inspectors were successfully smuggled past security screeners. The report suggested a clear threat to public safety.

Upon taking office, Admiral Neffenger learned that the screening deficiency was one of many shortcomings plaguing the agency. There were also problems with morale, training, oversight, management, internal connectivity, and external relations. And the traveling public disdained TSA. As Admiral Neffenger later reflected to us, "TSA is a daily reminder of terrorism and a system that failed. And it is intrusive. When you have a system that you are already inclined to dislike, you'll put up with it if you trust that it really is protecting you, but the minute you find out they can't do it, it collapses confidence in the system."

Admiral Neffenger was determined to investigate the causes of the breakdown and to fix them. First, he learned that TSA was understaffed. At the top thirty airports, TSA was able to meet only 60 percent of peak demand, causing long wait lines. To overcome that problem, the agency, before Neffenger arrived, had implemented a program called managed inclusion, which allowed a high number of passengers to be randomly selected to bypass standard screening. Instead, they were directed to the more streamlined TSA Pre-Check lanes. Screeners also received financial incentives to reduce wait lines. Although the program remedied the backup problem, it didn't fix the failing screening scores.

Ten weeks after taking office, Neffenger made his first pivot, leveraging the crisis prompted by the report to institute transformational change: he ended the managed inclusion program. Then, to reorient the agency to its core purpose, he required all airport TSA airport leaders, managers, and frontline security officers to participate in a new training: "Mission Essentials—Back to Basics." Neffenger's objective was to reinforce the agency's confidence, in particular the frontline transportation security officers. "I wanted to connect them to the mission so that they realized, they're the most important people in this organization because they're at the mission end. And the mission only gets done if the people are trained, connected, and involved and they feel empowered to do their job," said Neffenger. The new problem was that more careful screening, combined with screener understaffing, caused airport wait lines to balloon.

In the midst of these complications, on March 22, 2016, Neffenger arrived in Brussels for a meeting with European Union aviation leaders. His commercial flight reached the airport twenty minutes late. Just feet from the jetway, the pilot slammed on the plane's brakes. From the cockpit, the pilot was witnessing a catastrophic event that rocked the airport. Two bombs had detonated in the pre-screening area of the airport. Seventeen people died, and more than eighty were injured.

Panic unfolded inside the terminal; meanwhile, Neffenger's plane was held for hours on the tarmac. "I spent a lot of time looking out the window, watching. Airport and airline employees, emergency personnel, and passengers, all haphazardly running. It was clear that what was happening in the airport was catastrophic," said Neffenger.

The Brussels incident prompted Neffenger's next pivot. He returned to Washington the next day, even more determined to fortify the TSA aviation security mission. "The major takeaway for me was that we had to keep this from happening anywhere else. And in order to do so, we had to stop thinking of security as a series of checkpoints and barriers," said Neffenger. "We'd always tried to manage lines from the checkpoint, but the checkpoint is very different from the *approaches* to the checkpoint. And the approaches to the checkpoint are very much tied to the exposure of this public area, where the bombs had gone off. We later learned that the bombers hadn't planned to go through security. Their goal was to take advantage of the public area."

The dilemma was that those ballooning crowds were waiting in ever-longer screening lines. They were soft targets in exposed public areas, a clear security threat. Seattle, Minneapolis, Dallas, Atlanta—thousands of passengers were missing flights, and the airlines and airport operators were fuming.

The wait line problem reached crisis proportions two months later in Chicago, where passengers stood for up to four hours in security wait lines at O'Hare International Airport. Everyone—the mayor, aviation leaders, the public—was angry. On May 20, 2016, Neffenger flew out to Chicago. It was a moment to be present. "I knew that I had to get up there and that this was going to be a pivot point," said Neffenger. Some on his senior staff warned him not to go: he would get ensnared in the negative news cycle. Neffenger wanted to see the situation for himself and meet with the leadership in Chicago to determine whether TSA was providing the resources and training the front line needed. "I thought, well, there's no way to find out unless I go," said Neffenger.

The long wait lines in Chicago had sparked a media frenzy, and Neffenger became entangled in a swirl of suspicion and controversy. The *Washington Post* reported, "TSA Administrator Peter Neffenger May Be in Trouble." Airline executives were pressuring the White House and Congress. The public was furious.

Admiral Neffenger seized the opportunity to convert suspicion into swarm. What if the airlines, airports, and TSA worked together to both ensure security and advance screening process efficiencies? He was a presence at troubled airports. He reached out to industry leaders. And he took responsibility for turning the situation around. He crafted a massive collective pivot as he motivated everyone involved to turn "my" problem into "our" problem. And it worked.

The airlines pivoted with him. They offered to purchase and install new, more efficient screening technology. To speed lines, airports provided personnel to assist with nonsecurity tasks. Congress authorized new funding to expand on-duty hours for screeners. And airlines, airports, and TSA joined a new daily status call to share data on expected passenger loads. This way, screeners could be directed to service security lines at the height of an expected rush.

There had been stern warnings about the crushing security wait lines expected on Memorial Day weekend. Those lines never materialized. Neffenger had applied his meta-leadership sensibilities and forged the connectivity of effort needed to solve complex, interwoven problems with airport security.

Four months later, that collaboration coalesced into the first-ever TSA Public Area Security Summit. Though TSA had long been despised by the aviation industry, the agency was regarded now as a respected convener. Security leaders from the major airlines, cargo carriers, industry associations, law enforcement, and airports came together on a shared mission. Neffenger and his team of TSA leaders had coalesced a swarm.

One of Neffenger's senior leaders, Jerry Agnew, had just been through our meta-leadership course at Harvard before he shipped out to assist in the Chicago situation. He wrote us afterwards:

"Last week I was sent to Chicago to restore TSA to normal operations after the incredible operational challenges we faced the week previous. I can tell you first hand that I was fully aware when I reached the basement and at a couple of junctures began digging. One thing I found most helpful about understanding when you're in the basement was to remember that I was in a survival instinct mode, and the problems before me were bigger than myself.

"I employed every facet of what we learned at Harvard. I attempted to lead in every direction, searching for the connectivity that would make us all successful. I took a walk in the woods (several times a day) with air carriers, city officials, employees, you name it, anyone willing to walk and talk to find solutions to the multi-dimensional problem I was facing, and it worked, I believe, because I stayed with the concept you taught us of 'How can I make you a success?'

"Instead of trying to achieve my goals in negotiation, I sought an interest-based solution. In some cases it meant I may have gotten only 30% and sometimes less of what I wanted, and they may have gotten 70% or more, but it was effective. I continuously used the 3 zone Meta-Leadership principle to achieve results, especially when it came to strategy and execution, because it included my walk in the woods and the ideas they believed would make them successful. I sought the highest level of collaboration I could gain.

"You know it's kind of funny how this works, as I would move through the POP-DOC Loop and did my best to stay in the 3 zones, the leadership distractions began to disappear. It's almost as if you have the upper hand because those around you have no idea what you're doing. The pushback on changes, you wouldn't believe the number of times I heard 'we can't do that' come up in conversation. It all began to disappear. My executive circuits were fully charged and I was able to lead all of Chicago out of the basement. It wasn't until I had everyone going in the right direction, that I began to see a hybrid if you will of Swarm Leadership. I mean Hybrid because they are not fully there, but I did see them begin to understand their role and begin acting in it collaboratively."

As Winston Churchill said, "Never let a good crisis go to waste." By defi-nition, a crisis is a pivot point. It often pivots toward the worse, of course, though it can also pivot toward improvement. As a crisis meta-leader, cri-sis is your opportunity to shape something that otherwise would not have emerged. This was the lesson of the TSA experience.

You can never know when a crisis might hit. When it does, move method-ically through pivot after pivot, executing what you have learned and prac-ticed. Adapt what you do as the situation unfolds. As your proficiency grows, you develop even more routines and tools for your workroom. With time, your capacity to adapt grows, building confidence. The more you experience, the more the unprecedented becomes the routine. You collect familiar pat-terns and behaviors to call upon as you handle circumstances that you never before thought possible.

An example: Paramedics riding in an ambulance are trained to treat severely injured people at gruesome scenes. For victims, this could be a life-changing crisis. For onlookers, it is a traumatic event. For the paramed-ics, this is another day on the job, something sad which they have seen before and will again. They know how to handle it. They follow their routines.

Don Boyce is an alumnus of our Harvard executive crisis leadership pro-gram and a senior emergency response official. He is also a former New York City paramedic. In his early days in that position, when he arrived at an incident, he would first survey the situation to assess what he and others had to do. Pivot. No matter how shocking, he would then open his trauma, medical, or airway bag and quickly assess the inventory, making sure that he had what he needed. Another pivot moment. It was his routine for getting himself from the basement to productively saving lives. Those pivots offered momentary pauses to collect himself and formulate his plan of action. They reinforced his confidence that he could handle whatever the situation pre-sented. Although his tools have changed, he retains the leadership practice of synchronizing his mental preparedness with the material job that faces him.

One final point for your crisis meta-leadership: Leaders often are reluctant to tend to themselves. As you take care of others, don't forget to take care of yourself. When the moment is right, take a break—particularly in an extended crisis. Performance degrades over time, and working beyond your limits is a disservice both to yourself and to others.

On your break, your brain is working—busily processing all you are experiencing in the crisis. Shocked by what you have seen and undergone, you might need some time to collapse into the basement. Alone and away from your duties, let that happen. Cry if you need to. You are alone. At this moment, you are not leading. These moments fortify you when it is time to step back into your role.

You enhance team performance when you remember that your self-care is also a model for those who follow you. They too may be exhausted and emotional yet afraid to say so in front of you or their peers. Three weeks into the H1N1 response, the acting CDC director, Dr. Rich Besser, announced that he was taking a day off and encouraged others to do the same. Stepping away to rejuvenate was also a vote of confidence in those others he left in charge while he was gone.

In a crisis, be a role model for attentive, focused, and driven meta-leadership. Your job is to lead your followers beyond the crisis. Taking care of yourself is an essential part of taking care of others.

Questions for Journaling

- Reflect upon crises you've experienced. What did you do well? What could you have done better? How can you improve your capacities and insights during times of crisis?

- Your pivoting is a very personal process. What works for someone else might not work for you. What trigger scripts do you call upon, and how can you adapt and expand them to meet crises, both those you've experienced before and future crises that will be new to you?

- It is rare to think of crisis as opportunity. In your experience, what opportunities have been spurred by a crisis? What happened? How did leaders leverage the moment? What was the result?

THIRTEEN

SHAPING THE CHANGE

Meta-Leading Across the Arc of Time

This book's title includes the phrase "How to Lead *When It Matters Most.*" "When" alludes to the dynamic factor of time in whether "people follow you." Central to the meta-view of time is orchestrating it—seeing time, working with time, and leading in time. We present here both a way for you to think about time and a tool to make it part of your meta-leadership.

A crisis is often seen as one moment in time. It is more than that. A crisis builds, erupts, evolves, and is resolved over a period of time. Transformational change also unfolds incrementally. Time seems to move at light speed sometimes. By contrast, it can crawl or even seem to move backwards, as pushback reverses progress. Your meta-leadership responsibility is to remain balanced and resilient through the duration of the crisis or change. Doing so requires understanding and working with the complexities of time.

The outcomes of leadership practices are often measured in tangible operational metrics: money earned or saved; people affected, lost, or rescued; property damaged, restored, or removed. There are also intangibles at stake, among the most important of which is time. You can't see time. You can't change time. You can't go forward and you can't go backward in time. How you perceive and affect time often moves, motivates, or distracts those who follow.

The Arc of Time: Was–Is–Will Be

What you can do with time is use it, save it, waste it, and adjust it. You can get ahead of time or get behind it. Time and timing are powerful metrics and tools for the meta-leader.

When something happens can be as important as *what* happens. After a motor vehicle accident with horrific injuries, an ambulance arrives. If it arrives quickly, people live. If it's late, people die. Same action. Different outcome. Time is critical. A cyber-attack hits your organization and IT is called in. With a quick fix, data is saved and operations resume. If the response is slow, data is lost and operations collapse. Your company is about to introduce a new product line and the reviews are great. The new line fails, however, because your competition beats you to market.

As you understand, anticipate, and focus on time, you harness it to the advantage of what you hope and need to accomplish. Influencing the pace of events along with expectations and attitudes about them, meta-leaders perceive and shape a progression along a flexible "Arc of Time." When you are responsible for leading solution-building for a large, complex problem, involving many people, its urgency is experienced differently by the relevant stakeholders. There are diverging notions about *when* the steps in tackling the problem should occur.

Who does *what* and *when*? If some lag in their actions, others are frustrated. As a meta-leader, your job is synchronizing many different people, expectations, and activities to achieve a *timeline* suitable to the situation at hand. Time complexity emerges from differing positions, priorities, and sequencing, presenting you with a puzzle to solve. You work with the "gives" and "gets" of time: hurry it, slow it, and always gauge it.

The Arc of Time can be adjusted, adapted, and reoriented. A skilled meta-leader uses time to increase the pace toward a solution or slow it to ease the pressure to find one. Decisions, operations, and communications

are configured along a timeline. The POP-DOC Loop is a guide for mea-
suring, pacing, sequencing, and ordering the course of events over time.
Pattern recognition translates into predictions of what will, or what could,
happen next.

At the end of the day, that time is gone. On the human landscape, time
is limited. It ends. Value how you use it.

The official hurricane season in the United States runs from June 1 to November 30. In 2017, there were seventeen named storms between late April
and early November. Nature sets her own schedule. Ten of those storms were
hurricanes. They arrived consecutively, the most ever to do so in the Atlantic
Basin. It was the costliest season on record—more than $280 billion in dam-
age. Most of the damage resulted from three storms that battered communities in quick succession: Harvey, Irma, and Maria.

In late August, Hurricane Harvey hit the United States, the first Category 5 storm in a dozen years. The storm stalled over Houston and dumped
more than fifty-one inches of rain on the metropolitan area. Neighborhoods
were flooded. Across the city, people were trapped in flooded homes. Their
calls for assistance were overwhelming emergency response organizations and
their leaders.

There was a mass of people huddled in a Houston mega-shelter sur-
rounded by deep water and separated from supplies and volunteers. It took
high-profile military vehicles to make the deliveries. Leaders coordinated
humanitarian and business organizations in tandem with federal, state, and
local government agencies to deliver relief services.

Brad Kieserman, whom you met earlier, is vice president for American
Red Cross Disaster Services. He oversees the provision of shelter and food to
thousands of disaster survivors—an extraordinary meta-leadership challenge
given the immediate situation that summer with multiple hurricanes swirl-
ing across the southeast United States and Caribbean.

On Thursday, September 7, we observed Brad lead a sequence of three
conference calls. The first was with leaders in Houston, discussing how to
cope with the aftermath of Hurricane Harvey's devastation. The next call

was with people in St. Croix as Hurricane Irma roared directly overhead. The third call was with leaders in Florida. Since Hurricane Irma's direction was still unknown, shelters were being prepared on the state's east and west coasts and everywhere in between. Looming behind each of these discussions was the impending future: Hurricanes Jose and Maria on the horizon. Mother Nature's hurricanes were proceeding on their own Arcs of Time. Emergency response leaders were simply trying to get one step ahead.

From the American Red Cross Disaster Operations and Coordination Center in Fairfax, Virginia, all these different events ordered in sequence over an Arc of Time: the "was," the "is," and the "will be." Harvey *was;* Irma in St. Croix *is;* and Irma in Florida *will be.* The Arc of Time differed for each of these locales.

Brad's meta-leadership mission was to work with each location through the Arc of Time of its unique situation. Mindful of the big picture, Brad also grappled with the complexities of another challenge with its own Arc of Time: the allocation of resources across many simultaneous crises. For example, as waters receded in Houston (the crisis that "was"), it became possible to close the mega-shelter at the NRG Center—a large conference facility—and allow its owners to return to normal operations. Meanwhile, the Red Cross ERVs (emergency response vehicles) were still deployed across Texas, so capacity and supplies needed in Florida (the crisis that "will be") were depleted. Difficult resource distribution decisions were made for Florida, since the Red Cross couldn't supply all that was being requested. And in St. Croix, the shelter was surprisingly empty: the locals were so afraid of post-storm looting that they were taking the risk of weathering the storm in their soon-to-be-ravaged homes. Each scenario was different, yet all were happening in the same moment.

The situations through which you lead have beginnings, middles, and ends—unfortunately, not always in that order—across different people and places. One problem recedes and another begins. Your meta-leadership Arc of Time task is to see the wider time frames in which everything occurs. You can't control time though you can order and coordinate passage through it: the sequence, people, decisions, allocations, and priorities. Arrange the big picture in your mind so others can arrange it in theirs.

Working with the Arc of Time

The Arc of Time measures relative activity—more or less—across a relative stretch of time (longer or shorter). On a coordinate grid, the horizontal x axis is the passage of time. The vertical y axis is the relative activity and attention devoted to it.

To assess an event in retrospect, identify the beginning and ending points, then gauge relative activity at points in between. Distinguish the phases. To grasp an event as it unfolds, apply the POP-DOC Loop to look and move forward.

For example, if your office of ten people responded to a cyber-attack over a ten-day period, measure the hours per day devoted to addressing the activities and attention relevant to the attack. Just before the attack, they were low: the work of IT specialists was routine, and standard anti-phishing precautions were in place. When the attack was discovered and your network went down, defensive activity intensified and productivity declined. People identified the compromised data and reassembled records and files. As the situation returned to normal, attack-related activity and attention subsided. The Arc of Time outlines the time and attention devoted to the attack and distracted, nonproductive activity over those ten days, from low to peak to decline.

Charting the time itself is a management task. The meta-leadership pursuit is guiding the process that shapes the Arc of Time.

In most cases, you work with relative measures, not with specific numbers. There is a comparative spike of activity that increases with an incident, reaching its peak and then declining. A hurricane—a predicted event with notice—illustrates the point. As weather forecasters raise caution about the storm's impending arrival, activity mounts in preparation. Supplies are deployed, windows are protected, and people evacuate or ready themselves to take shelter. When the hurricane hits, the next phase, all attention is on saving lives, the peak. Once the danger recedes, action focuses on places where destruction is most severe and the need is greatest. Over time, the recovery phase turns to damage assessment and repair. The area eventually returns to normal and hurricane-related activity recedes. The Arc of Time initiated by a hurricane could span three years or more. The levels of activity during the rise, peak, and descent correlate with the areas where the greatest devastation occurred.

Leaders shape activities and experiences through the Arc of Time. Assessing the situation, you close gaps between what is happening and what needs to be done. You mount an uptick in attention and activity, planning, tracking, and further assessment as you lead through distinct phases. Enlisting the POP-DOC Loop, you strive for a good fit between requirements and actions.

For time: You assess the *when* of all this activity and attention. You distinguish the urgent actions that need to be taken *immediately* from the *long-term* actions that can be taken over time. Bringing out your Situation Connectivity Map, you sequence activity so that your stakeholders are working along coordinated and parallel timelines. You manage expectations for both the *when* and the *what,* knowing that the one thing you never get back in a crisis is time.

The sequence of phases depends on circumstances as you lead through time. For a predicted hurricane, the sequence is will be–is–was: the prediction, the hit, and the postdisaster reconstruction. For the destructive cyber-attack, the sequence is was–is–will be: the attack happened, the company is now in crisis, and the work to reconstruct its data will enable it to return to normal operations in the future. Time is relative to the situation you face and the many others stakeholders affected.

The people you met in prior chapters recognized time as a dynamic variable. It affected what they had to do, when it had to be done, and how they could go about it. They made unique Arc of Time calculations.

Admiral Thad Allen and project director Budge Upton both worked against the clock: each was facing a mandatory end point. Allen had a leaking oil well to cap; until that was accomplished, each day and each delay translated into more damage to the Gulf ecosystem and economy. He had to both speed the work of the engineers and manage the expectations of the public and politicians. This urgent Arc of Time ended when oil stopped spilling into the Gulf. Upton had a mélange of stakeholders to satisfy, each with distinct conceptions of what was most important in the museum addition. He had to lead them while orchestrating complex interrelated pieces of the project—different Arcs of Time—to finish simultaneously.

Dr. Rich Besser of the CDC had to buy time to learn more about H1N1 virulence before definitive public health advisories could be issued. In the meantime, the CDC announced interim measures designed to mitigate transmission and avoid disruptions to the economy. Frequent public announcements and adjustments in the advisories won public confidence. By contrast, waiting to take action backfired on Coca-Cola CEO Doug Ivester during the beverage contamination scare in Europe. By delaying a public appearance, he was perceived as insensitive by consumers and officials, and that perception damaged the reputation and profitability of the business.

Harriet Green of Premier Farnell created a sense of urgency in her first day on the job. Her message—that the company would have to quickly change in order to grow—upset some employees and motivated others. Over the next few months, that distinction helped to inform decisions about who would stay and who would go. Rich Serino faced angry North Dakotans impatient to secure funding to restore their communities after the flood. His words, in that moment, paused the urgent time pressure: "You saved lives. You made a difference. So thank you." He reframed both the conversation and the work. At that time, it was what people needed to hear.

Finally, in the wake of 9/11, Jimmy Dunne of Sandler O'Neill learned to carefully balance between two Arcs of Time: caring for company and family survivors as slowly and patiently as required by this sensitive work, while getting the business back on its feet with urgency and speed. Dunne transformed himself into the leader needed at the time and, in doing so, transformed the company. In only two months after 9/11, the firm was not only back in business, it was again profitable.

Time is a powerful parameter, both enabling and constraining what can be accomplished. Consider these reactions: "We have *ten weeks* to complete the project. Great!" "We have *only* ten weeks to complete the project? Oh no!" The value of time and what can be done with it varies by situation. When you see the big picture, you often must balance and align many Arcs of Time.

The mind-set, practice skills, and experience of meta-leadership help you perceive the uses and applications of time. When you do, time itself becomes a valuable tool and asset. For example, time can heal as you get distance from a painful event. However, if an unaddressed problem simply escalates and festers, the passage of time only makes matters worse.

Ask yourself: What are the time considerations in this situation? In the face of a complex problem or change that defies immediate solution, progress can be planned through prescribed steps—meetings, strategy, benchmarks, assessment, completion. Different people work at different paces. Time itself allows you to coordinate and mark forward movement, tracking both *whose* activities you're coordinating and *when* those activities must be synchronized. In crisis, time is short. Activities are streamlined. Don't waste time.

During crisis planning and preparation, time is your ally: protocols can be developed, contingencies examined, and training completed. With a long and slow Arc of Time, you can invest abundant time in adequately mitigating problems, amassing needed resources, fostering connections, providing training, and scheduling exercise experience. The better prepared and configured the system, the more adept the decisions, operations, and communications when time matters most.

During a crisis, time is your adversary: the longer the response time, the more lives are lost, along with property, confidence, and reputations. Your Arc of Time is short in an active shooter event: run, hide, fight—now! For business operations, a crisis disrupts the flow of material, services, funds, and information; unsettles interdependencies; and leads to unnecessary costs, missed sales, and cascading delays. If goods are out of stock when the marketing campaign hits, customers are angry, sales associates are stressed, and revenue targets are missed. That is a crisis. Businesses operate with intricately connected Arcs of Time that, when disrupted, create a cascade of troubles.

Whether ally or adversary, time sets very different meta-leadership parameters, opportunities, and requirements. In routine situations, people and operations advance just as they are supposed to—methodically, through incremental phases and achievements. Your leadership credibility and reputation build with steady progress.

To instigate change, you disrupt the course and pace of activity. You inject calibrated acceleration that reshapes the stepwise Arc of Time. Risks for you, and for the organization, increase as the stakes rise.

In a crisis, time speeds up dramatically: reputations can be made and credibility established in short order, and the high stakes amplify your actions. By the same token, your reputation can plummet with an avoidable high-profile misstep, as was the case for BP's CEO Tony Hayward, who, in the midst of the Deepwater Horizon oil spill, commented, "I'd like my life back." After eleven people died on the collapsed oil rig and thousands across the Gulf lost their livelihood, the callous and impatient comment cost Hayward his job.

Reputations can also recuperate after bad news, as happened for Starbucks after a racial incident in April 2018. A white employee in one of its Philadelphia shops called the police when two black men asked to use the restroom before making their purchase. When the police arrived, they arrested the two men for trespassing. It turned out that they were waiting for a business associate to join them before ordering.

Almost instantly, the story became national news. Protests sprang up. The hashtag *#boycottstarbucks* went viral on social media—accelerating on its own rapid Arc of Time. Time was flying by, and the momentum was with those accusing the company of racism.

To assert some control over the Arc of Time, Starbucks leaders' actions had to catch up to the speed of the social media trajectory. CEO Kevin Johnson apologized immediately. The company quickly reached a settlement with the men. Within days, the company opened restrooms to customers and noncustomers alike. A few weeks later, after consulting experts, all Starbucks stores in the United States closed for an afternoon of racial tolerance training.

By intentionally factoring time into its response, the company was able to retrieve its image and business. When leaders promptly acknowledge errors, sincerely apologize, and then direct a substantive response, they stanch the momentum of bad news and redirect it in a more positive direction.

Timing and Expectations

Time presents the meta-leader with one overarching imperative: avoid getting stuck in the now. Rather, see in one Arc of Time the past, present, and future; the variances in the "was," the "is," and the "will be"; the beginning, the middle, and the end. Everything eventually ends. Plan for it and how you will bring the Arc of Time to its conclusion.

Discern patterns. Anticipate how events and people evolve over time. Guide and influence that evolution. Can the pace be varied to either increase urgency or instill patience? Identify what can be done tomorrow that cannot be done today. Lest the situation deteriorate, prioritize what cannot wait and must be done now.

People commonly remember the commitments that leaders make about time with far greater specificity than their other promises. When Arc of Time reality falls short of expectations, disappointment sets in and conflict may erupt. Shape and manage time expectations assertively. Use specifics—"within the hour" or "next Tuesday"—rather than vague terms, such as "immediately" or "soon," whose interpretation can vary wildly. Assume that everyone has a watch and a calendar—and that they are calibrated differently. Consider how a leader used time in the 2010 mine disaster in Copiapó, Chile. The mine collapsed on August 10, trapping thirty-three workers more than two thousand feet underground. Once the workers signaled that they were all alive, a delicate and complex rescue mission was begun. The collapse and subsequent rescue efforts attracted worldwide media attention. Around the world, people were rooting for "Los 33."

In similar situations, many politicians would be tempted to promise immediate results: *We'll get them out as fast as we can.* Chile's president, Sebastián Piñera, however, set expectations for a long operation. He declared that they would be out by a specific date: Christmas. This strategic use of time relieved some of the political and media pressure that would have come with a highly anticipatory daily rescue watch. Setting the expectation for late December bought time for both the rescuers and the government. When "Los 33" were rescued and finally brought to the surface in October, there was widespread jubilation—they were safe! And because the rescue happened "ahead of schedule," everyone in the response, including President Piñera, was a hero.

As the Arc of Time approaches its conclusion, there are a number of transitions to navigate. So that expectations and experiences conform, each must be carefully negotiated and communicated. For example, ending a crisis response is both a logistical process and an emotional one. For those affected, the crisis has likely been a nightmare. Reestablishing their lives after the terrible ordeal has been a distant and hoped-for conclusion. For them, the return to normalcy is both a relief and a difficult adjustment. Responders, by contrast, may have experienced an adrenaline high during the crisis event that can be addictive. Withdrawal from that high can be a simultaneous relief and let-down.

Though the Arc of Time is complex, you teach yourself to perceive it, assess and understand it, and then nimbly shape it.

Balancing Across the Arc of Time

Your practice of meta-leadership is a complex exercise in balancing time. Not every decision, person, action, or operation has the same value. Herein lie your difficult meta-leadership calculations across the Arc of Time. What are your priorities? What happens now? What can wait?

This balancing is a continual activity and an ongoing quest. Spend your day on one activity and you have less time for others. Attract a new client and you have a critical question: do I expand time by hiring staff or recalibrate time by adjusting workloads? You balance resources, personalities, options, and investments along a continuum of priorities.

You lead in complex, dynamic environments where change is the norm. The balance you achieve is therefore temporary. Almost as soon as your practice is in balance, you are out of balance again. The challenge is to adapt, recalibrate, and adjust. Your job is to meld all your priorities into a workable, balanced arrangement.

This understanding of balance and balancing informs your meta-leadership thinking and practices. In Dimension One, the person, you balance individuals' emotions, attitudes, words, and actions, both those of others and your own. You likewise seek balance in Dimension Two, the situation. How will the velocity and direction of all the forces and counterforces affect your balance? For Dimension Three, connectivity, you link the activities of different silos and constituencies. In promoting connectivity, you have to balance the timing to get everyone together on the same schedule.

The presence or absence of balance is apparent through your meta-leadership lens. When people's activities and productivity are in balance, your interactions are smooth, engagement is high, and there is unity of effort. When that balance is off, people squabble for resources, priorities, and attention.

TSA Administrator Peter Neffenger faced the challenge at airports of balancing security and time. As you read in Chapter 12, there was significant conflict within the aviation industry over the long security wait lines. After the Brussels bombings, Neffenger realized that time had become his adversary: long wait lines at airports were presenting large and dangerous soft targets to terrorists. He met this challenge by turning time into an ally. He leveraged the urgency of this new danger to recruit the airlines and airports to solve the wait-line crisis together. This meta-leadership accomplishment turned old adversaries into allies and partners.

Your balancing objective is to guide people toward mutual success. You engage them in a coalition of the willing who are clear on the current state and have a strategy and plan to achieve a desired future state. What is broken and in need of a fix? What is waiting to be accomplished? Over the Arc of Time, manage your progress toward driving high achievement and sustaining it.

Life is filled with situations, some great and others awful. Victories and successes are fun, triumphant, and encouraging, while failures are disappointing and discouraging. Time is a factor in all of them. Only time will tell what is lasting and what is fleeting.

Naturally, it is far more difficult to rise above adversity than to celebrate successes. Loved ones die. People get divorced. Poor decisions are taken. Start-ups fail. Bankruptcies are declared. Hurricanes and tornadoes rip through communities. Illnesses wreak havoc. Mistakes are made. Accidents upend dreams and alter lives. Processing the lessons of adversity over time, however, builds an essential human quality: resilience. The truly resilient bounce forward through adversity to emerge stronger than ever, having absorbed insights, discovered strengths, and learned about themselves and the people around them. By virtue of the experience, they are better able to cope the next time they are hit.

Time has distinct qualities, depending on how old you are. Time is expectant for a twenty- or thirty-year-old who's looking forward to launching adult life and a career. A fifty- or sixty-year-old's life and career reflect ample acquired knowledge and a growing sense of legacy. Forty-year-olds sit at the middle of the trajectory of the human Arc of Time, benefiting from both their experience and their anticipation. These different views of time affect what feels like a long or short amount of time to you, what matters to you and what doesn't. As a meta-leader, you are probably bringing together people at these different stages of life with their varying agendas and priorities.

Resilience develops through these different perches in time. No matter what the challenge, resilience takes time. Time to heal, learn, and change. What is a crisis for one person may be a welcome and solvable challenge for another person. What might be a long-overdue transformation for one is a feared disruption for another. As you lead, your meta-view helps you weave together the diverse perspectives of different generations and different experiences.

Your life is a series of transitions through Arcs of Time: childhood, adolescence, adulthood, retirement, and whatever comes next. Each phase shapes you and signals your future.

We met Jirayut "New" Latthivongskorn while he was a student in our Harvard leadership class. New grasped his sense of purpose early in life and conveyed it to others. He's someone whose life mission found him, not the other way around. Despite setbacks, he found the resilience to keep going.

New's is a classic immigrant story with a familiar theme: personal dreams that collided with public policy obstacles. At nine years old, along with his parents and two siblings, he arrived in the United States from Thailand. They moved into a one-bedroom California apartment. Working long hours in a Thai restaurant, his parents urged New to study and work hard to get ahead.

Not long after arriving, the family faced a wrenching decision: return to Thailand or remain beyond the valid date of their visa. While the family did not fully understand the implications of staying, they did know they wanted a better future. They saw their Arc of Time, particularly for the children, stretching forward in the United States. "Will be" outweighed "was" and the risks of "is." They opted to stay.

Young and ambitious, New learned early about the contentious complexities of immigration policies that imposed wrenching choices and obstacles on him and his family. Through that experience, he discovered his identity as a leader.

New did well in school and enjoyed a normal childhood until his mid-teens. That balance was upended when his undocumented status created barriers to the typical rites of adolescent passage: obtaining a driver's license and getting a job. As California public universities have no citizenship requirements, he applied to five University of California campuses. Each school accepted him, and UC Davis offered a full tuition scholarship. New's sense of balance returned and he enrolled. The American dream for which he worked so hard was presenting itself to him.

Immigration problems again arose a few months before he was to graduate from high school. Shortly before he was to begin college, UC Davis withdrew his scholarship and told him to return when his status changed. Scrambling to start college, he enrolled at UC Berkeley, though without a scholarship. Resilient and determined to earn a degree, he worked to pay his way.

A creative writing project, designed for undocumented students, led to "a lot of unpacking and thinking about my immigrant identity." New felt a calling to join and lead on issues facing undocumented immigrants. He was a "Dreamer," so called because of a US immigration policy, Deferred Action for Childhood Arrivals, that recognizes the undocumented status of some immigrant children as the result of their parents' actions, not their own. New joined the fight for the first national Dream Act, a movement that captured his leadership passion. Disappointed but undeterred when the Dream Act failed in Congress in 2010, he pivoted to use his leadership efforts to help pass the California Dream Act, testifying at the state capitol. The state law passed in 2011 and expanded access to institutional and state funds to undocumented immigrant students.

Looking toward his future, New's aspiration was to be a doctor. That was a big and risky life pivot. Though unsure if his immigration status would render him ineligible, he applied to medical schools. He told us, "Undocumented med students were like unicorns. People kept telling me that they had heard of them, but no one could actually name one. I thought they didn't exist." New persisted and became the first undocumented student admitted to the University of California–San Francisco Medical School.

His success turned into his meta-leadership mission. With two peers, he cofounded Pre-Health Dreamers (www.phdreamers.org) to support undocumented students pursuing health and science graduate education and careers. What started as a quest for unicorns was transformed into a community-building movement. Pre-Health Dreamers grew to more than one thousand members providing peer-to-peer guidance, networking, resources, and advocacy. As we write, New Latthivongskorn is one of one hundred Dreamer medical students nationwide.

Six years after founding the organization and preparing to launch their own careers, New and his cofounders faced an Arc of Time dilemma. Should they keep the organization going or close it down, declaring victory in their initial mission? This was a pivot point at which personal Arcs of Time diverged from the organization's Arc of Time.

"I had thought about postfounder transition early on," he said. "I knew that an area where I wanted to work was developing leadership in others. Passing the baton was one way to do that." Although the founders remain involved in Pre-Health Dreamers, most of the work was transferred to a new team.

New Latthivongskorn's experience is a story of meta-leadership across his transitional Arcs of Time. He turned his personal story into his meta-leadership mission, connecting with others to translate his experiences into opportunities for other Dreamers. Demonstrating abundant resilience despite the obstacles he encountered, New navigated multiple pivot points, investing his passion and energy into a growing movement. You can learn more about New Latthivongskorn online in his 2018 TEDx Berkeley talk.

Human beings are naturally resilient. It is an inborn coping and survival skill. How that resilience manifests, however, varies greatly from person to person. For organizations and communities to be resilient, leadership is critical. New Latthivongskorn forged a pathway and then opened it to others. Leaders chart the way forward in the face of adversity. Meta-leadership practices provide a framework to drive that purpose.

Your meta-leadership test—during crisis, change, or when it matters most—is transcending your own personal resilience to promote resilience in your larger social circle. To amplify resilience across the network, you connect a broad range of collaborators who may be deep in the basement. You model, encourage, and spread calm and assurance that the calamity will be overcome and the changes will demonstrate progress. Over the Arc of Time, you build the critical mass of a resilient team, organization, or community.

A meta-leader always expects to meet a measure of failure along the way—hopefully modest and not catastrophic—and so failure must also be a part of your resilience narrative. If you are unwilling to periodically fail, you are unwilling to discover the new ideas and solutions that could reap exciting innovation and success. Learn from your failures. Pick yourself up. Turn failure into the fuel of your resilience. Winston Churchill opined, "Success is the ability to go from failure to failure without losing your enthusiasm."

Meta-leading for resilience does more than ensure survival. It rekindles movement—over your Arc of Time—toward a better future. It stokes the conviction that you and your followers will ultimately restore balance and prevail through your challenges. Meta-leading for resilience takes willpower, tenacity, trust, and great personal strength. You transmit hope, confidence, and commitment as you embody and raise your indomitable human spirit.

You live on the Arc of Time, a progression of "is–was–will be." As a meta-leader, you can be proactive about the *when* of what you do and the *where* of the places you go, taking others with you. To do so, balance the wide view of who you are, the situations through which you lead, and the many people who follow you and whom you follow. Over time, resilience is yours to achieve.

Questions for Journaling

⊠ Write a short resilience narrative about yourself. Complete the sentence: "A resilient me was . . . " Recall an event. Be specific. Then develop a second narrative: "A resilient me will be . . . " What behaviors will be in evidence? Who or what will you call upon? Who will you help? Are there gaps between your narrative and your reality? How will you close them? Then try this exercise with your family, your team, or your organization.

⊠ Chart an Arc of Time experience you have been through. Describe your experience and that of others through different phases of the event. What factors were in play during those different phases?

⊠ How do you manage time balance in your life? How do you balance work and family? Giving and getting? Listening and talking?

FOURTEEN

THE META-LEADERSHIP IMPERATIVE

You're It

It is time to launch your meta-leadership. As you apply and integrate the practice dimensions, appreciate their fundamental interdependence. What happens with one—the person, the situation, the connectivity—affects the others, as well your larger purposes and objectives.

In this systems view, people, events, and emotions are linked. They interact and interrelate. You are less likely to overlook important activity and people when you perceive these pieces as parts of a wider, comprehensive whole. As you see it, you help others see it too. With others, your collected strength is the moving power that animates your combined principles, practices, and ideals.

As a meta-leader, you will do more because you take a fuller view and have access to a broader scope of people, problems, options, and resources. Meta-leading your team, information becomes more readily available, expertise is more willingly offered, and tangible assets are more generously shared. Competition as a prime motivator is reduced because you and your followers define success less in terms of prevailing in turf battles and more in terms of achieving overriding objectives. The focus shifts to generating momentum for what you (plural) hope to achieve together.

Retired US Coast Guard commandant Thad Allen speaks of the importance of "peerage." This is your network of people to whom you turn for advice, perspective, or support.

Leadership is indeed lonely. There are times when you can't bounce questions and concerns off your boss or your trusted subordinates. Your colleagues in the organization may be too close. Your spouse may be too eager to take your side.

Turn to someone who has been in a situation similar to yours, who can offer unvarnished commentary. You know this person to be fair, honest, and trustworthy. Someone who has been in a similar situation is more likely to see what you are missing—and won't be afraid to tell you. Look for peerage before you need it. In high-stakes, high-stress situations, it is an invaluable resource. It is also a precious gift you can provide other leaders riding through a crisis of their own.

Incorporating the three dimensions of meta-leadership into a seamless routine may seem overwhelming. However, with accumulating experience, human brains intuitively build patterns and calculate how to navigate complex problems. These skills and perspectives become embedded in the mind's toolbox. With practice and greater familiarity, you will assimilate the dimensions of meta-leadership into your default guide for leading others. You will routinely ask yourself: What would a meta-leader do in this situation?

Learning and practicing the three dimensions demands focused attention, though eventually it becomes second nature. The more you do it, the more you become automatically mindful of your own reactions and keenly observant of others.

Dr. Richard Besser, acting CDC director during the H1N1 virus outbreak in 2009, was schooled in meta-leadership and trained to teach it.

During the H1N1 outbreak, with news of growing numbers of infected people in the United States, he shifted into crisis meta-leadership quickly. It guided the many interactions and decisions he faced.

"When I heard about this yet unspecified virus and its potential impact, I immediately turned to the meta-leadership dimensions," he told us. "I was not in the basement—or at least not for long. I had been part of many responses to infectious disease outbreaks. But I had questions: What is the situation? What are the people within the CDC telling me, and how are they handling the threat? I had to quickly lead up, getting the attention of Washington. Since the secretary of Health and Human Services was not yet appointed, I was soon leading up directly to the White House. There was a lot of leading across and beyond to do as well. I had to engage the Department of Education about school closings, the World Health Organization, and state and local health officials.

"Actually, being on top of the situation and mindful of the organizational connections helped me keep myself out of the basement," he noted. "Even though the influenza itself was out of our control, I was confident that I was on top of what I could be, and that gave me a greater sense of confidence and assurance. And I think that rubbed off on others, who themselves had building confidence that we could figure out this virus and then get ahead of it."

Rich Besser is now CEO of the Robert Wood Johnson Foundation. In this position, he isn't doing day-to-day crisis leadership. Nonetheless, he shared with us, "I use the meta-leadership framework all the time in my current work. First, I try to recognize when I go to the basement. It doesn't have to be a national emergency that sends you there. I take steps to recognize and recoup. Meta-leadership keeps me on my toes with the different groups with whom I work. As CEO of the foundation, I lead up to the board of trustees. I lead beyond to other philanthropies, government agencies, businesses, and communities. Building the necessary connectivity, the question is how to have influence well beyond our authority."

Besser continued: "Our mission at the foundation is help create a society in which all people have a fair and just opportunity for health and well-being. To be successful, we can't command and control. For me, a big part of being successful is practicing good followership. Part of being a good leader is seeing others moving in the direction you want and helping them in what they are trying to accomplish: what can we do to help make them a success? We don't own all the best ideas, though when we see good value, we want to help."

Through your meta-leadership, you are seeking a wider perception and a deeper understanding of people, their experiences, and what affects them. That understanding—through connectivity—allows you to find patterns of behavior, reaction, and response. The intersection between what occurs in your surroundings and its impact on people becomes clearer. You take and guide actions in this broad human panorama.

Commit yourself to lifelong leadership learning. Foster your passion and wonder. Learn from mistakes. Equip yourself with the knowledge to find and achieve your full potential. Make it a sustainable ingredient of your own development and the culture of your organizations. Your meta-leadership street credibility is built on what you accomplish. Aspire to your bigger vision.

We began with the game of tag. Let's turn the game around. Now that you're "it," it's your turn to tag and influence as many people as widely as you can. Be a force multiplier. Spark your curiosity and that of others. Be a thoughtful teacher and perpetual student. This is the vitality of your meta-leadership.

Find other "its" who share your passion and drive. Join them. Tag them and be tagged by them. Seek and integrate different perspectives. Forge unity of effort. Create a fresh balance of people and priorities. Marshal the power of networks to extend your meta-leadership scope and influence. Reach far.

Imagine the world, the community, and the organization you want to live and work in. Know what you hope to achieve. Across your Arc of Time, live in the short term and reach for the long term. With others, perceive, orient, predict, swarm, and act to devise resilient futures. Meta-leadership illuminates your mission and sense of purpose. Find it and thrive within and beyond it.

Understand and shape yourself and the society you inhabit. Challenge yourself and those about you. Journal your progress and obstacles. Chronicle your achievements. Devote yourself to the people who follow you and the people you follow. Arouse your senses to notice more and to understand deeply. Connect. Make things happen.

You're it!

Questions for Journaling

⚏ This is a reading exercise, not a writing exercise. Go back and read your journal entries and reflect on what you have learned through this process of reflection. This is *your* meta-leadership story. Contemplate it and celebrate what you have accomplished and what you strive to accomplish. Anticipate your ongoing meta-leadership story and its many yet-to-be-written chapters.

To find updates from your authors and to become part of the "you're it" community, go to www.youreitbook.com.

ACKNOWLEDGMENTS

Lenny Marcus: My appreciation to Jeremy Marcus, Una Lee, Kayla Marcus, and Eli Marcus for their loving inspiration, support, and encouragement. My thanks to Wendy Caplan for her help, perspective, and assistance on the long road to publication. And to our team here at the NPLI, who every day demonstrate what people can do when they truly work together.

Eric McNulty: Many thanks to my wife, Anne, for her patience and support throughout this process, as well as Cooper, my loyal Cockapoo, who sat attentively through many sessions of writing and editing and Bailey, my keyboard-loving cat.

Joe Henderson: I would like to thank my wife, Deb; my children, Christina, Nicholas, and Stephanie; and my grandson Jaxson, who will someday be "it"! I also thank the US Centers for Disease Control and Prevention, where I was allowed to put our meta-leadership model to the test.

Barry Dorn: I would like to thank my wife, Jan, and all of the first responders and other professionals from whom I have learned so much.

Although we four have written this book, we are part of an exceptional team at the National Preparedness Leadership Initiative at Harvard University. In particular, Peter Neffenger and Richard Serino, whom you met several times in the book, were generous with their time when they were leaders in the field. More recently, both have joined us on the faculty and continue to contribute their thinking and content development to our work. Together, we have written multiple teaching cases based on their experiences. Our work has also benefited from the talents and leadership of Dr. Gregory Ciottone and Dr. Suzet McKinney. We are supported by the indefatigable Regina Jungbluth and Andrew Schwartz, who have ably managed our complex and busy writing, travel, teaching, and training schedules. Our able research assistants, including Lisa Flynn and Jennifer Grimes, have been invaluable in helping us distill observations and data into useful cases rooted in scholarship.

Our work would not be possible without the support of our academic colleagues. At the Harvard T. H. Chan School of Public Health, they include Dean Michelle Williams, Dr. Robert Blendon, Nancy Kane, Nancy Turnbull, and Dr. Arnold Epstein. At the Harvard John F. Kennedy School of Government, we are honored to work alongside NPLI founding codirector David Gergen, General (ret.) Dana Born, Dr. Ron Heifetz, Dr. Arnold Howitt, Juliette Kayyem, Dr. Barbara Kellerman, Dr. Herman "Dutch" Leonard, Dr. Christopher Robichaud, and Laura Winig, among others. Dr. Max Bazerman is a valued contributor and friend from the Harvard Business School. Our understanding of neuroscience has been greatly aided by Dr. Srini Pillay of Harvard Medical School and Dr. Donna Volpitta. Andrew Heyward and his colleagues at the MIT Media Lab have enriched our appreciation of the evolving media.

In these pages, you met some of the generous people who have allowed us to interview and, in some cases, shadow them during high-stress, high-stakes situations. Our field insights would not be possible without them. In addition to those already mentioned, they include: Jerry Agnew, Admiral (ret.) Thad Allen, Muriel Barnier, Kellie Bentz, Dr. Richard Besser, Willow Brugh, Dr. Nicole Cook, John Crowley, Dr. Suraya Dali, James "Jimmy" Dunne, Harriet Green, Eden Hebron, Jim Hooley, Brad Kieserman, Muhtar Kent, Jirayut New Latthivongskorn, Ilana Lerman, Desi Matel-Anderson, Marc Mathieu, Professor Kobi Peleg, Galit Sorokin, Budge Upton, and Ethan Zohn.

There are many other people from whom we have learned much about what it means to lead. They include: Jane Cage, Darrell Darnell, Dr. Julie Gerberding, Alice Hill, William "Billy" Evans, General Steven Kwast, Matt Olson, Governor Deval Patrick, Julie Pierson, General Scott Rice, and Mark Sullivan, as well as the many participants in our NPLI executive crisis leadership programs and symposia.

Meta-leadership would have remained an abstract concept had organizations not allowed us inside to observe their leaders and test our ideas, and some have supported our research financially. They include: American

Airlines, American Red Cross, Boston Athletic Association, Boston Emergency Medical Services, Boston Police Department, the CDC, CDC Foundation, Federal Bureau of Investigation, Edelman, Federal Emergency Management Agency, Massachusetts Emergency Management Agency, Massachusetts State Police, National Council of State Boards of Nursing, National Counter-Terrorism Center, Office of the Director of National Intelligence, Robert Wood Johnson Foundation, Schlumberger, Transportation Security Administration, US Air Force, US Centers for Disease Control and Prevention, US Coast Guard, US Department of Health and Human Services Assistant Secretary for Preparedness and Response, US Department of Homeland Security, US Office of Personnel Management, US Secret Service, White House National Security Council, and the W. K. Kellogg Foundation.

No book comes into being through the efforts of the authors alone. Our devoted agent, Esmond Harmsworth of the Aevitas Creative Management Agency, shepherded us through this process with grace, humor, and boundless patience and perseverance. Carolyn Monaco of Monaco Associates thoughtfully educated and guided us through the many steps necessary to find an audience. This is a far better book thanks to the deft editorial insight of Colleen Lawrie of PublicAffairs and the sharp copyediting of Cynthia Buck. We are grateful to Josie Urwin and Miguel Cervantes of PublicAffairs for their tireless help with publicity and marketing. We also thank the team at Fortier Public Relations for their insights and assistance.

Finally, we thank you for reading this book and, more important, putting its concepts and tools to work. Our research, teaching, and writing are directed at better equipping those who lead as they face increasingly turbulent and complex times. You have an enormous responsibility. The world needs you now. You're it!

THE META-LEADER'S BOOKSHELF

We have referenced the work of many people throughout this book. We keep a regularly updated list of books, videos, and other resources we find relevant, useful, and interesting at www.youreitbook.com.

INDEX

Leonard J. Marcus, PhD, is founding codirector of the National Preparedness Leadership Initiative, a joint program of the Harvard T. H. Chan School of Public Health and the Harvard Kennedy School of Government, Center for Public Leadership. He is also founding director of the Harvard T. H. Chan Program for Health Care Negotiation and Conflict Resolution. He received his PhD from Brandeis University in 1983. He was a fellow with the Kellogg National Leadership Program from 1986 to 1989. He joined the faculty of the Harvard T. H. Chan School of Public Health in 1995. He coauthored *Renegotiating Health Care: Resolving Conflict to Build Collaboration,* winner of the 1995 CPR Annual Book Prize Award for Dispute Resolution. A second edition was published in 2011.

Eric J. McNulty, MA, serves as associate director for the National Preparedness Leadership Initiative and the Program for Health Care Negotiation and Conflict Resolution, both at the Harvard T. H. Chan School of Public Health. He is also an instructor at the Harvard T. H. Chan School. McNulty is a contributing editor at *Strategy+Business* magazine and has written for *Harvard Business Review* and many other leading publications and websites. He has served as editor at large and director of conferences for Harvard Business Publishing. He is the coauthor of the second edition of *Renegotiating Health Care: Resolving Conflict to Build Collaboration.* Eric holds a master's degree in leadership in the context of large-scale challenges, such as climate change and urbanization, from Lesley University.

Joseph M. Henderson, MPA, is a distinguished senior fellow at the Harvard T. H. Chan School of Public Health and is on the faculty of the National Preparedness Leadership Initiative. He retired from the US government in 2018 as a member of the senior executive service. He served for twenty-five years at the Centers for Disease Control and Prevention. Shortly after 9/11, he was the first director of the CDC Office for Terrorism Preparedness and Emergency Response. In his last executive position at the CDC, he was director of the Office of Safety, Security, and Asset Management. Henderson also served in the US Air Force.

Barry Dorn, MD, MHCM, is senior advisor of the Program for Health Care Negotiation and Conflict Resolution at the Harvard T. H. Chan School of Public Health and a faculty member with the National Preparedness Leadership Initiative. He was on the faculty of health sciences at Ben-Gurion

University of the Negev, Israel, and a clinical professor of orthopedic surgery at the Tufts University School of Medicine; he also held the position of interim president and CEO of Winchester Hospital. Dr. Dorn is among the leaders in the development of the negotiation and conflict resolution field. He is a coauthor of *Renegotiating Health Care: Resolving Conflict to Build Collaboration.* He has an honorable discharge from the US Army.

PublicAffairs is a publishing house founded in 1997. It is a tribute to the standards, values, and flair of three persons who have served as mentors to countless reporters, writers, editors, and book people of all kinds, including me.

I. F. Stone, proprietor of *I. F. Stone's Weekly*, combined a commitment to the First Amendment with entrepreneurial zeal and reporting skill and became one of the great independent journalists in American history. At the age of eighty, Izzy published *The Trial of Socrates*, which was a national bestseller. He wrote the book after he taught himself ancient Greek.

Benjamin C. Bradlee was for nearly thirty years the charismatic editorial leader of *The Washington Post*. It was Ben who gave the *Post* the range and courage to pursue such historic issues as Watergate. He supported his reporters with a tenacity that made them fearless and it is no accident that so many became authors of influential, best-selling books.

Robert L. Bernstein, the chief executive of Random House for more than a quarter century, guided one of the nation's premier publishing houses. Bob was personally responsible for many books of political dissent and argument that challenged tyranny around the globe. He is also the founder and longtime chair of Human Rights Watch, one of the most respected human rights organizations in the world.

．　　　．　　　．

For fifty years, the banner of Public Affairs Press was carried by its owner Morris B. Schnapper, who published Gandhi, Nasser, Toynbee, Truman, and about 1,500 other authors. In 1983, Schnapper was described by *The Washington Post* as "a redoubtable gadfly." His legacy will endure in the books to come.

[signature]

Peter Osnos, *Founder*